Sex Over 50

Sex Over 50

Sex Over 50

Joel D. Block, Ph.D.

A PERIGEE BOOK

A PERIGEE BOOK
Published by the Penguin Group
Penguin Group (USA) Inc.
375 Hudson Street, New York, New York 10014, USA
Penguin Group (Canada), 90 Eglinton Avenue East, Suite 700, Toronto, Ontario M4P 2Y3, Canada
(a division of Pearson Penguin Canada Inc.)
Penguin Books Ltd., 80 Strand, London WC2R 0RL, England
Penguin Group Ireland, 25 St. Stephen's Green, Dublin 2, Ireland (a division of Penguin Books Ltd.)
Penguin Group (Australia), 250 Camberwell Road, Camberwell, Victoria 3124, Australia
(a division of Pearson Australia Group Pty. Ltd.)
Penguin Books India Pvt. Ltd., 11 Community Centre, Panchsheel Park, New Delhi—110 017, India
Penguin Group (NZ), 67 Apollo Drive, Rosedale, North Shore 0632, New Zealand
(a division of Pearson New Zealand Ltd.)
Penguin Books (South Africa) (Pty.) Ltd., 24 Sturdee Avenue, Rosebank, Johannesburg 2196, South Africa

Penguin Books Ltd., Registered Offices: 80 Strand, London WC2R 0RL, England

While the author has made every effort to provide accurate telephone numbers and Internet addresses at the time of publication, neither the publisher nor the author assumes any responsibility for errors, or for changes that occur after publication. Further, the publisher does not have any control over and does not assume any responsibility for author or third-party websites or their content.

PRINTING HISTORY
Reward Books trade paperback edition / April 1999
Perigee trade paperback revised edition / August 2008

Perigee trade paperback ISBN: 978-0-399-53436-2

The Library of Congress has cataloged the Reward Books edition as follows:

Block, Joel D.
  Sex Over 50 / Joel D. Block [Susan Bakos].
      p.   cm.
  Includes index.
  ISBN 978-0-7352-0058-6
1. Sex instruction.   2. Middle aged persons—Sexual behavior.   I. Bakos, Susan Crain.   II. Title.
HQ31.B569   1999
613.9'6'0844—dc21   98-42503 CIP

PRINTED IN THE UNITED STATES OF AMERICA

10 9 8 7 6 5

PUBLISHER'S NOTE: Neither the publisher nor the author is engaged in rendering professional advice or services to the individual reader. The ideas, procedures, and suggestions contained in this book are not intended as a substitute for consulting with your physician. All matters regarding your health require medical supervision. Neither the author nor the publisher shall be liable or responsible for any loss or damage allegedly arising from any information or suggestion in this book.

Most Perigee books are available at special quantity discounts for bulk purchases for sales promotions, premiums, fund-raising, or educational use. Special books, or book excerpts, can also be created to fit specific needs. For details, write: Special Markets, Penguin Group (USA) Inc., 375 Hudson Street, New York, New York 10014.

Contents

INTRODUCTION

The Best Years of
Your Sex Life

Sex does change as we age, and that is the good news. Performance anxieties and many common sex problems occur far more frequently in the young than in those who are old enough to know better. Men and women are still vital, alive, and sexy at 40, 50, 60, and beyond; and they're sexually confident and experienced, too. As long as we don't lose our zest for life, we don't lose our lust for lovemaking either.

Couples at 50 are on the threshold of a richer, fuller, and more mature sex life than they have enjoyed in the past. Adults-only sex not only can but *will* be emotionally satisfying and thrilling physically. Although physiological changes dictate that we make certain adaptations to our lovemaking styles, *we are also the beneficiaries of some potent sexual benefits at midlife.* They include:

- Greater sophistication about our own and our partner's sexuality
- Increased capability of communicating our sexual and emotional needs without fear of looking silly or being rejected or misunderstood by the one we love
- Improved sexual responsiveness in women and a corresponding improved ability to control ejaculation in men

- Greater willingness to experiment with sexual variations

- Lessened inhibitions and increased ability to have fun during lovemaking

- Far greater technical proficiency as a lover

Many of the sexual problems couples experienced in their youth are naturally resolved at midlife. Premature ejaculation, for example, is a young man's problem; some ejaculate in as little as 30 seconds after insertion. By the age of 50, most men's ejaculatory responses have slowed down considerably, to at least the average time of 2 to 5 minutes of thrusting and sometimes much longer. Simple remedies can resolve minor problems that occur naturally at midlife, such as vaginal dryness in women.

As we age, we evolve sexually; and the sexual maturation process makes lovemaking a far more enjoyable overall experience at 50 than it was at 20. Typically, men and women cross sexual and psychological paths at midlife in a process psychoanalyst Carl Jung described as the *contrasexual transition.* Women become more independent and assertive, less in need of reassurance or approval from their partners. Men become more nurturing, more comfortable with intimacy, and better able to share themselves. Older men seek the warmth and closeness in sex that women may have waited decades for them to discover. Each partner becomes more like the other in patterns of sexual response.

We know more about ourselves and our intimate partners at this point in our lives than we did when we were young. At 50, we can be bold and tender lovers, unafraid of our passion and our lover's desires. We are more likely to be empathetic, able to feel and understand our partner's feelings, sexual and otherwise. Couples who relegate sex to the storage closet of their life together because they are no longer young are giving up just when the real prize is within their grasp.

Why do some couples make the transition to a higher sexual level whereas others use aging as an excuse for shutting down?

- Some people subscribe to a series of myths about sex over 50 that lead them to believe passion is the exclusive province of the young.

- Others fail to recognize that physiological changes present opportunities for better sex, not obstacles to it.

- Some fail to adapt their lovemaking styles to accommodate their changing needs and particularly their improved abilities as lovers.

- Many allow boredom, stress, or dissatisfaction with other areas of life—jobs, finances, child rearing, extended families, physical signs of aging—to stifle their sexuality.

In 2000 MetLife Mature Market Institute reported that baby boomers—over 76 million of them—represent more than a quarter of the U.S. population. The boomers, unlike many in the generation preceding them and with an estimated spending power of over a trillion dollars, will not go quietly into the sexual darkness. They don't and won't consider themselves finished with sex because media images of sexuality are predominantly youthful ones.

In fact, some advertisers are beginning to get the message that older isn't neutered. Vanity Fair, the lingerie company, reassessed their ad campaigns when market researchers discovered many of the women who purchased their products were 40, 50, and older, considerably older than the teen models hired to display the wares. Now there are exceptionally beautiful Vanity Fair models in their 30s, 40s, and 50s, some of whom display fine lines and graying hair.

Advertisers have increasingly devoted more energy to romancing the older consumer as more boomers cross the 50 mark. That flattering attention will, in small increments, increase the collective sexual self-esteem of those of us who are no longer young. Whether you are pushing 50 or on the far side of it, you'll benefit from boomer power in the marketplace. New trends in healthcare promise to keep lovers feeling and looking as fit as possible, too. There has never been a better time for the mature lover.

Sex Over 50 helps you make the transition to a deeper, richer, more sophisticated sexual relationship by giving practical advice for overcoming negative attitudes and providing specific erotic directions for upgrading your lovemaking skills. You really are getting better as you get older. You now have much more to offer your partner.

While treasuring the special joy that was youth, you can still embrace the beauty of the present and look forward to discovering the hidden erotic treasures in your future.

CHAPTER ONE

Create a Sexy Frame of Mind

Sex begins in the brain, the most important sexual organ of all. Before you can have great sex, you have to believe you can have it—which means changing any thinking that stands in the way.

"I thought I was too old for sex," says Jane, a 50-year-old who came to this conclusion after going through menopause, surviving one daughter's wedding, and seeing the other daughter leave home for college. The combination of an empty nest and menopause convinced her she was too old for sex, though her husband certainly thought otherwise. "No periods, no contraception necessary, no girls coming home at all hours of the day or night," Jane says, laughing. "My husband thought we were in prime time for sex. 'Are you crazy?' he asked me. 'Don't you recognize liberation when it tickles you in the genitals? We can act like kids again.'"

She resisted his playful mood at first. When he walked around the house naked and encouraged her to shed her own clothes, she was embarrassed, not aroused. Fortunately, he was able to convince her she wasn't too old when they took a romantic second honeymoon cruise around the Greek islands. Over dinner, he lavished attention and compliments on her. Alone in their flower-filled cabin, he massaged her body with scented cream before making love to her, very slowly. After a few days of sexual pampering, she felt young again—desirable and filled with desire.

What if he'd shared her mind-set or hadn't been so persuasive in changing it? "I was ready to close up shop," Jane admits. "Maybe I would have been ready to open it again in six months or a year, but think of the time we would have lost. Now I would say to other women: Ask yourself why forty (or fifty or sixty) should be the cut-off age? Don't you still have feelings of physical love and desire for your husband? Aren't you still capable of experiencing pleasure?"

The 12 Myths About Sex Over 50—And the Corresponding Truths

Some of our most cherished sex beliefs are myths. Though we have access to more accurate information about sexuality than any society in history, we still subscribe to many sex myths, especially about aging. A previous generation believed that love alone—or the penis alone—would transport a woman to sexual ecstasy. Now the majority of couples know clitoral stimulation is necessary for most women to achieve orgasm, a key ingredient in the definition of *sexual ecstasy*. But, like Jane, they may still believe one can be too old for sex.

Our relentlessly youth-oriented culture entered an attitude-adjustment phase more than two decades ago when the first baby boomers turned 40. The generation who refuses to grow old the way their parents did is redefining middle age, and the new definition includes sex. Now, as the boomers age, the process of rethinking continues. Actresses and models in their 50s and 60s, women such as Meryl Streep, Diane Keaton, Jane Seymour, Jamie Lee Curtis, and Sally Field, are still considered sex symbols. (Aging men such as Clint Eastwood, Harrison Ford, and Michael Douglas have always been.) *Playboy* magazine has done tasteful nude photo spreads of women over 40, often considerably over. But our private attitudes about sexuality and aging have developed through a complex process that combines elements of socialization, learning, and personal experience; current media images represent only a part of the equation. Many men and women can admire Meryl or Diane and still believe that 50 is too old for sex when they think about their *own* lives.

Myth 1: The Quality of Sex Declines for Both Men and Women as They Age

Sexual responses are different, not worse, after 50. A man may not have the hard erections he had at 21, but he is capable of sustaining an erection longer and knows how to use a semierection to tease and stimulate his partner. More important, he can enjoy the slower buildup of sexual tension and use the added time to bring her to orgasm before intercourse. At midlife, men can finally be sensual beings, capable of enjoying a wider range of touch and sensation beyond friction applied to the head of the penis. Sex is no longer driven by the immediate needs of the penis and becomes a whole-body experience. Plus most men find that giving satisfaction is as thrilling as experiencing it.

Often women are not comfortable taking the sexual initiative until they are in their 30s. As they age, their sexual assertiveness increases as does their enjoyment of intercourse. A shift in a woman's hormonal balance, beginning in her late 30s or early 40s, increases her libido and her ability to have orgasms.

Once in their 50s, men and women achieve a level of emotional maturity and sexual self-confidence that make it possible for them to enjoy a superior intimate relationship. The quality of sex definitely improves and continues to remain high for decades.

Myth 2: If a Woman Does Not Lubricate Sufficiently or a Man Does Not Become Erect Immediately, He or She Is Not Aroused

Sexual arousal does not necessarily manifest in immediate physical changes. Insufficient lubrication in a woman is probably a result of hormonal changes, not lack of desire. The situation can be corrected through the use of lubricants (such as K-Y jelly), hormone creams, or hormone-replacement therapy that is natural and safe. In older men, desire does not always immediately translate into an erection. Some men report feeling desire throughout their bodies rather than localized in their penises.

Myth 3: Erection Problems Are Inevitable and Incurable Without Medical Intervention

Men often interpret natural physiological changes as being problems. They think they are not hard enough because they aren't as hard as they were at 19. Or they overreact to an occasional failure to get or maintain an erection. By the time he is 40, nearly every man has experienced a bout of erectile dysfunction, and many men unnecessarily fear these erotic disappointments will inevitably become regular occurrences. Healthy, physically and sexually active men can continue to achieve erections into old age without medical intervention. According to the National Institutes of Health, only 15 to 25 percent of men over 65 have erectile dysfunction severe enough to preclude intercourse; and the majority of the problems are caused by over-the-counter or prescription medications, illnesses such as diabetes and hypertension, or alcohol abuse.

Myth 4: Female Desire Declines Dramatically After Menopause

Many women report an *increased* sexual desire after menopause. In one survey of women over 50 conducted by the Robert Wood Johnson Medical School in New Brunswick, New Jersey, a whopping 72 percent reported no complaints—including declining desire—about their sex lives. When postmenopausal women do have less interest in lovemaking, the causes are typically a hormone imbalance or negative thinking. Each can be easily resolved. In addition, desire at any age is affected by many other factors, including health and fitness, relationship issues, and general stress.

Myth 5: Once a Man Is No Longer Aroused by the Mere Sight of His Wife, He Will Have Great Difficulty Making Love to Her

The older a man gets, the less likely he is to have an unassisted erection—in other words, to become erect merely by looking at his partner or another arousing female. That doesn't mean he isn't aroused or isn't interested in making love to her. After age 35 or 40, a man needs direct penile stimulation to get an erection. When midlife men have difficulty making love, the cause is more often rooted in relationship conflict than in the physical appearance of aging bodies. As men become more psychologically in tune with women, they also find their feelings have become a more important factor when it comes to sexual expression, something that may have happened to them rarely if at all when they were young.

Typically, young men are ready to go, despite the state of the relationship, short of it being a total disaster. The good news is that when midlife men express those feelings rather than keeping them inside, they become more passionate.

Myth 6: Men Peak in Their Teens

Men achieve erection more quickly in their late teens than they ever will again in their lives. Those erections are also harder than they'll be once a man is old enough to know what to do with them. If male sexual performance is judged purely in fast and hard erectile terms, the peak is indeed young. But isn't it more realistic to view sexuality in broader terms? A man can't be truly said to have peaked until he has become a good—even great—lover, with ejaculatory control and the ability to please his partner in many different ways; and that's unlikely to happen at age 19.

Myth 7: Women Peak in Their 30s

For most women, sex does gets better in their 30s, but their level of responsiveness doesn't plateau and then level off in later years as many people mistakenly believe. Women's increased ease with their bodies and confidence in lovemaking continues to grow throughout life. And a woman's orgasmic capacity, including the ability to have multiple orgasms, is undiminished by age.

Myth 8: Youthful Orgasms Are More Intense

Too many of us believe that sex is only for the young and beautiful. A corollary of this belief is the assumption that sexual ecstasy is more intensely experienced by the young. Not true. Women often report that orgasms are more intense after the age of 40. Although men may notice that the force of their ejaculation isn't as strong in midlife as in youth, they will also feel a more diffuse orgasm in other parts of the body, including the entire genital area, not merely the head of the penis.

Myth 9: Men and Women with Heart or Other Problems Should Avoid Sexual Activity

A study of 1,600 people conducted at Boston's New England Deaconess Hospital found that the risk of a heart attack during sex was roughly equivalent to the risk of a heart attack from getting out of bed in the morning. According to Dr. Robert Butler, former director of the National Institute on Aging, heart attacks during intercourse account for less than 1 percent of all coronary deaths—and 70 percent of those occur during extramarital liaisons, when the stress level can be assumed to be higher. Sexual activity is actually good for all of us. Lovemaking has many physical and psychological benefits, from reducing stress to preventing depression.

Myth 10: Sex Has to End in Orgasm

Both men and women can find satisfaction in lovemaking that doesn't end in orgasm. Sometimes couples are tired or rushed, yet want to kiss, caress, and fondle each other. Orgasm isn't a goal that must be reached each time. In fact, some mature lovers deliberately make love without orgasm to intensify the experience when they do have one.

Myth 11: Oral Sex Is for the Very Young

According to studies cited by *The Janus Report on Sexual Behavior* and *The Kinsey Institute New Report on Sex*, couples are more likely to have oral sex at 40 than at 20. Younger people have more inhibitions about performing sex acts, including fellatio and cunnilingus. They are also more likely to be unsure of their erotic skills and hold back because of performance anxiety, something older women suffer, too.

Myth 12: Intercourse Is the Only Kind of Sex That Counts; Anything Else Isn't Sex

That intercourse equals sex is a modern Western concept. In the ancient Indian text the *Kama Sutra* many forms of lovemaking were celebrated. Is it coincidence that the Eastern erotic acts became popular again when the boomers entered their 40s? Most of us learned as teens that foreplay was the kissing, caressing, and touching a man had to do to get a woman ready for intercourse. *Loveplay* is a better word, encompassing all the ways men and women have of giving each other sexual pleasure. By midlife, a man craves this touching, kissing, and caressing as much as a woman does, requires it for erection, and may sometimes be satisfied with oral or manual lovemaking and even intercourse that does not end in ejaculation. There is so much more to sex than intercourse.

Overcoming the Mental Obstacles
to Great Sex

The obstacles to great sex are not age-related factors. Anyone at any age can suffer from boredom, be too busy for sex, or let duties get in the way of pleasures. But some people use age as an excuse for failing to surmount the following obstacles to sexual pleasure:

- *Simple boredom.* If we don't seek out new challenges and experiences at midlife, we can fall into a state of ennui, an emotional comma induced by familiar, safe, and repetitive patterns. Boredom is not conducive to passion.

- *Assigning low priority to romance and lovemaking.* Members of the sandwich generation, those of us caught between the needs of growing children and of aging parents, not to mention jobs, can feel guilty about planning a romantic evening together instead of taking care of others.

- *Allowing daily life stresses and time demands to stifle desire.* Many of us feel too tired, too tense, too busy, too wound up for sex.

Men are as apt to find their libido trapped under one of these three big rocks as women are, and they may have more trouble acknowledging the real problem. (Another myth: Women lose interest in sex before men do.) For her 50th birthday, Anne gave herself a career change, turning from a corporate job to running her own decorative-arts business. Rather than being inspired by her energy and enthusiasm for life, her husband was alternately baffled and annoyed by those qualities in her. He was comfortable in blaming external circumstances for his own lack of energy, enthusiasm, and sexual desire.

"John turned fifty six months after I did; and he gave himself a case of the blues instead of a celebratory gift," she says. "He felt trapped in a job that hadn't challenged him in years, yet he was certain he was too old to do anything else. Whenever I suggested any kind of change, from professional to personal, he had excuses for not trying anything new.

Our sex life suffered, too. He teased me about being a 'horny old broad' when I tried to initiate lovemaking, but he was insistent about pushing me away."

Another woman might have allowed rejection and criticism to dampen her own ardor. When one spouse loses interest in sex, he or she typically brings—or attempts to bring—the other down to the same level. Apathy loves company. A change in attitude is the first step toward surmounting the mental obstacles to great sex. If changing your own negative attitudes can be difficult, how is it possible to help change your partner's thinking?

Five Steps for Overcoming the Obstacles

1. *Open a discussion.* Get your partner to talk about why he or she believes there is no time for romance, no room for change, no reason to feel like a sexual being at this point in life. Saying the reasons out loud forces us to examine them for validity. Anne insisted that John both talk and listen to her. At first she didn't challenge his opinions and attitudes. "I knew he would mull over what each of us had said in his own time," she says. "If I'd forced him to respond to my thinking, he would have rejected it."

2. *Agree to remove critical language from the discussion.* Neither partner can accuse the other of being horny or sex obsessed, hinting that such a state is inappropriate to one of a certain age, or of being frigid, impotent, or over the hill. Each partner should be able to express a desire, or lack of desire, for sex without fear of being judged or ridiculed.

3. *Be clear about your motives.* Do you want more sex? A better, closer relationship? Are you concerned about helping your partner pull out of a funk? "I wanted more for both of us," Anne says. "At first he thought I was being selfish, wanting more sex at a time when he didn't think he could meet my needs. I was able to convince him I wanted more than sex for us. I wanted him to be alive again and for the two of us to enjoy these golden opportunity years together in every way."

4. *Test the validity of your attitudes.* Is it a fact or an opinion that one can be too old for sex? A fact or an opinion that duties and obligations

must always come before pleasures? Present your partner with some facts about midlife sexuality and ask him or her to consider them. Examine your own attitudes and prejudices, too.

5. *Be open to change, not merely sexual change.* Trying a new intercourse position, renting an erotic video, making love in the morning instead of at night or introducing some other change into your lovemaking routine may not be the place to start. You wouldn't begin an exercise program with a half hour of aerobic activity if you hadn't been physically active in months or years. Start with easy changes, such as trying a new restaurant, having mango and kiwi instead of a banana in the morning, or buying a brightly colored shirt or blouse.

"I got John to agree to sign up for some continuing education classes with me," Anne says. "Our first course was on wine. John became something of a wine aficionado in no time at all. Just having a new interest made him more lively in bed. The night he suggested we take our wine into the bedroom, I was hoping we wouldn't drain our glasses before making love; and we didn't."

Removing Boredom from Your Life

Boredom, more than anything else, dulls desire. A 25-year-old awash in ennui may still function sexually; but as we get older, our sex lives increasingly reflect what is happening in the rest of our lives. You can't live a routine no-habits-changed-in-years life and have passionate sex. Lasting passion is not an end in itself, something achieved by following the sex-guidebook numbers; it is a consequence of living an adventurous life, in bed and out.

To remove boredom from your daily existence, you have to live a counterphobic life, which means working against your fears rather than giving in to them. Here are five tips for doing just that.

Acknowledge Your Fears
Take a piece of paper and write down your fears in escalating order of importance, from fear of spiders to fear of sharing embarrassing intimate

information with your lover. What do all fears have in common? They represent loss, such as loss of control, of power, of esteem, or of love. Some fears are healthy, such as the fear of walking alone in a dangerous neighborhood after midnight. Most fears hold us back. Don't be discouraged and give up. Tell your partner you need support, not ridicule. Insist. It's that important.

Beside each fear on your list, note what you are afraid of losing. Then ask yourself, What is the worst thing that can happen to me if my fear is realized? Face that scenario. Imagine yourself dealing with it. If you are afraid of driving alone at night, picture yourself stranded in a car with a sudden mechanical problem. Then picture yourself taking out your cell phone and calmly dialing for help while you wait in your car with the doors locked and flashers on. You will survive. How reasonable is it to assume that the worst will happen anyway?

Share your fears with your partner, who undoubtedly knows what some of them are but may be surprised at others. A man might be avoiding sex because he fears performance failure, something his wife doesn't suspect because she thinks she no longer excites him. When he shares his vulnerability with her, he gives her more than the gift of trust. He tells her she's desirable.

What if your partner doesn't understand your fears? Or even laughs at them? That's possible, of course, but is it likely? If it does happen, remember that one who ridicules another's fears probably has more fears of his or her own.

Eliminate Guilt

How does guilt interfere with the ability to lead a counterphobic life? Guilt can stop you from taking a risk. The guilt-ridden have a multitude of reasons for not taking the chance they suspect will improve their lives. A man stays in the family business rather than pursuing a career of his own because his parents need him. A woman sacrifices her educational plans to support a husband's goals and later to carpool the children to every activity that interests them. The couple puts sex and romance at the bottom of their priority list because they feel guilty about doing anything selfish, indulgent, and not for the benefit of others. For the guilty, self-denial has become a habit and is thought of as a virtue. It isn't.

Denying self in the name of duty only makes one less—less of a person, a full and loving partner, a parent, an adult child, a sibling, and a friend. Don't confuse *selfish*—"I want what I want at any cost"—with *I am worthy, I count.* When you deny yourself pleasure, you give less to the people you are sacrificing to serve because you have less to give. Make a list of everything you've given up—including lovemaking—because you would have felt guilty if you hadn't. Do these sacrifices make sense? Examine your life. What do you want that you haven't let yourself try to have? Guilt is a comfortable excuse, and it's time you threw away that security blanket.

Stop Being So Cautious

There are two kinds of caution: physical and psychological. They can overlap, for example, when a couple won't try anal sex or light bondage or spanking—practices that excite them *both* in fantasies—because they might experience initial discomfort or look silly. For some people, physical risks such as Bungee jumping, are exhilarating, whereas psychological risks, such as sharing hidden fears, are very frightening.

If you were raised by cautious, fearful parents who warned you against every possible accident or injury, you probably grew into a cautious, fearful adult unlikely to leave home without an umbrella on a mildly overcast day. At middle age, you may be leading an unnecessarily restricted life, protecting yourself from every imagined hurt. Is it possible to experience thrilling sexual passion inside that cocoon? Not likely.

Start throwing caution to the wind. Take a walk in the rain. Share a secret about yourself. Head out for a weekend trip without planning every aspect of it. If a little voice inside your head says, "I can't/shouldn't do that," tell it to shut up.

Push Back Your Personal Boundaries

We all have limits and rules that constitute our personal boundaries. In addition, we draw a set of imaginary lines around our possibilities and don't let ourselves dream or plan, reach or hope beyond them. Some people have too many rules; and their limits are narrow and confining, the lines they've drawn are too far within the limits of what they might achieve. By midlife, they have become rigid people who can be approached only in certain ways, like the potentates of small countries. Pushing back the boundaries may be difficult for them, almost physically painful, but it's ultimately liberating.

You can push back your physical boundaries in small ways. A man who isn't comfortable with public displays of affection might hold hands with his wife while walking down the street. A woman who hasn't put on a sexy dress in years can buy one, wear it to a party, and flirt with her mate. Hug a friend, express a painful feeling, admit a mistake to your son or daughter. Ignore the initial discomfort and push the boundaries back so the people you care about can come a little closer. Sometimes extending yourself outside the imaginary lines takes a little more effort, like asking for a raise, applying for a promotion, or changing jobs.

Take Risks

Risk taking is the backbone of an exciting, passionate life. Without risk, a life doesn't stand tall and move forward with vigor. Ironically, at midlife when many have a secure financial and emotional base from which to take more risks, they shut down and take fewer. This is why some men and women who have achieved financial success seem so curiously dull and flat when cornered in conversation outside the office. Risk is essential to continued personal growth. People who remain interesting and sexy are risk takers in all areas of their lives.

That doesn't mean you have to register for a skydiving class, take up mountain climbing, or quit your job without having another one lined up. The high-stakes risks are often emotional ones. Admitting fear, expressing anger, or daring to be vulnerable can be a huge leap of faith across a scary chasm. Taking such a risk leads to change; and the move is fearful because there's no guarantee that the ensuing change will be for the better. When taking a risk, we let go of something: a sense of security, a false belief, a protective habit, a tenuous investment or relationship. What will we get in exchange? Maybe something wonderful, and maybe nothing at all.

A risk that will improve your sex life is *not* having unprotected sex with a stranger on a business trip but is telling your long-term partner about a previously undisclosed erotic fantasy or wish. On the other hand, going back to school, joining a gym, or confronting a buried issue in your family of origin could also have unforeseen erotic benefits. If you felt sexier when you were young, you also took more risks then. Do you see the connection? Life was more exciting, and so were you.

Tying It Together

"My libido began limping like a guy with an old football injury [when I was] in my late forties," says Ron, a chemical engineer. "I attributed the situation to aging, though my wife, only a few years younger, was more interested in lovemaking.

"For years I'd been employed by the same small firm. One day, I was told by someone in the field whose judgment I valued that I was considerably underpaid for my job given my years of experience and level of performance. When I told my wife, who is an investigative reporter, she researched the subject and told me how poorly compensated I really was. She and my best friend began hassling me to ask for a raise or look for another job. I countered that there were advantages to working for this small firm, but I was rationalizing. I was really afraid of asking for a raise, afraid of having my boss tell me that I was worth only what he was paying me.

"But my wife and my friend kept up the pressure, so I finally had the talk with the boss. He said he'd get back to me. For two weeks, he said nothing. I felt better about myself for asking, but when he didn't respond in a timely fashion, I realized I'd have to ask again. By this time, I wasn't getting any outside pressure. Asking was something I wanted to do for myself.

"He offered me a good raise. If he hadn't, I was prepared to begin looking for another job, something I'd been afraid to do before. The real surprise to me was the lasting effect this incident had on my libido. I felt more sexual after asking for that raise than I had in years; and the feeling persisted."

As soon as Ron began working against his fears, he changed his life. His lack of libido was an indicator that he hadn't been happy for a long time. He'd kept himself strictly within a tight set of boundaries, living at a level of discomfort he associated with safety, which perversely felt like comfort to him. In pushing those boundaries, he freed his libido.

Five Tips for Creating a Sexy Mind-Set

- Pretend that you're dating again and sex is a delicious possibility, not a certainty. After a couple have been together for years, they each know when the other is in the mood for sex. One partner makes a move, gauges the other's response, and knows if the answer is affirmative or negative. Not knowing creates erotic tension.

- Rather than squashing erotic thoughts unless they can be carried to completion, indulge in fantasies of lovemaking when you know you won't have the opportunity to do it. In youth, people encourage and enjoy their fantasies, which is one reason they always seem to have sex on the brain. Later, they sternly shut down sexual thoughts until it's time for sex. The result? The erotic hour arrives; and the sexual thoughts remain suppressed.

- Laugh together. Laughter unlocks the emotions. It is an erotic elixir more potent than good wine.

- Learn how to tease your partner, visually and verbally, to create desire. Mother said, "Don't be a tease," but Mother was wrong. In the early stages of sexual attraction, men and women tease each other with suggestive comments, seductive gestures. Later, they become overly direct, eliminating the playful aspects of their sexual relationship.

- Take care of your body through exercise, a healthy diet, and vitamins. You'll get this message more than once here because it's important.

SIZZLER #1

We're Still Sexy

"Grandparents!" Jill said. "She's six months along now; and I still can't believe it. I'm happy, of course, but…" Her voice trailed off. Steve reached across the bed for her hand. It was limp and cold in his. "Grandparents," she repeated. "We're old, Steve. Old."

"I don't feel old," he said, a suggestive note in his voice. "I couldn't wait for the kids"—his term for their son and daughter-in-law—"to leave so we could be alone. We didn't make love once the entire ten days they were here." Or how long before that? He couldn't remember, but he did know that Jill's disinterest in sex dated back to the day they'd been told they were going to be grandparents.

She caught the suggestion, took her hand from his, and rolled over so that her back was to him. He moved to her side of the bed, fitted himself against her back, and put one arm around her, his hand resting against her stomach, gently rounded and softly warm to his touch. She flinched lightly. How long had it been since she'd teased him that she didn't dare turn her back on him if they hadn't made love in a few days. He liked to enter from behind. Her ass had always been beautiful to him. Sometimes when she bent over, he had to resist the impulse to fall to his knees and bury his face in her cheeks. He wanted to worship his wife's body; she was a goddess to him.

"I'm tired," she said. "Sleep well."

Sleep well! His wife was consigning them to a sexless old age in their early 50s. And he was supposed to sleep?

Steve tossed and turned that night and, as a result of his frustration, developed a plan. He called it "Operation: We're Still Sexy." The next morning, he got up before she did, hurriedly showered, and then took the kitchen calendar off the wall and slipped it into his briefcase. When he got to the office, he asked some colleagues to help him come up with the names of sexy celebrity grandmothers and grandfathers. They included Lonnie Anderson, Raquel Welch, Sean Connery, and Clint Eastwood. He skipped lunch and went to a newsstand where he bought magazines featuring these stars. Back at the office, he made a new calendar: The Sexy Grandparents Calendar.

Jill laughed when he hung it up, but it was a good laugh. She liked the calendar. Over the next several days, he bombarded her with small romantic gifts and cards. His behavior toward her was tender and affectionate, but he didn't push for sex, even when she pressed her body against his in the night. One day, he brought home an expensive midnight blue silk kimono. And finally, he gave her the pièce de résistance: A day spa for two. When he'd called to arrange their day of total pampering at a local spa that advertised couple days, he'd asked the receptionist to book them with other mature couples. Steve wanted Jill to see other older women reveling in their sensuality, to notice the quiet passion he was sure she would see simmering in couples who had taken the time to be together in a different way.

As they lingered over their spa luncheon, sipping champagne while wearing thick white terry robes, she reached across the table and stroked his hand. "I haven't felt this good in years," she said. "I can't thank you enough for planning this day."

"You'll think of something," he said lightly. Beneath the robe, his penis grew hopefully stiff.

That night she put on the midnight blue kimono and curled up beside him on the sofa. Stretching her torso languorously like a cat, she whispered, "I'm not wearing any underwear." He put his hand between her legs. The silk of the cloth gave way to the softness of her inner thighs. He caressed her skin and slowly moved his hand up her leg. She sighed happily, leaned forward into his arms, and kissed him passionately. His thumb parted her labia. She was moist, hot, anticipating him. "I want you," she said.

The words thundered in his ears. He lowered his face and slowly licked her clitoris until her breath came in that short, jagged pattern he knew so well. *We've still got it,* he thought, as she began to come for the first time that night.

CHAPTER TWO

The Building Blocks
of Passion

In Chapter 1, I encouraged you to throw out those tired old negative sex attitudes with the nonrecyclable trash. You're *not* too old for sex. Both you and your partner are capable of experiencing a rich and rewarding erotic life together. It is possible to become joyously sexual again even for partners in a sexless marriage. You have a new attitude. How do you move up and out of the sexual doldrums now that you believe it's possible to do so?

Begin by replacing the old attitudes with new ones. Attitudes are like emotional building blocks. Your old foundation was made of negative building blocks. Use new positive building blocks to build a new sex-positive foundation for your life. Those positive building blocks, the emotional qualities that lead to great sex, include the following:

- *Sexual self-esteem.* People who have enjoyed good sexual relationships before age 40 usually have sexual self-esteem, but it may be at low ebb now. These individuals are relatively free of sex guilt and confident about their desirability and erotic skills, yet at midlife they may suffer a setback rooted in body-image anxiety or misinformation about the effects of aging on sexuality.

- *Enthusiasm.* Enthusiasm for life and for lovemaking is contagious—and so is the lack of it. One partner's loss of the zest for life typically has an effect on the other.

- *Optimism.* Optimistic people tend to see the challenge in change, whereas pessimists look for the downside. To a pessimist every setback, from failing to get a promotion to failing to get an erection, is a catastrophe. Optimism is an energizing sexual force.

- *Playfulness.* Sex is one way that adults play. When couples complain that sex isn't fun anymore, they have stopped being playful with each other. Put the play back in your sex life, and the orgasms will follow.

The negative feelings, the building blocks of your old foundation that sap sexual energy are the following:

- *Anger.* People who can't acknowledge or express their anger typically try to suppress it. What else can they do with it? Eventually, stored anger dulls sexuality. People who are chronically angry stifle their sexual feelings and alienate their lovers.

- *Guilt.* As noted in the previous chapter, guilt is not a sensuous emotion. Whether you feel guilty about having sexual desires, participating in certain activities, or taking time away from duty for lovemaking, it will cost you. The price of guilt is diminished sexual satisfaction and decreasing opportunities for sex.

- *Depression.* Nothing dulls desire as effectively as depression. A man or a woman who is deeply or persistently unhappy about other areas of life isn't likely to have good sex until the underlying causes of the depression are resolved.

- *Fear.* Fear leads to protective behavior that makes it difficult to be intimate, vulnerable, and playful with a partner. When we're fearful, we create avoidance patterns rather than reach out to connect.

Tear Down the Old Foundation and Create
a Positive Sex Foundation

"I prided myself on never refusing my husband sex even when I was angry at him," says Fran, 49 and married to Morris for 24 years. "Shortly after our twentieth anniversary, I started to lose interest in sex, but I never said no. I faked orgasms. I thought I was doing my share.

"Two years ago he came home from a real-estate brokers' convention in Boston and confessed that he'd had a fling with a woman he'd met there. I was devastated, then furious. How could he do that when I'd always been so accommodating to his needs?"

Morris told her he'd been "insulted" by her sexual accommodations. He wanted to be wanted, not tolerated. She was, he said, "emotionally flat," in bed and out. When she told him he hadn't given her an orgasm in years, he responded that he'd suspected she had been faking for years. "You never broke a sweat," he accused, "and your orgasms were too perfectly timed to coincide with mine. How real is that?"

For 6 weeks, they alternated between not speaking to each other and sharing heated, angry exchanges in which each told the other how unsatisfactory they were as sex partners. Repressed anger, mild depression, fear of aging, and an accompanying loss of sexuality were the building blocks of both their foundations, but they didn't yet recognize it. Some couples in similar situations would either get divorced or stay together in a sexless marriage. Fran and Morris were lucky.

"Looking back, we see the explosion of anger on both sides as a positive thing," she says. "We got rid of a lot of feelings that we'd been keeping inside. Our big advantage, however, was in having the right confidants. He talked to his brother, and I talked to my best friend. Some brothers and friends might say, 'You're right and your spouse is wrong.' They helped us see the other person's side.

"My friend Lorraine told me that Morris was right when he said I'd become emotionally flat. Hearing it from her was like a splash of cold water in the face. She also said it took a lot of courage for him to confess his infidelity to me, and she was right. That fling was his act of desperation."

When they were a little calmer, Fran and Morris were able to examine some of their emotional issues, such as anger and depression, and their underlying sexual attitudes. They had both assumed a female orgasm was a gift a man gave a woman, like handing her a single red rose. That had put all the responsibility for her sexual pleasure on him and thus encouraged her to fake as a way of rewarding him for his effort. (A nice girl says thank you even if the rose is a little wilted and hasn't much fragrance.) It is not surprising that he had concerns about his sexuality he'd never shared with her. Would he have trouble with erections soon? And how would he handle that when and if it happened? They both had misconceptions about sexuality and aging and harbored secret fears about performance and desirability.

"When I noticed his erection wasn't as hard as it used to be," she says, "I thought he was a little turned off by my body because my breasts aren't as perky as they used to be either."

Voicing these concerns brought them closer together. When they made love for the first time after his infidelity, they were more vulnerable to each other than they could ever remember being. They both regard that lovemaking session as a new beginning.

"I'm learning to speak up," she says, "to tell him when I do or don't want to make love, to be more comfortable about asking him to touch me the way I want to be touched. I read an article advising women to touch themselves during lovemaking, and I tried that. Before everything happened between us, I would have felt silly masturbating with my husband next to me in bed. I would have been embarrassed. But it was exciting for both of us and liberating for me."

A crisis of fidelity led Morris and Fran to tear down their old foundations and begin to build new ones, something you and your partner can do without a motivating trauma.

How to Build Sexual Self-Esteem

Studies have shown that people who have high self-esteem live longer, healthier lives; continue to enjoy sex throughout their lives; and are optimistic about the future. At midlife, most of us suffer an occasional blow to our esteem. We look in the mirror and recoil at the image of our mother (or father) looking back at us. Wrinkles, sagging skin, receding hairlines—this is not the stuff of romantic legend as we learned it when we were sure our parents never had sex except for the purpose of procreation. A man may have trouble getting erect or ejaculating, a woman in lubricating sufficiently for intercourse. How we feel about our bodies affects our sexuality, and rare is the person of any age who hasn't experienced feelings of angst rooted in body image or performance issues.

"I stopped feeling sexy after I caught a glimpse of myself in the bedroom mirror while making love," says Kim, 49. "I looked at my image and thought, 'Who is this old fat broad on top of that man and why is she letting everything hang out?' Not a flattering self-analysis, but it seemed true to me."

Kim's partner, with whom she lives, did not share her negative evaluation of her body. Men typically are more forgiving of women's figure flaws than women are. They are capable of lavishing admiring attention on her good parts and putting the less attractive ones in soft focus, like selective photographers. A man often looks at a longtime partner, especially while lovemaking, and sees not the woman she has become but the woman she was when they first met. But her physical appearance was a problem to Kim, one that interfered with her sexual enjoyment. For her, a diet-and-exercise program was the first step toward restoring sexual self-esteem, and it may work the same magic for many midlife people. Toning the body and improving appearance can have an aphrodisiac effect on most people of any age.

The following sections introduce other methods for restoring your confidence.

Challenging Your Inferiority Feelings
Midlife inferiority feelings come from four major areas: physical appearance, sexual performance, financial status, and worldly accomplishments.

The great majority of people do not have model bodies, perfect hair, and ideal faces. Why compare yourself to Cindy Crawford or George Clooney? At age 40 we castigate ourselves for having fallen from a state of physical grace few of us ever attained in the first place. Set reasonable, attainable physical standards for yourself. Improve what you can and be accepting of your physical imperfections. Even models know they aren't perfect and are often unhappy with certain body parts.

Although men are susceptible to insecurity about their physical appearance, women have more concerns in this area. When it comes to sexual performance, however, men take the number one position. Though most middle-aged people are more enlightened about gender and sexuality issues than they were when they were on the brink of adulthood, they nonetheless were indoctrinated in the belief that women's sexual role is to attract, and men's is to perform. That message is imbedded deep within the psyche. Her biggest fear is losing the ability to attract; his is losing the ability to perform. Both have to let go of impossible, often imaginary, standards and replace them with reachable goals.

"I finally stopped competing with my adolescent self," one man said in explaining how he overcame the feelings of sexual inferiority that had begun to paralyze him after 40. "My ejaculate doesn't shoot powerfully. You can't hang a cowboy hat on my erection anymore. But I'm a better lover than I was then. I was more impressed with myself at nineteen than my partners were with me. A woman would rather have a tender lover than watch a young stud in action."

Some men who never considered themselves "young studs in action" may develop sexual anxiety more rooted in their fiscal performances than erectile abilities. In our time, corporate downsizing has created a sizable pool of unemployed or underemployed middle-aged men and women. Job loss and the perceived failure of achievement can affect a woman's sexuality, too. Increasingly, women measure themselves in terms of money and position earned. Rare is the older adult who can weather downsizing or being passed over repeatedly for promotion without experiencing at least a temporary loss of sexual desire.

How can you challenge those inferiority feelings and begin to restore desire?

- Stop idealizing your youthful self. When you look back in time, try to retrieve the memories of the insecurity and callowness of youth. Haven't you evolved into a better, more loving person? Most of us have.

- Make a list of your attributes and strengths, sexual and otherwise. It's a much longer list than you thought it was, isn't it?

- Whether or not your job provides self-esteem benefits (such as good pay or other less tangible compensations), look outside the workplace. Volunteer. Go back to school. Take up an artistic pursuit. Develop a hobby into a paying enterprise. Consider supplementing your income with consulting work. A woman forced into early retirement at 50 used her severance package to start her own mailorder bonsai business and has never been happier.

- Help your partner build his or her self-esteem. As one grows stronger, so can the other.

Accepting Yourself

It is surprising that studies show middle-aged and older people are actually more comfortable with their bodies than are younger people, particularly women. We may not love what we see at 40, but we don't loathe it the way many do at 20. After a certain point, most of us learn how to practice personal forgiveness when we look into the mirror. If you have achieved this level of body comfort, work at extending the concept to the rest of you. Accept your personality quirks, small character flaws, and less-than-sterling résumé with as much equanimity as you accept a slightly crooked nose, a receding hairline, or a few extra pounds.

Look over your list of attributes again. Juxtapose it with the little debit column you carry in your head. Doesn't the balance tip over to the positive side? At midlife especially, self-acceptance is necessary to continued growth, change, improvement—and to a good sex life.

Paying Attention to Your Partner's Sexual Self-Esteem Needs

What's the best sex advice for a woman whose partner has lost his erection during lovemaking? Encourage him to please her. Nothing takes a man's mind off his own perceived shortcomings like his partner's pleasure.

The same advice applies to either a man or a woman with low sexual self-esteem: Take your mind off your own perceived shortcomings by lavishing erotic attention on your partner. Put your own feelings aside and do something to boost his or her sexual self-esteem. Compliment appearance. Give an unrequested back rub. Nuzzle a neck and murmur kind words about the scent and feel of your lover's skin. Say, "Lie back and let me make love to you; I want to do all the work this time." When you make your partner feel more desirable, you feed the cycle of desire shared by both.

Four Sexual Self-Esteem Exercises

Masturbation

Many people place masturbation after marriage on their internal list of sexual shoulds and shouldn'ts. Reasoning that sex is something you do with a partner unless you don't have one, they believe only the single person should masturbate. Women are more prone to make this assumption than are men and may even regard masturbation as a form of cheating.

Masturbation is a normal, healthy form of sexual expression for everyone, male or female, married or single. Through masturbation, we learn about our sexual responses, too. A man can teach himself better ejaculatory control by practicing techniques while masturbating. A woman can learn how to reach orgasm via masturbation if she's had orgasmic difficulties. Women who are comfortable with masturbation are more likely to help their partners please them because they know when, where, and how touch is needed.

As the ultimate form of sexual self-love, masturbation also serves a higher purpose. Lovingly stroke yourself. People who feel worthy of self-love are more apt to consider themselves desirable to their partners.

The Indirect Request

Help your partner please you by providing more nonverbal guidance. Some couples lose interest in sex because lovemaking becomes mechanical—in other words, they have been making love in the same way for years. The patterns of arousal and response that once worked for them may have become dulled over time.

Maybe he would like to take her head gently in his hands and guide it to his penis at just the point when she typically stops manual stimulation in preparation for intercourse. Maybe she would like to put his hand on her vulva and show him how to massage her in a new way. Habit, fear of change, and uncertainty prevent us from translating wishes to realities.

Be bold. Lead your partner in a different direction. Then be enthusiastic in your response to change.

The Direct Request
Ask your partner for what you want. Just as your self-esteem rises when you ask for a raise, request redress for a wrong, or state a unique opinion, so does your sexual self-esteem increase when you make a direct request. What do you want? More oral sex, more stroking and caressing, more variety in practices and positions top most people's sex wish list. Share yours with your partner.

What stops couples in long-term relationships from making the direct request? Fear of looking silly, of being refused, of being judged, or of having the other suspect infidelity. "Where will she [or he] think I'm getting these ideas?" silences some of us; but in our society, we are exposed to enough sexual information and imagery to negate that excuse. You got the idea from a book, a magazine article, a movie, a glossy advertisement for an expensive perfume. Now express it.

Practice Enlightened Sexual Self-Interest
Be sexually self-interested. Nothing is more exciting than an excited partner. Here are some suggestions for raising your own temperature:

- Don't have sex to please your partner if you're not in the mood. Ask to be seduced.

- If your partner is not in the mood for sex, masturbate where your partner can watch, if this is acceptable. Ask first.

- Ask him or her to devote a lovemaking session to pleasing you alone.

- Splurge on sensuous accessories for your own pleasure, such as bath oils, scented creams, lingerie meant to arouse you, not necessarily him. Maybe all your silk undies are black, for example, because he likes black. Buy something in *your* favorite color. If you're hot for a red lace bra, for example, go for it!

Why Enthusiasm Encourages Passion

Enthusiasm for life in general and work, hobbies, family, spiritual, and other pursuits in particular make one more passionate. Lust for life leads to lust in the bedroom. If there is a great fallacy in our approach to sexual problems it is the isolating of sex from the relationship, from the rest of life. Only in the young and intensely hormonally driven does sex happen regardless of what else is going on. They can more easily turn on and find their way to orgasm; you can't anymore. The disaffected midlife man or woman, disillusioned and discouraged, is not going to be an exciting lover, no matter what his or her partner pulls from a little bag of sex tricks.

People who have lost their enthusiasm for life have set up negative patterns for living and loving. As they begin to have less and less interest in their jobs, families, and relationships, employers, coworkers, relatives, friends, and partners have less and less desire to interact with them. These patterns lead to having less sex, which diminishes the desire for sex. The cycle of giving less, receiving less, and wanting less becomes habitual.

If you're caught in the habits of less, you have to do something to put the vitality back into your life.

The Hidden Sexual Potential of Optimism

Some people lost their enthusiasm for life as a natural result of losing their sense of optimism. They have allowed negative life experiences, difficult challenges, rejections, or setbacks to quell their sense of hope in the future. By middle age, the habit of pessimism has begun to take a toll on sexuality.

Optimism goes much deeper than believing the glass is half full. Optimism is characterized by the following:

- Assigning *temporary* causes to *particular events*. A pessimist says, "I can't get an erection; I must be impotent"; an optimist says,

"I can't get an erection because I'm tired and ate and drank too much tonight; I'll try in the morning."

- Being *specific* rather than *global*. A pessimist says, "Jim didn't call after our first date; I'm a loser"; an optimist says, "Jim may not be interested in a relationship with me, but there are plenty of other men."

- Assigning *external* rather than *personal* explanations for things. A pessimist says, "Sue didn't like me"; an optimist says, "Sue may not be ready for a relationship."

Numerous studies show the connection between optimism and achievement. In one study, students who had hope for academic success overcame a bad test score and were able to raise their grade by the end of the term, whereas those who expressed little or no hope after the initial failing grade didn't recover from it. In the business world, people with high hopes set higher goals and continue working toward them when they suffer setbacks. Optimism gives us more than solace when times aren't good; it plays a role in reducing anxiety, alleviating the emotional distress accompanying many life events, and motivating us to achieve personal and professional goals.

The habit of optimism has powerful sexual benefits. If you are pessimistic about the effects of aging on sexuality, you'll likely suffer sexual problems at midlife. On the other hand, if you're optimistic about your continued sexual future, you probably won't have difficulties or will certainly be able to work around them. What you believe is possible (or not possible) often is.

"In the past five years I've been treated for diabetes, mild heart disease, and a prostate problem," says Robert, 65. "Every time I had a medical situation, someone told me that meant the end of my sexual potency. I never believed that; and it never happened. I get erections. My wife and I have intercourse and enjoy that as we do other variations of lovemaking.

"I will never be an impotent man."

Robert is a born optimist. A tendency toward optimism (or pessimism) may well be inborn, but you can develop optimism, too. If you are practicing the steps for leading a counterphobic life given in Chapter 1, you're already on the way to adopting a more optimistic view of life and sexuality.

Five Tips for Making Sex More Playful

Injecting some elements of play into lovemaking, passion's final building block, will help make your new sex foundation sturdier.

- *Don't take your clothes off.* Remember groping, making out, dry humping? Remember being so desperate for your lover's body that you didn't take the time to remove clothing, only pushing aside the necessary items? Start kissing on the sofa and recapture those feelings.

- *Combine food and sex.* Even grown-ups like to play with their food occasionally. Take food to bed with you. Feed each other. Get more creative than that.

- *Paint your bodies.* Use water-soluble finger paints or body paints—some come flavored—to decorate each other's nude body. Paint yourselves to look like the members of some exotic tribe and make love the way you imagine they might.

- *Wear a mask.* Not a rubberized Nixon mask but something light and feathery. Use the feathers to tickle your partner during oral sex.

- *Eroticize your environment.* Create a romantic, erotic bedroom and bathroom. Put poetry and erotic fiction on your night table. Buy leisure clothing and fragrances that arouse you and your partner. Indulge in flowers and other accouterments of gracious, sensual living.

Conquering the Three Emotions That
Sap Sexual Energy

The three emotions that can deplete your sexual energy are anger, guilt, and despair. You've seen how these emotions dampen ardor and squelch passion. You can, however, conquer them by taking the following simple cognitive behavioral steps:

1. *Acknowledge.* On a conscious level, tell yourself the things your unconscious already knows. Anger, guilt, and despair are often stored below the conscious surface, where they can do the most damage. Don't tell yourself, "I'm not angry at my partner for treating me badly, I'm just annoyed." Admit it! You're angry.

2. *Address.* What is behind your feelings of anger, guilt, or despair? Look at your emotions as objectively as possible. What causes the feelings? How long have you had them? What can you do to change them?

3. *Express.* Talk to your partner about your feelings. Don't blame everything on the other person. That will only create a defensive response.

4. *Resolve.* Some issues can be resolved by negotiation with your partner, and some issues are yours alone, like the sex guilt you brought into the relationship. Work on your own issues. Fix what you can and learn to live with the rest.

5. *Release.* Let go of old feelings, old resentments, old arguments. Release them into the atmosphere as if they were helium balloons going up into the sky.

Overcoming Five Fears That Steal Passion

The five fears counteractive to passion are these:

• *Fear of intimacy.* For some people, intimacy is associated with early memories of an overly involved or protective parent. They may subconsciously fear losing their own identity in an intimate relationship as an adult. Rather than risking being overwhelmed by a partner, they protect their vulnerability by shutting down emotionally.

- *Fear of rejection.* Men may fear sexual ridicule, especially at midlife when performance anxieties increase. Women may fear abandonment, again especially at midlife when younger women are perceived as a real threat to the relationship. Ridicule and abandonment are devastating forms of rejection.

- *Fear of performance failure.* Although stronger in men, the fear of performance failure also strikes women. What if she isn't as good in bed as another woman might be? Will she lose him?

- *Fear of hidden (possibly kinky) sexual desires.* At midlife, kinky desires come more readily to the surface, as people come to terms with who they are and what they want. A repressed desire for sexual variation can become an almost unbearable itch at this point. For some, a search for sexual innovation is part of the quest for eliminating boredom.

- *Fear of (unseemly) passion.* Men and women who have subscribed to the sexual myths are sometimes afraid of their own passion. Do they look foolish? Is their behavior inappropriate, even perverse?

You can overcome these fears by relinquishing the sex-negative myths, leading a counterphobic life, and following the cognitive behavioral steps listed in this chapter.

SIZZLER #2

Sex Play

Exciting sex was not on Helen's agenda. Nor on her husband Jim's. Married 30 years, they had recently suffered the deaths of both their mothers, helped one daughter through a difficult divorce, consoled another after a miscarriage, and endured the humiliation of downsizing on their jobs. As Helen said often to friends, they were emotionally tired.

Jim suggested they needed to learn how to laugh again. "If we don't," he said, "we'll turn into miserable old farts nobody wants to invite over for dinner." Helen laughed at that remark, and she had to admit laughing felt good.

It was the week before Halloween so Jim made his usual stop at a discount store to buy candy for the neighborhood children and their grandson. On a whim, he picked up a handful of masks, too, a glittering sequin and feather mask on a stick for Helen; the ubiquitous mustache, nose, and glasses; a rubber monster face; and a Batman mask with accompanying headgear.

"I've always fancied myself the Batman type," he said to Helen when he came in the door wearing that mask.

"I'm more the Marx Brothers type, don't you think?" she teased, pulling the mustache, glasses, and big nose out of the bag and putting it on her face. While preparing dinner together, they played with the masks, inventing dialogue to go with their new identities. Helen vamped when she held the sequin and feathered mask in front of her face. "We should wear these for the trick-or-treaters," she said, and he agreed.

"Why stop at masks?" he said. "Remember how we turned the porch into a Halloween display when the girls were small? Let's do it again. The kids will love it."

They shared a lot of laughter while planning and putting together their Halloween fantasy. Though they had for months and by mutual unspoken consent avoided anything but the kind of brief and occasional sexual contact they'd referred to as "necessary quickies" in happier days, they began touching each other more often, especially when they were laughing together. On a crisp afternoon, Helen watched from inside as Jim created a scarecrow to place on the porch. Bits of straw clung to his sweater and his hair. She was overwhelmed with the desire to pluck them away and went outside to join him. As she pulled the straw from his hair, he looked deeply and tenderly into her eyes. They kissed with their eyes open.

By Halloween night, the front porch was filled with lighted pumpkins and piles of apples. Ghosts and smiling witches hung from the ceiling. The bemused scarecrow and his pal the Tin Man, a masterpiece of aluminum foil and cardboard, stood guard on either side of the steps. Jim wore the Batman mask and headgear with his tuxedo, part Bruce Wayne, part Batman, he explained. Helen, an elegant witch, wore a long black dress and held the silvery mask in front of her face. The living room was softly lit with candles of all shapes and sizes, and a fire blazed in the fireplace. With the light at Helen's back as she answered the door and distributed candy to the little ones, Jim thought she had never been more beautiful. A small boy shyly told her she looked like the beautiful and good witch in *The Wizard of Oz*. The compliment made her glow.

When the lights were out in the pumpkins, they sat side by side on the sofa, sipping red wine and sharing memories of holidays past. They laughed repeatedly at the familiar family stories. Then Helen put down her glass, picked up her mask, and again played the vamp.

"My Wayne," she said in a throaty voice. "I'd love to see your bat cave."

They walked arm in arm to the bedroom. Slowly they undressed each other. They teased each other with their hands and lips and tongues, building up the desire in delicious increments as they hadn't done in a very long time. Erotic requests tumbled from their mouths. "Please kiss my pussy," she begged. "Touch my cock," he whispered. "Put it between your breasts." The words aroused them to greater heights.

Finally, she put her hand on his penis and said, "I want you to fill me up. I want you to take me, own me, possess me now." He felt exactly like Batman when he did.

CHAPTER THREE

Take Charge of Your Sexuality

Imagine a couple lying side by side together in bed after having told each other an hour earlier they were too tired and stressed for sex. She's reading a novel; he's watching an old black-and-white movie on television. An erotic passage in the novel arouses her. If he were paying attention, he would see her nipples briefly stiffen beneath the silk of her nightgown. Like the heroine, she wants to be taken "hungrily" by a man whose "desire cannot be refused." Beside her, he watches the screen intently. A woman in a low-cut gown leans across the table so the man seated opposite can light her cigarette. Her breasts sway seductively forward. Under the sheets, he feels a slight stirring in his penis, a movement that quickly subsides. After a while, she puts her novel on the table, turns out her light and tells him good night. He falls asleep before the movie is over. Sometime in the middle of the night he will awake, reach for the remote control, hit the off switch, go back to sleep.

In a way, both husband and wife are like Sleeping Beauty. Each would like the other to wake him or her from this sexually somnolent state. Maybe they harbor unspoken anger and hold private grudges. Maybe they are simply bored, with themselves and with each other. The flames may have died down, but the fire is still alive, buried inside each of them.

Are you waiting for your partner to rescue you sexually?

Stop waiting. After reading this chapter, you will be able to take charge of your own sexuality and stop hiding behind the stress excuse, the intimacy fear, and/or the need to control. Light your own fire, and your partner will get caught up in the flames. You are about to become an irresistible sexual force.

The Sex and Stress Connection

Stress isn't all bad. Can you envision a life without tension? Americans tend to overreact to every perceived threat to their physical or psychological health, and they make too much of stress. Too much stress or, more likely, an inability to handle a reasonable amount of stress can have a negative effect on libido and sexual performance. Couples who avoid lovemaking opportunities, pleading stress, will find at midlife that they aren't very interested in sex when at last they have the opportunity for the perfect island vacation of their dreams.

The primary sources of stress are money, jobs, the responsibilities of parenthood, household chores, health issues, extended families, and marriages or other intimate relationships. Typically, people respond to stress in both active and passive ways. They may cry; snap at others; exercise; eat; drink; or take time out from the world through reading, going on a nature walk, or playing with a pet. Others seem sanguine in the face of every emergency yet develop health problems such as fatigue, headache, neck or back pain, irritable bowel syndrome, or nausea. Many people let stress get a choke hold on their libido.

Some people function well under stress, and they may consider sex a good outlet for tension. But, although stress can be an energizing factor, motivating one to exercise or tear into that mess in the attic, basement, or garage to relieve tension, it is more likely to have a debilitating effect on sexuality for most of us. During periods of unusual stress, even loving couples with a good sex life probably experience a lack of desire.

"My husband completely lost interest in sex while his construction business was going into bankruptcy," says Sharon. "We didn't make love for six months. At first I was understanding, then irritable, then really worried. I wanted him to see a counselor but he wouldn't. Eventually, he found a job and began putting his entrepreneurial failure behind him, and we had sex again. He didn't tell me until long after the fact that he hadn't wanted to make love to me because he was afraid he wouldn't be able to perform. I wish I'd known that at the time."

A man who is already under great stress may avoid sex because the added pressure of sexual performance may be more than he can handle. His partner feels rejected, and she begins avoiding opportunities for sex, too. They are careful to go to bed at different times, develop headaches or stomachaches late in the evening, or choose the eleventh hour to make long-distance phone calls to chatty relatives or friends on the opposite coast. For other couples under stress, sex seems like another chore, one they can put off until later.

Couples who are too stressed to make love only add to their stress level by the habit of erotic avoidance. They may feel guilty for not making love. Unresolved and perhaps unrecognized sexual tensions begin to mount. Without lovemaking to smooth the rough edges of the relationship, they find each other more irritating and annoying as the days go by. The stress level increases again.

How can you remove the stress from your sex life? Take a look at the following ideas:

- *Never put sexual pressure on a spouse who is under extraordinary stress.* Death of a parent, loss of a job, and other major life traumas almost inevitably take a sexual toll. Be patient and understanding. Offer affection without strings.

- *If sex has become a chore, suspend performance criteria.* Forget intercourse. Don't count orgasms. Agree to touch, stroke, caress, and fondle—with no goal in sight. Touching can be as satisfying as intercourse and will often lead there without the pressure of the goal.

- *Reduce some of the tension in your life.* Do you chronically over-schedule free time? Make too many outside commitments and promises to family and friends? Cut back. Consider relaxing your housekeeping standards or hiring occasional help if you don't already have it. Simplify meal preparation with smarter shopping, easier menus, family participation. Divide household responsibilities equitably among family members.

• *Make it possible for your partner to move toward you but not away from you.* Stressful events can being couples closer together, but stress can also trigger two distancing responses: withdrawal and smothering. The stressed partner may withdraw, leaving the other feeling rejected. Or the partner under stress can feel smothered by the other's solicitousness. Be supportive without something, and don't respond to withdrawal by pulling back yourself.

Seven Sexy Stress Busters

Here are some proven ways to reduce stress:

• *Hit something.* Buy a punching bag. Or a pair of soft bats. Or designate two pillows as your stress removers of choice. Take turns hitting the punching bag or whacking the bed with the pillows. You'll eliminate some of the tension from your body and probably share a laugh at the same time.

• *Practice erotic touching.* Touch your partner everywhere and anywhere except the genitals, from shoulder kneading to full-body massage. Too many couples touch only when they are signaling their intent to have sex.

• *Take regular joy breaks, brief sensual/sexual interludes.* Plan a joy break at least once a week. Don't be inhibited by fear of looking foolish. Joy breaks include a candlelit bubble bath, dancing together in the living room, and having breakfast in bed.

• *Practice deep-breathing exercises.* Get into a comfortable position, perhaps facing each other. Take a deep breath. Let it out slowly. Relax your body. Repeat as necessary. Look for books on meditation for more varied and advanced breathing exercises.

- *Do something physical.* Plan a shared physical activity, such as biking, hiking, or swimming, at least once a week. Exercise is a natural tension reducer.

- *Do something spiritual.* You need not attend organized religious services. For example, some people find a nature walk to be a spiritual experience.

- *Take turns letting each other off the hook.* Everyone needs a day, a night, even 2 hours free of obligations. Give each other regular mini-vacations during which one partner handles all the chores, calls, and family demands.

The Intimacy Fear

You may have noticed this couple sitting at a table in a restaurant. Well-dressed, middle-aged, attractive, the man and woman exchange few words. When they speak, they look *past* each other as often as they look *at* each other. They are together, but they don't connect. Most observers would rightly guess they're married and have been for many years. You've seen them. In fact, you and your partner may be them.

Some couples don't make the transition to a deeper level of lovemaking at midlife because one or both of them are afraid of becoming truly intimate with each other. They are together, but they know how to connect only through the genitals. Without recognizing it, they got stuck at the level of hormonally driven sex and are ready to give up on each other now that the wake of the roiling hormones has subsided. Sexual passion isn't dead between them, but it has to be reached through a different path. If they don't find that path, the couple will have few alternatives: boring sex, no sex, changing partners.

"When Matt and I got married twenty-five years ago, we lived in the hot zone," says Beth, 49. "Passion was everything to us. We sustained a high level of pure physical passion longer than our other married friends did, but gradually things began to change for us, too, around our tenth anniversary. He had the first affair; and then I had one. The excitement generated by the affairs, the tearful confessions and angry recriminations, the dramatic reunions made our relationship hot again, but we couldn't sustain the heat.

"Eventually he did the predictable thing. He left me when I was forty for a woman half his age. Exhausted from being the drama queen, I went into therapy, where I learned we could probably have saved our marriage and our sex life if we'd been vulnerable and open to each other. But we didn't; and I've moved on. My second marriage is different, better. We are more connected to each other on all levels than Matt and I ever were. At almost fifty I'm having the best sex I've ever had—and, in my case, that's saying a lot. This time the sex is deeply emotional."

Passion doesn't always predict pleasure. Beth shared explosive, orgasmic lovemaking in the early years with Matt; but some women, with matching passion and equally avid partners, don't have the orgasms. When we envy the very young, we often forget that women in their 20s are less likely to be orgasmic than older women, that men in their 20s are more likely to have problems with premature ejaculation, that both genders have less erotic sophistication than their elders. Beth, easily orgasmic, was lucky, but even she says the sex is better now, the second time around in a marriage with a man who shares more than his genitals. What does that tell you about the erotic power of intimacy?

Being open with a longtime partner should be easy, but it isn't for many people. Years of squelching their anger, denying their guilt, and suppressing their emotions have left them afraid of being honest. To be honest is to be vulnerable. What if your feelings are rejected? What if your partner harshly judges and withdraws? Emotionally disrobing in front of another person is more frightening than physically disrobing, yet more necessary for great sex at midlife. That kind of intimacy will seem less fearful to you if you learn how to conquer your fears.

Four Ways to Master Midlife Intimacy Fears

- *Comfort yourself.* Don't make your life harder than it needs to be. Rather than waiting for your partner or someone else to notice you need a break, take it. *Comfort* doesn't mean binging on food, drink, or another substance but finding ways of helping yourself feel calmer, quieter, and soothed.

- *Stop taking your partner's behavior personally.* A partner's tension, anger, or sadness may have nothing or little to do with you, and you aren't responsible for solving all of his or her problems. And don't assume your spouse's unhappiness or frustration is signaling, "No lovemaking tonight, dear." Admittedly it's difficult *not* to take a partner's angry, defensive, or sullen behavior as a form of rejection. A good strategy is to try talking the issue out. But, so that you avoid "catching" the negative mood, keep telling yourself: This isn't about me. I didn't cause it, and I'm not responsible for fixing it.

- *Turn off your own negative thoughts that inhibit sexuality.* You may be angry about something that happened at work or unhappy with your body after a weight gain. Such negative thoughts make you too angry or uptight to be loving. Your partner may be more accustomed to making assumptions (reading you, often incorrectly) then to asking questions. He or she may thus interpret your negativity as a keep-away sign rather than a cue to ask, "What's really bothering you?"

- *Use your vulnerability to be a better lover.* At midlife, we may be more comfortable with our own vulnerability and can, therefore, be more understanding of and comfortable with a partner's insecurity and doubt. *Expose* rather than *protect* yourself emotionally. This openness will allow you to touch your partner in a more intimate way.

Let Go of the Need to Control

Before you can take charge of your own sexuality, you have to stop trying to control your partner. Few of us ever do really control our partners' behavior—sexually or otherwise, though we expend a lot of energy in trying. Maybe you think your sex life would improve if your partner took the initiative more often or were more willing to try different positions or make love at the times you would prefer or would wear high heels to bed or brought home flowers.

Let it go. Work on yourself. Your own growth will excite your partner.

The more you become a complete person—instead of half a couple—the less you will need to control your partner.

Try the following methods for letting go:

- *Own your own issues.* Stop blaming your partner for your mistakes, bad behavior, or problems with your family of origin. These are your problems and your issues, and the solutions are yours to find.

- *Don't personalize your partner's anger, need for privacy, or mood swings.* Grant him or her the space to resolve personal issues, too.

- *Stop judging your partner.* And don't accept judgments from your partner either.

- *Don't lecture.* Too many married couples behave like each other's parent, nagging about the chores, the checkbook, work, and personal goals. Is there anything sexy about a nagging parent?

- *Don't insist that your partner change so you can.* Change yourself. Let your partner be.

Ten Tips for Creating an Electric Sexual Atmosphere

You *can* improve the quality of your sexual relationship. Rather than thinking that your lovemaking would be better if only your partner would do something new or different, take positive steps to becoming a better lover yourself.

- *Make time.* Don't wait for your partner to set aside the time. Plan a romantic evening. Ask him or her out on a date.

- *Stay as fit and healthy as possible.* Aren't you more attractive when you do? Don't wait for your partner to join the health club with you. Get started on your own.

- *Be fully present in every erotic encounter.* Banish thoughts of chores, duties, responsibilities, and don't watch the clock. Focus on your sensations and your partner's responses.

- *Communicate your feelings as well as your needs.* Make the difference clear. "I feel…" statements do not mean "I expect…" or "I need…"

- *Give positive feedback, both verbally and in nonverbally.* Compliment appearances. Say thank you for kindnesses and favors. Caress your partner's neck when he or she is tired.

- *Take responsibility for your own pleasure, sexual and otherwise.* A man does not give a woman an orgasm. A woman can't intuit when a man wants to be touched in a different way. Communicate.

- *Don't think of sex as work.* You don't have to live up to the average numbers you read in a magazine survey. Sex is not a chore. Nor is it an athletic event with points for orgasms.

- *Keep a sense of humor, in bed and out.* Laughter has been shown in various studies to promote physical and psychological healing. If you can laugh and can make your partner laugh, nothing will seem all that terrible.

- *Have the courage to explore new areas of being together, to say the things you've been holding back.* Express your fears. Show your vulnerability.

- *Expand your definition of sex beyond intercourse if you haven't already.* I'll discuss some ideas later in the book.

How to Become an Erotic Consumer

"Every now and then a relationship needs a jolt of the new," says Todd, 52, and married to Janey for 30 years. "My wife is game to try a lot of things other women aren't, including white-water rafting, fly-fishing, and going up in a hot-air balloon; but she is more reluctant when the adventure is an erotic one.

"I really wanted her to wear lingerie for me. She kept saying she wasn't that kind of woman. I know she thinks the twenty pounds she's gained over the years make her less appealing to me, but she couldn't be more wrong. I like her body better now. It's softer, rounder, more womanly. I love her dimpled knees, which she can't fathom.

"Then my daughter-in-law gave her a beautiful silk robe for Christmas. She loved the feel of it, and she let me make love to her while she was wearing it. I bought her a set of silk tap pants and camisole to match the robe; and she surprised us both by loving those, too."

If you've never or rarely purchased erotica or sex toys, rented videos, or bought lingerie or other items of sexy clothing for you or your partner, now is the time to become a sophisticated shopper. These items can inject a note of play into lovemaking, introduce new ideas, open the lines of communication, and spark desire. Never mind the budget. Sometimes you can't afford *not* indulging yourself. In the past, some couples may have refrained from visiting the X-rated section of the video store or the sex-toy shop because it was nearly impossible to find quality among the schlock. Many of the toys, like foot-long dildoes and edible panties, were of the gag-gift variety. In addition, most of the video material was designed for male arousal, not female, and much of it was crudely produced.

Bookstores and video stores now have an unprecedented selection of erotica written by and for women, including the most highbrow and hard-core material available. Videos in both the entertainment and sex-instruction categories are increasingly produced by women and marketed to both women and couples. Sex-toy shops have gone upscale, selling everything from expensive body oils and creams to pasta in the shape of penises. You can even find elegant corsets; leather whips; and gold and silver jewelry meant to be worn in pierced nipples, belly buttons, and genitals.

What if your partner balks at the introduction of videos or sex toys into the bedroom?

- Start with erotic reading material. Erotic thrillers available in paperback include *In the Cut* by Susannah Moore, *Topping from Below* by Laura Reese, and *Suspension* by Robert Westfield. Amazon.com or the Literary Guild always has a selection of erotic books if you don't feel comfortable buying them at the mall. Take turns reading a chapter a night to each other in bed.

• Rent sexy films that you may not have seen in the theater, such as *Original Sin* with Angelina Jolie and Antonio Banderas, *Unfaithful* with Diane Lane, and *Uncovered* with Kate Beckinsale. Check out video guides for other ideas.

• Don't pressure him or her into watching a video or trying a vibrator. Ask. Suggest. If the answer is no, say, "Okay, but I'm going to enjoy this myself." Don't accuse your partner of being a sexual prude.

• But don't be deterred from pursuing your own independent pleasures.

• If a reluctant woman consents to watch a video, choose one aimed at couples, with a more romantic story line such as those produced by Candida Royalle's Femme Productions. Don't rave about the actresses' bodies. Many women compare their own bodies to those on-screen and feel inferior.

• If a reluctant man agrees to vibrator play, treat the toy as an adjunct to, not a replacement for, his penis. See page 63 for suggestions on how you can give each other pleasure with a vibrator.

• Buy lingerie cut to fit and flatter her figure. And don't forget him. Buy some silk boxer shorts or, if he is trim and fit, perhaps a silk bikini or g-string.

• Leave catalogs from the following good sex-toy stores on the night-stand—and then order them from Good Vibrations or Adam & Eve (for more information, see page 320). The ubiquitous Victoria's Secret lingerie catalogs are also a good source for gifts and inspiration.

Develop Your Own Erotic Lesson Plan

"My husband is always working on perfecting his golf swing," a woman complained, "but he hasn't changed his lovemaking style in twenty-eight years."

Her husband needs to apply the principles of the counterphobic life to his sexual technique. Yes, technique does matter. Anyone who says it doesn't probably needs a few erotic lessons. No amount of loving, caring, and sharing will bring a woman to orgasm unless either she or her partner makes sure she gets adequate clitoral stimulation.

Sex education is not just for the young. Lack of knowledge is a contributing factor to sexual boredom in midlife couples. Many are unaware of how the physiological changes associated with aging can be used to their advantage in lovemaking. They continue to have sex in the same old way they've been having it for years and wonder why they're bored.

Why shouldn't we apply the same creativity to our sex life as we do to other pursuits? Think about the way you make love now and then imagine how you would like to make love. What did you see in the fantasy? Is there any reason it can't be made real?

In later chapters, you'll learn some new techniques for cunnilingus and fellatio, ways to adapt the standard intercourse positions to changing bodies, and many other things. For now, develop your own lovemaking goals. Know what you want: This book can take you there. Here are suggestions for developing your lesson plan:

- *Make it personal.* This is not a list of suggested changes for your lover to make to please you. What can you do to increase your own pleasure and your mate's?

- *Be aware of the physiological realities associated with aging, but don't be unnecessarily limited by them.* You can't learn to have the erections you had at 19, but you can learn to make better use of the erections you do have.

- *Be specific.* Rather than "I want to perform cunnilingus better," say, "I want to learn new ways of using my tongue, lips, teeth, and the tip of my nose to increase her arousal, prolong her excitation phase, and induce a stronger orgasm."

- *Look beyond the genitals.* Remember there is more to lovemaking than intercourse, genital play, or even orgasm.

- *Build on your strengths.* If you're a great kisser, you can be equally adept at oral sex. And if you give a wonderful back rub, you can learn to bring your partner greater pleasure through manual stimulation.

- *Take your partner's needs and desires into consideration.* What would constitute his or her idea of better lovemaking? If your partner has desires you've never explored, can you learn how to do that comfortably and safely now?

- *Expand your erotic horizons.* What have you been afraid or ashamed to try—and why? In later chapters, you will learn the facts about anal sex, bondage, spanking, and light S&M, and you may decide they are worth trying as an occasional alternative.

Try making a to-learn list that includes at least a couple and maybe as many as ten objectives. Items in the list can be as simple as learning how to give an erotic back rub or perfecting the art of the whispered endearment. Either will likely create sexual excitement in a long-term relationship, if for no other reason than that it introduces the element of surprise.

The Take-Charge Lover

Jessica prided herself on being a sensitive woman. At 55 years old and 10 years into her second marriage to a slightly younger man after being widowed, she had grown accustomed to responding to the emotional needs of her husband Brian, her grown son and daughter, granddaughters, stepchildren, and even other relatives and close friends before they had to articulate those needs. Especially now that she was retired from her university teaching position—an early retirement ostensibly taken for the purpose of writing the book she was letting languish largely in her mind—Jessica felt, then endlessly analyzed her feelings and those she projected on others before acting. She was, in fact, becoming sexually paralyzed by her own sensitivity.

"We don't make love very often," she told her best friend. "When we do, it's routine, tepid. Brian is so tense around me. I know he's unhappy about some aspect of our relationship, but I don't know what it is. When I ask him to talk, he says there's nothing to talk about. Everything is fine."

"Maybe it is," her friend responded. "There's more to his life than your relationship. Maybe he is worried about his job or turning fifty or any number of things."

"Then why won't he share his concerns with me? And why doesn't he want to make love very often anymore?"

"Because you put everything in the context of 'you'?" her friend posited, stunning Jessica with what she perceived was criticism.

That blow was followed by her daughter's advice: "Stop overanalyzing everyone, stop living through others, and"—harshest of all—"stop believing 'sensitivity' makes you better than the rest of us." Hurt, Jessica retreated into her own work. She didn't initiate sex, but waited for Brian to take charge. He didn't. Feeling better about herself now that she was working again, she began to feel dissatisfied with her sex life, not because unsatisfying marital sex might reflect on her inability to meet his emotional needs but because her own sexual needs weren't being met.

She wanted more sex. How was she going to get it? Obviously, demanding an explanation for his lack of interest wasn't the answer.

First, she became more affectionate with Brian. She took his hand when they walked; rubbed his shoulders or neck when they watched television together, occasionally leaned her head against his shoulder at a movie, while seated side by side on a restaurant banquette, or riding together in a cab. Her easy affection seemed to relax him.

One night she shyly asked him if he would masturbate her to orgasm. At first he seemed uncomfortable with the request, but he did comply. After bringing her to several shuddering orgasms, he was clearly aroused. She kissed him and, offering her profuse gratitude, fell asleep in his arms. The next morning she woke early to the delicious feeling of Brian's erection moving rhythmically against her buttocks.

"Are you awake?" he whispered.

"Umm," she replied, moving her body against his, in tune with his urgency.

His hands massaged her breasts, her clitoris. She angled her hips, to make his entry easier. Shortly after he penetrated her, she began coming. After his own orgasm, he clung to her, their sweaty bodies bonded together.

"You're so hot these days," he whispered appreciatively in her ear.

Later that morning she left a message on his voice mail telling him how much she'd enjoyed their time together. That afternoon she received flowers, a dozen yellow roses, her favorite. Brian followed that by calling to make a dinner date with her.

They made love again that night. For several days afterward, Jessica felt like a woman embarking on a second—no, third—honeymoon. After their passion was reestablished, Brian confided in her about some problems he'd been having with one of his major clients. Her best friend and her daughter had been right: Her "sensitivity" had been perceived by her husband as a suffocating demand for attention on her part. When she got involved in her own life again and went after her own sexual satisfaction without trying to understand his reasons for withdrawal, she turned him on.

"I can't believe how much you turn me on these days," he told her. "You've changed."

She smiled enigmatically and put his hand on her crotch.

CHAPTER FOUR

Games for Mature Lovers

"Several years ago, I realized my lovemaking wasn't having the same effect on David anymore," says Elizabeth. A professional couple in their 50s, the two have been married for 20 years, the second marriage for both. "I thought he was tired of me, maybe there was another woman. After 50, a woman thinks everything that goes wrong can be blamed on her sagging breasts. I stopped initiating sex. When he suggested making love, I agreed, but I was holding back. I felt tentative, insecure. I couldn't let go."

"I knew she was holding back, but I didn't understand why," David says, taking up their story. "Finally I just asked her. I'd learned from going through one divorce that it's better to ask what's wrong before you inadvertently make it worse by stumbling around in the dark, pretending there are no obstructions in the path."

Elizabeth told him she knew she wasn't turning him on anymore. He vehemently denied that was true. "If I excite you, why does it take you so long to get an erection?" she demanded. "It didn't before." David gave her a lesson in the facts of midlife.

"My rhythm has changed," he says, "and I like the change. Now that she understands and has adapted to the slower pace of my arousal, she likes it better. I respond more slowly but more fully than I did."

Reading Your Partner's Sexual Rhythms

As previously noted, some normal changes in arousal and sexual performance patterns are associated with aging in both men and women.
Things are different now; they aren't worse, just *different*. These changes
don't lead to a loss of pleasure, unless a couple misreads and misunder-
stands them. In some ways, a man and a woman who have been together
for many years need to get sexually reacquainted at midlife. If she continues to treat his penis like a gun that might go off at any minute while he
holds on to the innocent belief that she always prefers cuddling to intercourse, they aren't reading each other's rhythms.

After age 40, a man probably does not get an immediate, strong erection, and the intensity of his need to ejaculate may diminish. Some men
may no longer need to ejaculate every time they have sex. (In a later chapter, I introduce men who describe how they can have orgasms without
ejaculating.) Most men report their need for both affection and more
prolonged caressing during lovemaking increases. A woman's sexual
response cycle speeds up as a man's slows down. One of the hurdles standing between this couple and great sex is simple misinformation. Once a
woman understands that her partner's slower arousal patterns are not a
negative reflection on her lovemaking skills or desirability, she can relax.
And once a man understands that his partner can be more easily aroused
and satisfied than she was in the past, he can relax, too.

"This is really the best time in our sex lives," Elizabeth says, "because
I don't have to worry that he will ejaculate while I'm performing fellatio
or come too soon after we begin having intercourse. Sex has a more luxurious feel now. I can give him blow jobs like I never could before. I never
feel rushed to have my own orgasm. There is time for everything."

How to Flirt Shamelessly with Your Mate

At midlife the tempo of the seduction dance changes, too. Take advantage of the new beat by putting more energy into the pre-arousal phase of
lovemaking. Too many married couples in every age group skip this part

altogether. They think it's enough to kiss or cuddle briefly before sliding a hand suggestively down the other's body or even to ask with no erotic preliminaries, "Do you want to?"

Consciously flirt with your mate whether you have the opportunity for sexual activity or not. Flirting is really nothing more than letting the other know she or he is attractive and appreciated, with no demands or expectations implied. It keeps the spark alive. If you've forgotten how, here are the four elements of flirting for lovers:

- *Eye contact.* How often do you look into each other's eyes while talking? Hold a gaze longer than a nanosecond? Seek your lover's eyes; and lower your voice a bit as you hold them. The gaze need not be soulful or studiedly romantic. Let your eyes convey warmth, amusement, and a hint of erotic availability.

- *Body language.* Don't sit across from each other at a table or beside each other on the sofa with arms and legs protectively crossed. Use open inviting body language.

- *Light verbal bantering, with sexual innuendo.* In a gently suggestive tone, praise your mate's physical appearance. Be witty if you can. Tease, but don't criticize in the guise of teasing.

- *Touch.* Use sparingly, like spice in food. Touch your lover's hand or arm to emphasize a point while speaking. Run a finger down his or her cheek, stroke your thumb across a hand, brush a leg under the table with your foot.

How to Behave Like a Teenager in Lust

Young lovers and for that matter lovers of any age who face repeated and/or prolonged separations know the joys of delaying intercourse and even orgasm. When preserving virginity or waiting until a suitable period of courtship had passed were the conditions under which most of us chafed, we played arousing, teasing love games. Such play can work for you and your partner now. Agree to a moratorium on penetration for a while.

Ratchet up the sexual tension over a period of days or weeks. Intercourse will seem like a holiday.

Three games teenagers play—and we played when *we* were teenagers—are petting, dry humping, and outercourse, all of which stop short of the act. Why not briefly return to the glory days of youth? Tell your mate you've been revirginized and won't go all the way.

- *Petting.* The object of the game for the boy was to get his hands inside her bra and panties. For the girl, it was holding the elastic line. Tongues in mouths are more than acceptable. They're mandatory. He touches her a lot more than she touches him. Get in an upright seated position. Start with a clench.

- *Dry humping.* He's lying flat-out on top of her in the backseat of the car, her parents' sofa, the floor (preferably carpeted), or she's lying on top of him. They move together simulating intercourse. If she has an orgasm from the friction, he's a stud. But if he comes inside his jeans, they're both a little embarrassed. He should stop the rocking motion when he feels ejaculation is imminent and substitute the flat of his hand pressing against her vulva.

- *Outercourse.* Clothes may be loosened and pants pulled down in the heat of the moment, but the underwear stays on. He rubs her clitoris through her panties. She may take his penis in her hand if it spontaneously falls out the slit in his shorts or briefs. He may continue rubbing her until she has an orgasm. If she masturbates him to orgasm or allows him to come on her stomach, she loves him.

Be a Tease

There is simply not enough play in sexplay. By midlife, the average couple has become far too serious about sex. Teasing is something they, particularly she, might have done to one another a very long time ago. Now teasing is what they tell each other not to do to the dog or the grandchildren.

Stop being so forthright about sex. Tease your partner. Torment eventually gives way to delight. You do remember delight, don't you?

Here are some teasing games to get you started:

- *The feather tease.* Chinese courtesans once used peacock feathers to tease their titled lovers. You can use any feather—peacock, ostrich, the ones attached to gift-shop pens. Tickle and caress your partner's genitals with the feather. A silk scarf can be used in the same way. Experiment with other fabrics or soft household items, such as those dishwashing implements made of soft fingers or a sponge on a handle.

- *The visual tease.* You're dressed, running 10 minutes late, hurrying out the door. Your partner is still getting dressed or lingering over breakfast. On your way out, flash him or her. Yes, flash. Quickly expose a breast, hike a shirt to show an inner thigh, unzip and let the penis show. When you want to make love, use visual-seduction techniques. Put a little jiggle in your walk. Stretch out your silk-stocking-encased legs. Let her watch as you slowly unbutton your shirt. Show what you like about your body and *then* dim the lights.

- *The verbal tease.* Make promises you aren't going to keep—yet. Tell him what you're going to do with his penis. Then make him wait until next time. Tell her exactly how you're going to make her come, and then make her ask for it in very specific terms.

- *The breast tease.* Men love women's breasts. For many men, making love to a woman's breasts is a fantasy they'd like to make come true. If you're unhappy with your breasts, buy a sexy push-up bra and leave it on. Take his penis between your breasts and let him have intercourse with your cleavage.

- *The penis tease.* Use the end of your penis to tease her nipples, inner thighs, clitoris, labia. The silky texture of the head makes the penis more effective than a rose petal at stroking and stimulating sensitive places. *A bonus:* Stimulation works both ways. Your penis may get harder than it normally does when you use it as a teasing device.

Improving Her Oral Lovemaking Skills

"Like a lot of baby boomer women, I learned how to perform fellatio by practicing on a green banana with a copy of *The Sensuous Woman* by J in one hand," says Delia, 48. That book, first published in 1969 and reissued many times since, was outrageously bold in its day. "The author made fellatio sound like fun, not an onerous marital duty or a sin, and I took enthusiastically to instruction."

When Delia got married a few years later, her husband, Andy, was delighted with her oral skills. Now, she says, he gently pushes her head away when she tries to perform oral sex on him. She doesn't understand what's wrong. How could a technique he once considered perfect suddenly not work? Andy's response pattern has changed. Though he enjoys receiving oral sex as much as he ever did, he doesn't get an erection as soon as she takes him into her mouth when he's flaccid. He probably doesn't want to disappoint her if it takes him too long to achieve an erection.

By adapting your fellatio technique, you may be able to bring your partner to erection more quickly or help him get a harder erection than he has been getting lately. But it isn't necessary to perform fellatio endlessly. If your jaw gets tired, alternate oral with manual stimulation.

The New Basic Fellatio Technique
Follow these steps for better oral sex:

1. Spend more time kissing, licking, sucking, and caressing his inner thighs than you did in the past.

2. Put his balls carefully in your mouth. Pull down gently with your mouth. With your thumb, massage his perineum (the area between the anus and the base of the scrotum) lightly.

3. Either with his balls still in your mouth or not, depending on what is comfortable for you, lovingly stroke his penis from the head down to the base of the shaft. The downward stroke is more

arousing to most men than stroking up the shaft. Spend more time stroking than you did in the past. While stroking, again lick, kiss, and suck his inner thighs.

4. Get into the most comfortable position, which might be the basic penis/mouth (P/M) position: the man lying on his back, the woman kneeling at his side at a right angle to his body. Take his penis gently in the palm of your hand and run your tongue around the head to moisten it.

5. Circle the head of the penis with your tongue, then work your tongue down the shaft, licking lightly with the tip. Repeat the stroke while massaging his testicles, gently pulling them downward. Alternate the testicle massage with a perineum massage (see page 61). Do not be concerned if he doesn't become erect.

6. Follow the ridge of the corona, the ridge surrounding the base of the head and the most sensitive area of a man's penis, with your tongue while massaging the shaft with both hands, the penis sandwiched between them. Keep the fingers together. Use the palm of one hand and the backs of the opposite fingers to create a rolling pressure, a slightly firmer pressure than you used on him in the past.

7. Wet your lips and stretch your mouth to cover your teeth, forming a ridge on top and bottom. Grasping the penis firmly in both hands, repeatedly move your mouth down toward your hand at the base of the penis and back up to the head, varying the speed.

8. When your mouth is tired, vary the routine by repeating steps 5 and 6. Keep a firm grip on the penis at all times.

Fellatio Variations

THE DEEP SUCK: Some men say their erections grow stronger with the deep suck. Gradually suck into your mouth the full length of his penis—the slower the better. Move your tongue around the shaft as you're sucking in. Once he is all the way in, pull in the sides of your cheeks to create suction. Relax the back of your throat. Give the penis several hard sucks. Open your mouth to release the suction. When you close your mouth, pull in the sides of your cheeks again before sucking.

If you can, tease the corona with your tongue while you're sucking. With practice, you may be able to lick the corona down the shaft. To stop the gag reflex, swallow frequently. Also, it may help to keep your tongue flat against his penis.

The famed deep throat is nothing more than the deepest suck. Linda Lovelace's trick in the X-rated film of the same name was to position her head so that her mouth and throat formed one long continuous passage, easiest done by fellating him while you're flat on your back with your shoulders at the edge of the bed and head thrown back. Experiment to find the right angle for you. Here's another position that works: Straddle him and kneel over his penis, facing his feet. Your throat and mouth will be at the right angle to accommodate his entire penis.

FLICK AND SWIRL

- *The butterfly flick.* Flick your tongue back and forth lightly and rapidly across the delicate corona. After several flicks, run your tongue from the base to head, then flick it up and down the same path, before resuming your ministrations to the corona.

- *The silken swirl.* Continually circle the penis with your tongue while sliding it in and out of your mouth. Combine with the butterfly flick.

THE JADE FLUTE

- For the jade flute, hold his penis firmly at the base in one hand. Hold the head in your mouth. Purse your mouth into a slight O and suck the head while playing up and down the shaft with your finger pads.

- *Some general hints:* Don't use your teeth. Remember that you can and should devote more time to fellatio than you did in the past. Concentrate most of your attention on the top third of the penis, which is the most sensitive part. The head and coronal ridge are the most responsive areas of the penis; on the shaft, the raphe, the seam running down the underside of the penis, is the only very sensitive part.

Improving His Oral Lovemaking Skills

"When we got married twenty-seven years ago, we were very much in love, but our sex life was disappointing to both of us," says Roger, 51. "I had a problem with premature ejaculation. Foreplay was quick and not inventive. Anita rarely had an orgasm. We had a family before we knew how to give each other pleasure, which is a little sad.

"We didn't discover oral sex until we'd been married for ten years. Her sister gave us a copy of *The Joy of Sex* as an anniversary gift. It was a revelation. I immediately loved performing cunnilingus. Anita was reluctant at first, but after her first orgasm this way she was a convert. When she started going through the perimenopausal phase, she would sometimes pull away when I started to go down on her or take my head away before I'd hardly begun. I read some of her menopause books and guessed she had concerns about losing her sex appeal after menopause.

"I was wrong. She was more sensitive than she'd ever been and was embarrassed by that. I find it an amazing, delightful turn of events. I can give her multiple orgasms via cunnilingus now. She goes higher than she ever has. It's incredible."

Sex surveys done in the past 25 years show increasing numbers of couples engaging in oral sex, with the rise in cunnilingus particularly marked. One of the most popular sex books, a manual for men on orally pleasuring a woman, is *She Comes First* by Ian Kerner. Sales of Kerner's book are testimony that, like Roger, men are pleased to learn that they can be more confident of giving a woman an orgasm via cunnilingus than by any other route.

At midlife, being a gentleman is easier than it was. If a woman felt some embarrassment about receiving cunnilingus, she, having been liberated from youthful hang-ups, may be embarrassed no longer. With erotic senses heightened, she may have an orgasm after minimal oral contact, allowing her partner to practice more sophisticated patterns of stimulation to tease her to the brink and bring her back repeatedly. For the first time, she may be able to have multiple orgasms.

The New Cunnilingus Technique
Now for the guy's turn to practice better oral sex:

1. Stroke, massage, nibble, suck, kiss, lick, and otherwise tease her body, avoiding the genital area until she is fully aroused. Pay special attention to her breasts and inner thighs. Massage her aureole with flat open palms, then play with the nipples as you kiss slowly down to her navel. Lick her inner thighs. As you are licking one side, use the finger pads of one hand to spider walk, up and down the opposite inner thigh.

2. Caress her perineum as you use your fingers to part her outer vaginal lips, making her clitoris accessible. Lick and suck the area surrounding the clitoris. Some women at midlife reach orgasm after initial licking and sucking of this area.

3. Cover her venus mons, the point where the clitoris begins, with your mouth. Suck, using *gentle* pressure. Some women enjoy having this area nibbled lightly, which is nothing more than letting your teeth touch the flesh, then pulling back, touching again and pulling back. No biting. Other women find this too much pressure. Remember that she may like more pressure, or less, than she did in the past. Vary your technique and gauge her response.

4. If her clitoris is well back inside the clitoral hood, exert minimal pressure with your fingers along the side of the hood to lift and expose the clitoris.

5. Indirectly stimulate her clitoris by putting your lips around the sides. Hold them in a pursed position as you suck. Alternate the sucking with licking of the sides of the clitoris and surrounding tissues. Her clitoris may be so exquisitely sensitive now that she won't be able to tolerate direct stimulation—or, on the other hand, will

be highly orgasmic this way. Pay attention to her as if she were a new partner whose responses can surprise you.

6. When she is nearing orgasm, you can vary the sensation by covering the clitoral area with your mouth. Suck around the sides of the clitoris. Stimulate her labia with your hands or stroke her inner thighs or tease her nipples or alternate those stimuli.

7. Try gently inserting a finger into her anus during cunnilingus. (Be careful not to put that finger into her vagina later.) Or stimulate her perineum.

How to Give Your Partner Manual Pleasure

Don't focus exclusively on the genitals. Touching that isn't programmed to lead directly to intercourse is often neglected in relationships. Couples use touch sparingly when they aren't stroking to arousal. Yet the need to touch and be touched varies in intensity from person to person and within the same person at different ages and stages of life. For many people at midlife, touch becomes increasingly important.

"The skin is one continuous erogenous zone," says John, 61, a retired movie-set designer living in California with his third wife, Juanita. "I didn't appreciate that until I took a workshop in erotic massage to surprise her on our twentieth anniversary last year. She was really surprised. First we got into the hot tub together. Then after serving her champagne and strawberries, I oiled my hands and began massaging her from head to toe. I started by gently kneading the base of her neck, then making long gliding strokes down her body to her buttocks, which I caressed.

"Combining the basic strokes the instructor taught us and adding a few fancy erotic techniques I picked up from one of the books on the recommended reading list, I gave her an experience she was begging me to repeat in a few days. Sometimes we make love afterward and sometimes I masturbate her to an orgasm. I enjoy giving her pleasure this way at least as much as she does receiving it."

In our haste to reach the genitals, we forget that our entire bodies have erotic potential. Before moving on to erotic massage, you and your partner might benefit from going back to square one. In the initial stages of sex therapy, couples are instructed not to have intercourse. Instead they are given homework assignments, series of pleasurable sensuous interactions called *sensate focus* or *nondemand exercises*. The acts are not demanding because they are not expected to lead to intercourse. Derived from the more varied and subtle arousal techniques taught by Asian sexologists hundreds of years ago, sensate focus is a good first-touch step.

Here is a variation on the basic technique: One partner lies belly down. The other uses the hands and lips to kiss, caress, and stroke the skin. Each concentrates on the feeling of touch and nothing else. The partner being stroked can ask for a change in pressure or speed.

The Erotic Massage

Unlike the typical invigorating massage that can sometimes include the painful kneading of knotted muscles, an erotic massage, focused on skin not muscle, is softer and the pace more languid. Use small amounts of lightly scented oil, warming the oil in the hands before rubbing into skin. Combine the following strokes in a pattern pleasing to your partner:

- *Glide.* Run your hands smoothly in long strokes that blend seamlessly together. Best for large areas of the body, such as the back, thighs, and legs.

- *Kneading.* Be careful not to be too vigorous and use sparingly. You are trying to arouse, not loosen tight muscles. Most effective on the buttocks.

- *Spider legs.* A highly arousing touch. Use the pads of your fingers as if they were spider legs wandering up and down your lover's body. Keep it very light and teasing.

- *Single-finger stroke.* Most effective on delicate areas such as eyelids and ears. Also thrilling on the throat. Simply run one finger very lightly along the skin.

- *Walk of love.* Walk your fingers around your lover's body. This touch is most exciting when you move from one erogenous zone to the other. Move more slowly and apply more pressure than in spider legs.

- *Love bites, pinches, and slaps.* An occasional bite, pinch, slap, or squeeze—*always* done lightly in the spirit of play—intensifies the arousal for some people. Slaps are particularly effective on the buttocks because they bring the blood closer to the surface, making the flesh more sensitive to the touch. Some men and women enjoy having their nipples teased by love bites or pinches—and some *hate* it.

- *Nipple stroke.* Use the palm of your hand to brush lightly over nipples, his as well as hers. Gently rub the nipples between your fingers. Blowing over the nipples after they've been wetted with saliva creates a pleasant tingling sensation.

- *Breast stroke.* Women can use their breasts on any part of the male anatomy. Press your breasts against him. Use the nipples to tease with light touches. Hold your nipples against his. Or take your nipples in hand and rub the tips against the tips of his.

Manually Stimulating the Male Genitals

1. Lightly stroke the perineum with fingertips.

2. Move your fingers to the back, bottom, and front of the scrotum in a quick, almost tickling fashion. Then cover the same ground in soft caressing touches. Alternate tickles and caresses.

3. Fondle his testicles tenderly.

4. Grip his penis with palms and fingers firmly near the tip and move your grasp smoothly down the shaft toward the base. Use the fingertips of the other hand to stimulate the head. Firmness of touch is the critical factor. Don't be too gentle.

5. Run a fingertip along the underside of the erect penis, outlining the head and the corona.

6. Lightly pump the shaft up and down while caressing the head.

The Perineum Massage

Some older men, or men who have become adept at holding back their ejaculation, may have prolonged intercourse to the point at which ejaculation is difficult. For many of them, the perineum massage induces orgasm. Try it, and don't be dismayed if it doesn't have the desired effect. Male response varies widely.

With the flat of your hand or your thumb, massage the perineum while continuing intercourse, manual stimulation, or fellatio. The key lies solely in the force of your pressure. Exert firm, but not harsh, pressure as you massage.

Manually Stimulating the Female Genitals

1. After using the glide on her thighs, stroke her labia using the single-finger stroke.

2. Lightly stroke above, below, and at the sides of the clitoris.

3. As she becomes aroused, use a soft vibrating side-to-side motion, which is achieved by placing finger pads on either side of the clitoris, touching gently, and vibrating the finger pads.

4. Alternate the sensation by moving finger pads farther apart and/or vibrating more quickly or more slowly.

5. Place one thumb lightly at the root of her clitoris and stroke her labia or inner thighs with the other hand.

The G-Spot Massage

Some women claim they don't have a G spot, can't find it, or have found the supposedly miracle place to be just another cluster of cells, not an erotic hot spot. Others swear they have wonderful orgasms if it's manipulated properly. The G spot, named for German gynecologist Ernst Grafenbert, who rediscovered it in the 1940s, was known to the authors of the *Kama Sutra*, who reported that stimulating the area produced a pleasurable response.

Locate the spot by inserting your index finger into her vagina, the back of the finger against the wall near her back. Move your finger in a tickling or "come-here" gesture. The rough patch of skin—which may be somewhat spongier than the surrounding tissue—is the G spot. The size and shape of a small bean, it is located about 2 inches inside the vaginal opening on the front wall of the vagina, the side toward the belly button. Massage the G spot in a smooth, rhythmic motion.

Bear in mind, every woman's body is different. Some women enjoy G-spot stimulation whereas others don't. Rather than get caught up in G-spot response issues, focus on how you treat each other when you are not having sex, because that will affect your level of satisfaction far more than G-spot exploration.

The Joy of Mutual Masturbation

"Ryan wasn't in the mood for sex one night, so I asked him if he would mind if I masturbated in bed," Jessica says. She and Ryan, both in their 40s, have been lovers for 7 years. "He feigned nonchalance, but I could tell he was titillated. I'd wanted to do this for years, but I was afraid I'd look funny or be too self-conscious to have an orgasm while he was watching me. Suddenly my inhibitions were gone. I wanted to show off. I was confident of my ability to have an orgasm any time I wanted one.

"I sat up with my back against the headboard, my legs open, bent up at the knees. First I massaged my nipples, slowly, slowly, with the flats of my hands. I took each nipple between my fingers and twisted gently, then massaged with the fingers. Moving my hands down toward my genitals at a leisurely pace, I caressed my body. By the time I parted my lips and placed two fingers in a V position alongside my clitoris, Ryan was watching me with glazed eyes.

" 'Touch your penis,' I told him, and he obeyed me in an erotic trance. We masturbated to climax, watching each other, watching ourselves, catching glimpses in the dresser mirror. It was an intensely erotic experience that energized us for days afterward."

Many women, particularly when young, find the idea of masturbating in front of their partner unappealing or intimidating. They think masturbation *should* be private or that couples *shouldn't* masturbate at all. Many men, no matter their age, rate watching a woman masturbate at the top of their sex-wish list. Fortunately, at midlife more women are willing to experiment with this very private form of exhibitionism. In this—as in so many other ways—the genders come together.

Why mutual masturbation?

- Watching each other fondle the genitals from a slight distance is a unique, intensely arousing experience.

- Each partner's excitement feeds the other's, creating a higher level of arousal than either would experience masturbating alone.

- The gift of masturbation increases intimacy between partners.

- It allows both partners to explore their own bodies at their own pace while being stimulated by their lover's presence.

- There's no clearer way to show a partner how you would like to be touched. If your needs have changed and your partner's lovemaking hasn't, give a little show rather than a talk.

- And it's the safest sex if you're having an affair, becoming intimate with a new partner, or if one or both is recuperating from an illness or surgery that makes other forms of lovemaking more problematic.

Five Top Vibrator Tips

For more variety, introduce a vibrator, first by using it on yourself during mutual masturbation and gradually adding it to the occasional lovemaking session.

- Most women reach orgasm with a vibrator by pressing it against the clitoris, not through vaginal insertion. Experiment by varying the pressure and speed. If the vibration is too intense for direct contact even at low speed, move it to the side of the clitoris or wear silky panties.

- Men can enjoy vibrator play, too. Start on low speed. Run the vibrator along the shaft, then press it against the base, the scrotum, and the perineum. Experiment with higher speeds and firmer pressures.

- First use the vibrator to massage your partner's body. Use it on the back, arms, legs, neck. Move slowly to the genitals, just as you would if you were using your hands in a full-body massage. Take turns massaging each other.

- A man can combine penetration and vibrator use during intercourse. Hold the vibrator on her clitoris while slowly thrusting into her vagina with your penis. He can also use the vibrator while manually stimulating her. Hold it against the back of his hand as he strokes her labia and the sides of her clitoris.

- A woman can use the vibrator to vary stimulation while caressing her partner's genitals in manual loveplay. Hold a vibrator against the back of her hand that is cupping his scrotum or holding his penis.

SIZZLER #4

The Love Game

When they were young newlyweds almost 40 years ago, Cal and Maggie made up for what they lacked in sophistication, experience, and erotic expertise with boundless enthusiasm and passion. Now they overcome the erotic lethargy that can accompany long-term relationships by using the sexual skills they've developed together. Sometimes they make love, Maggie says, and other times they play sex games.

"The intensity and purity of sexual passion in youth is a beautiful thing," Maggie says. "But we have idealized that phase of lovemaking in this culture. There are other beautiful things. Cal and I have become consummate sexual-game players. Sometimes lovemaking is about a tender union of souls. Sometimes it's not. We use props and costumes, play roles, and experiment with the occasional sexual variation, such as spanking and bondage."

A favorite game is the pick-up. They arrange to meet at a bar and agree that they will pretend not to know each other. The partner who arrives second has to play the pick-up artist. The last time they played, Cal was waiting in a lobby lounge in an expensive Chicago hotel. The ambiance was elegant. A long, highly polished mahogany bar was flanked by a mirrored and richly carved back bar. The drinks were expensive. The clientele looked well off. When Maggie took the bar stool one over from Cal's, he pretended to ignore her, affecting the expression of world-weary ennui worn so well by the rich and celebrated.

Though she doesn't smoke, Maggie pulled a cigarette from her tiny handbag. She pretended to search for a light before turning to Cal and murmuring, "I can't find a match. Do you have one?"

"No one smokes anymore," he replied, half turning away from her.

In response, Maggie made a half turn toward him. She uncrossed and recrossed her still fabulous legs. And she simply looked at him with a bemused expression on her face until he couldn't resist looking back at her.

"I was quite sure you were aware of me," she said, pitching her voice seductively low.

"It would be hard to miss those legs," he said.

"Are you a leg man?" Maggie asked. She put a manicured hand on one knee and slowly moved it up her thigh, exposing a little more leg encased in sheer black stocking as she did. Lowering her head and raising her eyes, she looked at him from beneath the broad brim of a stylish black hat.

"I can be," Cal said, deliberately not meeting her eyes, but keeping his gaze on her leg.

"I'll bet you can," she said. "Are you staying in Chicago long?"

"I live here," he said, turning to face her now, his leg brushing hers. "And you?"

"I'm here only to collect an inheritance," she said. "My lover died."

He raised his eyebrow and grinned. That was a new one. He put his hand on top of hers, the hand that was still resting on her thigh.

"Let me buy you a drink," he said, and she knew she had him.

An hour later, they were groping each other passionately in his car, which was parked in the hotel garage. They were going to "his" place. She was, she said, a little drunk and ready to toss her "virtue" aside.

"I like it hard and hot," he whispered in her ear. "How about you?"

For an answer, she took his hand that was covering her breast and squeezed his fingers until they compressed her nipple tightly. A shiver ran up her spine. He roughly pushed aside the fabric of her V-necked dress, reached inside her black-lace bra, and found her nipple. As he thrust his tongue deeply into her mouth, he twisted her nipple. She moaned appreciatively.

Before he started the car and began the drive home, he shoved her skirt up, exposing her genitals. She was wearing a garter belt and stockings, no panties. At every stoplight, he insinuated a finger into her vagina. By the time he pulled into the garage at "his" apartment building, she was wet.

Inside the apartment, with a panoramic view of the city before him, he took her the way, he said, "a man takes an expensive slut": From behind, as she was bent over the sofa. Her orgasm was both profound and prolonged. He deliberately stopped himself from ejaculating because, he knew, after they had changed clothes and driven back to the hotel to get her car, they would make love again, playfully yet more tenderly.

CHAPTER FIVE

Improving Intercourse

"I have always loved the feel of my man inside me during intercourse," says Monica. "When I was in my twenties and early thirties I almost never had an orgasm during intercourse, but I still enjoyed it because of the feeling of closeness you can't get from anything else. Now, at fifty, I am often orgasmic during intercourse, partly because I have orgasms easier, but mostly because I am more comfortable with stroking my clitoris.

"Intercourse is also better because foreplay lasts much longer now. My husband isn't in the rush he once was. He needs the time to get a good erection and be ready for intercourse. He needs the foreplay even more than I do."

Traditionally, the period of lovemaking known as *foreplay* has been considered something a man has to do for the woman to get her ready for intercourse. Presumably he is always ready. That was never quite true, and by midlife it is definitely quite untrue. Studies and surveys show that women enjoy intercourse now more than they did when they were younger, while men enjoy other forms of loveplay more than they did. Older men want and *need* more touching, kissing, caressing, and stroking before they are ready for intercourse.

Seven Tips for Hotter Loveplay

- *Start on warm*. Sex begins in the brain—for everyone. The mental fires need tending, particularly for the couple who've been together a long time. Get in the habit of indulging your fleeting sexual thoughts and fantasies, rather than banishing them until a suitable hour. Start thinking about lovemaking well in advance. Share your erotic thoughts briefly and graphically with your lover during the day if you can. Even the busiest executive has a few minutes to make or receive a husky-voiced call.

- *Get romantic*. The details are more important now, and typically the couple is paying less attention to them. Set the stage for love-making in little ways. Is your bedroom a haven for romance? Consider fresh decor, softer lighting. Add fat candles in glass or pottery containers, plants, fresh flowers, photos of the two of you when you were younger. Bring each other small gifts. Perform unexpected favors.

- *Go slower*. Begin making love in the living room, at the dining table, or in the restaurant. Start by paying close attention to each other. Remember how flattered you were when your lover listened carefully to everything you said? Flirt. Later, when you begin making love in earnest, kiss and caress each other's entire bodies, but not the sex organs yet. Sucking a finger or toe is sexy.

- *Lavish attention on his other erotic zones*. Don't go straight for the penis. Many men have sensitive nipples, scrotum, and perineum. Stimulating these areas orally or manually may make it easier for him to get an erection when you do take his penis in hand.

- *Give her an orgasm, manually or orally*. She usually can orgasm more easily than when she was younger and is more likely to have multiple orgasms. Giving her the first orgasm takes the performance pressure off, and watching her come is very arousing, possibly arousing enough to make his erection harder.

- *Spend more time stimulating his penis.* Some men have trouble getting and sustaining a good erection because their partners continue to treat their penises gingerly. He is unlikely to reach the ejaculation point too quickly. Grasp him firmly. Don't let go too soon.

- *Experiment with varying touch and rhythms.* Use a little more or less pressure than your lover expects. Arouse your partner, then back off at the point where you typically build up the stimuli. By teasing, you increase the level of arousal. Your lover never knows if you will continue stroking or stop and change the pattern. His or her excitement is increased by anticipation. It's also a lovemaking style that invites the other to make verbal and nonverbal requests.

The Intercourse Positions

Although there are really only six basic positions for intercourse, each can be varied to provide different sensations. No one position is inherently better than the other, and complicated certainly doesn't mean better. If you have looked through the *Kama Sutra*, you may have wondered, "Is this really possible?" Some of the more elaborate and distorted positions may be possible for gymnasts, but they couldn't be maintained comfortably by anyone for long. More important, they probably wouldn't lead to a scintillating genital connection.

One need not be an athlete to have erotic command of several positions. The overweight; the aged; and even those with a bad back, trick knee, or tennis elbow can find pleasure in intercourse. Put each suggested position to this simple feel-good test:

- Can you comfortably get into the position and hold it easily enough so that you won't be distracted by trembling muscles or minor pain? If not, how could you adapt it with the help of pillows or bolsters?

- Is this position conducive to female orgasm? The majority of women don't reach orgasm via intercourse alone. Does the position allow her or her partner room to stroke and caress her genitals?

- Is it visually stimulating to your partner without being embarrassing to you?

Most people are restricted in their choice of positions more by habit than by necessity. They have intercourse in the same way they have always done and wonder why it has become routine and boring. In the following sections, I describe the basic positions and their variations and offer tips and hints for each.

Female Superior Position, or Woman on Top

- *The basic step and some variations.* The man lies on his back as the woman straddles him and lowers herself onto his penis. Some men put a pillow under their buttocks to raise their hips for a more efficacious angle or easier entry. To change the angle of penetration and give her greater control of thrusting, she can lean back or forward, resting her hands on the bed behind or in front of her. In the final moments of intercourse before orgasm, she may flatten herself out on top of him, clench her thighs together, and roll her clitoris into him.

- *The pros and cons.* Many women find they are more apt to reach orgasm in this position than in others. The woman has greater control over the angle and degree of thrusting and can get more clitoral stimulation. She or her partner can easily provide manual stimulation of her breasts and clitoris. Many men say it is the most visually stimulating position because they can admire her breasts and see her face when she reaches orgasm. Sexually passive women find it difficult to assume this level of control.

- *The midlife secret.* Body-image anxiety stops some women from getting on top. If his reassurances aren't enough to allay her concerns, she can wear a bustier, camisole, a short silk robe or nightie, or any sexy piece of lingerie that makes her feel more appealing. A man and woman don't have to be completely nude to make love. Clothes can give a woman confidence, even in bed.

Comments: "This is a great position for a woman who knows how to excite a man," says Shelley, a 50-something bride who says her sex life is better now than when she was younger. "Make eye contact with your man, especially when you come. My husband told me that his first wife always closed her eyes when she came. He felt cheated because she hid her vulnerability from him. Use your hands. A man gets very aroused watching a woman touch herself during intercourse. And, be a little dominant when you're on top. Lean over and tweak his nipples occasionally. Or take his wrists and push them over his head."

The Missionary Position, or Man on Top

- *The basic step and some variations.* Legend has it that Pacific Island natives named this position after the missionaries who used it exclusively. Unfairly maligned, the man-on-top position may be the most common one for intercourse in the Western world. The woman lies on her back with her knees bent and legs opened outward. Some women place a pillow under their buttocks or the small of the back to make penetration easier or the angle of penetration less deep or more arousing. The man largely controls the speed of thrusting. For very shallow penetration, the woman can lie on her back with her hips at the edge of the bed so that her legs hang over the sides, feet touching the floor, with the man standing and leaning into her between parted legs. For deeper penetration, she can, in the classic position, open her legs more widely and bend her knees, either keeping her feet on the bed or placing them on his shoulders.

- *The pros and cons.* One of the face-to-face positions, the missionary position promotes intimacy, encouraging deep thrusting and full penetration. A couple can also kiss during intercourse. This is generally considered the best position for male orgasm. A man may choose to switch to it when he is ready to ejaculate if he doesn't get sufficient friction from thrusting in another position. If she is the partner more interested in lovemaking or he is suffering from fatigue or back problems, another position, requiring less masculine authority, would be a better choice.

- *The midlife secret.* By keeping her feet on the bed, knees bent, or placing her feet on his shoulders, she can create the effect of a tightened vagina. That may enable him to remain inside her with a less-than-firm erection. It may also cause him to become more erect.

Comments: "The missionary is a good position for older couples," says Marilyn, 54. "It's bad only if you use it exclusively. My husband and I like to finish in the missionary position after having intercourse in at least one other position. We put a pillow under my buttocks. I put my feet on his shoulders. The pillow and the right positioning of my legs enable us to get good penetration for him to reach a climax. With my feet on his shoulders, I have room to stroke my clitoris. Often now we can have an almost simultaneous orgasm this way. When he has a semierection, we use the position differently. I keep my feet on the bed, knees bent, and hold the base of his penis as he thrusts."

Rear Entry

- *The basic step and variations.* The woman is on knees and elbows, her hips elevated. The man kneels and enters her vagina from behind. She can kneel at the edge of the bed with the man standing behind her. To elevate her hips at a steeper angle, she can rest her chest on the bed. In America, the position is often referred to as *doggy style*, which connotes negative images for some people.

- *The pros and cons.* Men tend to like rear entry better than women do, though both can move freely and vigorously. Women complain about lack of intimacy—no eye contact—and worry about how their buttocks look from the rear. Actually, they look better in this position than when a woman is standing nude with her back to her partner. The arched position smoothes out the sags and bags. It is an excellent position for manual clitoral stimulation by either partner. Some women claim the G spot is more easily stimulated during rear entry, too.

- *The midlife secret.* With her chest lowered to the bed, the position has an elongating effect on her vaginal barrel, creating a tighter fit. His erection will feel more powerful to both of them.

Comments: "My wife didn't like the rear-entry position very much until recently," says Paul. "She is more assertive and enthusiastic in her sexual participation than she was. Now she says the rear-entry position makes her feel powerful. She pushes back against me, matches me thrust for thrust. We really go at it in this position, especially if I stand behind her and she lowers the front half of her body to the bed. I love looking at her ass. Intercourse is hard and hot, like it was when we were young, only better because it lasts longer."

Side by Side

- *The basic step and variations.* The couple lie side by side facing each other. One puts a leg over the other. In a variation, often called *spoons*, the man faces the woman's back, her buttocks angled against him. Each are bent slightly at the knees and waist. He may put one of his legs between hers and enters her vagina from behind. In another adaptation, the *scissors*, the man lies on his right side, with the woman lying next to him on her back, her right leg between his thighs and her left leg on top.

- *The pros and cons.* This is a warm and intimate position for a couple who are too tired for vigorous sex. It's also a good starting position for intercourse. They can caress and fondle each other's genitals easily. On the other hand, deep penetration isn't really possible.

- *The midlife secret.* She lies half on her side, half on her back, drawing up the leg on which she is lying. The man faces her. In this position, penetration is limited, but the couple can make very good use of a semierection. She can stroke her clitoris with the head of his penis and vary that with partial insertion.

Comments: "We call the side-by-side position our 'maybe we will and maybe we won't' position," says Iris, 40 and married for 15 years to a 61-year-old man. "It feels good to us to get into this position and stroke each other as we talk. We've found we're able to say things to each other in this position that we haven't said before. The unpressured physical intimacy encourages sharing of thoughts and feelings as well as bodies.

Sometimes we get excited and move on to more active lovemaking, and sometimes we fall asleep this way."

Sitting

- *The basic step and variations.* The man may sit in a chair with his feet on the floor or on the bed, his ankles tucked under his legs toward his groin. The woman sits astride him. He holds on to her buttocks. She has her hands on his shoulders and her legs around his waist or she may squat over him, keeping her folded legs to the sides of his body. Or they may sit facing each other in the middle of the bed, legs wrapped around the other's bodies. She will probably need to sit on a pillow to elevate herself for easier entry and a better angle of penetration.

- *The pros and cons.* This can be a very intimate position because of the close eye contact the partners share. Her clitoris is easily accessible to him for stroking. But it may be difficult for partners with chronic knee problems to hold the position comfortably.

- *The midlife secret.* The sitting position is probably not a part of the average couple's repertoire, which makes it an excellent choice for introducing change into a lovemaking routine. The eye contact makes a deeper intimacy almost unavoidable. This may be the erotic jolt your relationship needs. Place stacks of pillows behind your backs.

Comments: "My husband has a very large penis," Ginny says, "and we have always found the sitting position a good one. We can see his penis going in and out of me, and the position limits the depth of penetration. It still works for us. He gets more aroused when he can watch himself having intercourse. I find that more arousing now, too, than I did. I have become more of an erotic visualist, which surprised us both."

Standing

- *The basic step and variations.* He enters her from the rear while she is standing, slightly bent forward. To achieve insertion, the man will probably have to squat while the woman lowers herself on to him. He can help by supporting her with his arms wrapped around her. If she is supported by balancing against a wall or piece of furniture, better yet. His hands are freer to roam from her breasts to her clitoris. Or in another version, if he can hold her, she can put both legs around his waist, her back against the wall, as he cups her buttocks while energetically thrusting.

- *The pros and cons.* This is a great position for spontaneous lovemaking after a physically fit couple have fondled and caressed each other to the point of near orgasm. Who hasn't had, or imagined having, a quickie in an airplane restroom or the bathroom of someone else's house, her back pressed against the wall, his pants around his ankles? It's not, even for the young, a position meant to be held for long.

- *The midlife secret.* In the movies a strong young actor lifts up the actress, holds a hand under her buttocks, and supports her while he thrusts. In real life she can sit on a bar stool, kitchen counter, or other surface of the right height while he stands, her legs wrapped around his waist. The exciting elements are still there for dramatic, urgent lovemaking.

Comments: "A couple times a year I have to make love standing up, if for no other reason than to prove I can still do it," says Denny. "My wife is accommodating. The position dictates a quickie. The last time we did it, she really got into it. I don't think some kinds of sex work for young women. I tease her about being a horny old broad at forty. A woman has to be forty before she thinks sexually like a man."

The Dynamics of Thrusting

There's more to intercourse than position. Coital dynamics—the style, angle, and depth of penetration and the speed and force of thrusting— define the experience as much or more than the position does. The hard, deep, and regular thrusting pattern considered the ideal in Western society

leads to ejaculation in minutes, if not seconds. A man can prolong intercourse by varying the thrusting pattern. There are also ways in which
women can change the coital dynamics.

Taoist sex manuals devote a lot of space to techniques for prolonging intercourse and withholding ejaculation. At midlife, a man can readily adapt some of them to his own lovemaking style. He may also find
that changing the coital dynamics helps him maintain an erection during
intercourse.

The names of these thrusting patterns may sound a little off-putting.
Try them anyway. They've been working for thousands of years. Each
method can be used in any position. Concentrating on the count will dis-
tract a man from performance concerns if he has them.

- *Eight-slow, two-fast thrusting method.* The depth of penetration
  varies during the slow strokes from shallow to deep. The two fast
  strokes are deep. Exhale on the outward strokes. Inhale on the
  inward strokes.

- *Nine-shallow, one-deep thrusting method.* The Taoists believe the
  number nine holds powerful *yang,* or male, energy. During the nine
  shallow thrusts, the penis enters only 2 or 3 inches into the vagina,
  which is supposed to create a vaginal vacuum. The deep thrust
  forces the air out of the vagina, making the penis feel more tightly
  held. Some women may feel G-spot stimulation from the shallow
  thrusts.

- *Japanese set of nines.* He performs nine shallow thrusts, withdraws,
  pauses, and enters again. Then he performs eight shallow thrusts,
  followed by one deep thrust, withdraws and pauses. Next are seven
  shallow and two deep thrusts. The set continues in this manner
  until he takes nine deep strokes, which is supposed to bring her to
  orgasm.

"I was skeptical," says Michael, who was dragged to an Eastern
erotic-arts weekend workshop by his wife in search of a cure for the sexual blahs. "I thought I would feel silly counting strokes. It sounded like a
game. Well, I was wrong.

"Changing the thrusting pattern was very arousing for her. She had an orgasm during intercourse for the first time in months. I also found increased pleasure. When I use these methods, I don't lose my erection. I feel more powerful, too. We both think my erection is harder."

Her Coital Dynamic Power

The man isn't the only one who influences coital dynamics. Varied genital movements during intercourse create different kinds and degrees of stimulation for both the woman and her partner. She can change the dynamics most easily in the female superior position by controlling the angle and degree of penetration and the speed of thrusting. But she can get different sensations in every position simply by shifting her body so that his penis enters her vagina at a slightly different angle. Women who achieve orgasm during intercourse may consciously or unconsciously do this.

The following techniques are taught in Tantric workshops:

- *Oval track.* Typically, a woman moves up and down in the female-superior position. She can vary that dynamic with the oval track. In the movement down onto his penis, she leans forward slightly and pushes her pubis a little to the back, stimulating her clitoral area with his shaft. On the upward movement, she leans slightly backward and pushes her pubis a little forward, stimulating her G spot by the head of the penis.

- *Pause.* In any position, at the moment of his deepest penetration, she grasps his buttocks, holding him tightly and prolonging the moment of contact. This is even more effective if she has a strong pubococcygeal (PC) muscle—a muscle found on the bottom of the pelvic floor (see page 80 for ways to strengthen this muscle).

- *PC flex.* She times the flexing of her PC muscle with her partner's thrusting. She keeps the muscle relaxed until his penis is inside her vagina. Then she contracts it. Vary the flexing in intensity and duration.

"I always wanted to be more active during intercourse," says Kathryn, Michael's wife, "but I didn't know how to do it until we took that workshop together. Simple changes in your movements, like the oval track, produce big results. By using the pause or the flex, I can help Michael maintain his erection.

"We have extended the concept of subtle change to other areas of lovemaking. We've been experimenting with different ways of kissing and caressing, for example. Like many couples who've been together for a few decades, we thought we knew everything about each other's bodies, but we didn't. I would recommend learning a new sex trick to any couple. The technique is not an end in itself. It's more like the key to a door opening into a bigger room of pleasure. The willingness of both partners to learn something new has an energizing effect on the relationship as a whole."

Six Secret Hot Spots—And How to Ignite Them

Most people know that a woman's clitoris (and the surrounding tissue) and the head of a man's penis are the most sexually sensitive places on their bodies. Her clitoris is a small pink organ, often compared to a tiny penis because of its shaft-like shape, located at the point where the inner labia join at the top of the vaginal opening. The head is the part of the penis set off from the shaft by a thick ridge or crown, the coronal edge, also sensitive to touch.

Many men and women have a number of other hot spots that, when stimulated, produce pleasurable sensations and often orgasm. Though referred to as *spots*, the term isn't precisely accurate. They are more like areas than spots—not magic buttons but places particularly susceptible to erotic touch. Some sexual positions hit more of them than do others.

As men's erections lose some of their firmness and women lose some of their vaginal tone (see page 81 for some exercises), the same old positions may not work in the same way because the spots aren't being hit. Intercourse isn't thrilling anymore? That could be why. The good news: Hot-spot combustion can almost always be rearranged.

His Hot Spots

- *F spot*. The frenulum is that loose section of skin on the underside of the penis, where the head meets the shaft. This area is highly sensitive to touch in most men. Some men can be brought to orgasm if the F spot receives intense stimulation during intercourse.

- *R area*. The R stands for the raphe, the visible line along the center of the scrotum, an area of the male anatomy typically neglected during lovemaking. The skin on the raphe is similar to the skin of a woman's labia: very sensitive.

- *P zone*. The perineum, that area an inch or so in size between the anus and the base of the scrotum, is often neglected by Western lovers. Rich in nerve endings, the perineum can generate a tremendous erotic response in many men.

Her Hot Spots

- *G spot*. On page 61 I described how to locate and massage the G spot. Consider the quest for the G spot a treasure hunt, not a sexual-performance test. Some women report no unusual sensitivity there.

- *U spot*. Unlike the G spot, the U spot, for urethra, has received minimal press since its discovery as a possible trigger for orgasm was reported in 1988 by Kevin McKenna, an associate professor of physiology and urology at Northwestern University Medical School. Because urine is expelled through the urethra, we typically don't think of this tiny area of tissue above the opening as a sexual pleasure point, but it is. The U spot is just above the clitoris.

- *AFE zone*. The anterior-fornix erotic zone is across from the G spot on the opposite vaginal wall. Think of a sofa facing a chair: The sofa is the larger AFE zone and the chair is the G spot. Not marked by a change in tissue texture, as is the G spot, the AFE zone is indistinguishable at first touch from the rest of the vaginal wall. You'll know you've found it when her vagina begins lubricating from stroking that spot alone. Stimulate it first by sliding a finger up and down the area. Then move from the AFE zone to the G spot and back again. Stroke the AFE area in clockwise and then counter-clockwise motions.

Don't forget the private hot spots, the places unique to each of us. Try the backs of the knees, the ears, the throat, the inner thighs, and the instep.

Midlife Hot-Spot Adjustments

- In the female-superior position, she can improve the hot-spots connection by leaning slightly forward or slightly backward to change the angle of his penis with her movements.

- In the rear-entry position, she should elevate her hips to a steeper angle. By doing so, he should get more friction on his F spot and R area.

- In the missionary position, she should keep her feet on the bed with the knees bent or wrap her legs around his neck to intensify the connection with both of your hot spots. Experiment with the placement and size of the pillow(s) under her back or buttocks to change the connecting patterns of the hot spots.

- Modify the side-by-side or spoon position to the scissors position.

- In any position, experiment with pillows and bolsters to change the angle and depth of penetration, which is the key to improving the hot-spot connection.

Four Additional Ways of Enhancing Intercourse at Midlife

- *Strengthen the PC muscle—his and hers.* The PC muscle is located on the pelvic floor, running along the perineum, the area in men between the testicles and anus, and in women, the area between the lower tip of the vulva and anus. A strong PC muscle helps both men and women achieve stronger orgasms. Her vagina will feel tighter to him because she will be able to use that muscle to grip his penis during intercourse. He will have better ejaculatory control. In addition, a strong PC muscle can correct mild urinary incontinence in women. *Kegels*, named for Arnold Kegel who developed the exercise in the 1950s, are used to strengthen the PC muscle. Here's how:

1. Locate the PC muscle, which, as noted above, is part of the pelvic floor in both genders, by stopping the flow of urine. Practice stopping the flow of urine several times to become familiar with the sensation that locates the PC muscle. Stopping the flow of urine is only done to become familiar with the sensation. The Kegel squeeze, described below, is *not* done while urinating.

2. Start with a short Kegel squeeze. Alternately contract and relax the PC muscle 15 or 20 times at approximately one squeeze per second. Exhale gently as you tighten only the muscles around your genitals (which include the anus), not the muscles in your buttocks. Don't bear down when you release. Simply let go. Do two sessions a day, gradually building up to two sets of 75 per day.

3. Add a long Kegel squeeze. Contract the PC muscle and hold for a count of 3. Relax between contractions. Work up to holding for 10 seconds and then relaxing for 10 seconds. Start with two sets of 20 each and build up to two sets of 75.

4. Add a push out. After you work up to 300 repetitions a day of the combined short and long Kegel squeezes, add the push out. After releasing the contraction, push down and out *gently* as if you were having a bowel movement with your PC muscle. Repeat: *gently*, no bearing down.

5. Now create Kegel sequences that combine long and short repetitions with push outs. After 2 months of daily repetitions of 300, you should have a well-developed PC muscle. You can keep it that way by doing 150 repetitions several times a week.

• *Alternate intercourse with others forms of lovemaking.* Too many men think that they have to continue thrusting to climax once intercourse has begun, a belief that creates undue performance pressure at midlife. Alternate intercourse with oral and manual stimulation. The lovemaking experience will last longer. She will likely be more orgasmic. And a waxing and waning erection won't seem like a problem.

- *Change positions.* Changing positions changes the coital dynamics and alleviates muscle strain. The sensations are different. Lovemaking lasts longer without putting stress on muscles and joints.

- *Use your hands.* By midlife, women are less self-conscious about asking for additional clitoral stimulation from their partners or touching themselves as needed. He shouldn't be afraid to ask her for more manual support either. If she grasps the base of his penis during intercourse, she may be able to help him maintain an erection. Also some men find perineum massage during intercourse very stimulating (see page 61 for tips).

Take Me, I'm Yours

Damp tendrils of hair clung to her face and neck. The red flush of orgasm covered her chest. As her breathing subsided, she reached across the space between them and put her hand on his penis. He took it away from his semi-erect organ and muttered, "I'm too tired to come tonight, baby."

A sophisticated lover, Tracey knew that sex was more than intercourse. When she and her husband, Ned, were young, they had rarely made love without having intercourse. Now in their early 50s, they often did. Too often, Tracey thought.

Mutual masturbation and oral sex were Ned's preferred ways of making love. Often, after a prolonged session of what she considered foreplay, he brought her to orgasm with his hand or mouth, and then rolled over on his back as he had tonight. The "rollover" was his signal that he didn't want to, or couldn't, enter her.

"I miss feeling you inside me," she murmured.

"Tracey," he said, and she caught the warning note in his voice.

He didn't want to talk about whatever was wrong. Holding his hand, she pretended to fall asleep. Soon his light snoring told her he really had fallen asleep. She slipped out of bed and grabbed her robe, which had fallen to the floor. Pulling it around her, she walked softly down the long hallway into the living room. She curled up on the sofa where she eventually fell asleep. He woke her the next morning.

"Have trouble sleeping again?" he asked, tenderly stroking her cheek.

She wanted to tell him why, but she kissed his hand instead. Dismissing her sleep problem as caused by job anxiety, she hurried to take a shower while he made the coffee. Another day of avoidance had begun.

A few days later, Ned, lying beside her, asked, "Are you feeling amorous tonight?"

"Maybe," she said.

He held his penis in one hand and put the other against her crotch.

"Here," she said, taking his penis into her own hand, "let me do that."

Expertly, she stroked his member until it was standing at half-staff. His ministrations to her labia had sufficiently lubricated her for entry, especially for a soft entry. Tonight, she was determined, they wouldn't masturbate each other to orgasm side by side. She wanted him inside her, and she was going to take control and put him there.

She turned on her side. Still holding his penis, she kissed him deeply. Then teasing his lips and tongue with hers, she gently straddled him without letting go of his member.

"Umm," he murmured.

She sensed a note of concern beneath the pleasure, but she persisted. Holding her hand firmly around the base and lower part of his penis, she used the head to tease her clitoris. His excitement grew with hers. When she was very hot and moist, she carefully inserted his penis holding on with her hand. As long as she held him, he wouldn't fall out. She could feel him simultaneously relax in his body and stiffen in his penis.

Flexing her PC muscle, she gripped the head of his penis. He grinned at her. She was showing off her muscular expertise, and he liked it. Then she pulled a little more of his penis inside her. As he grew harder, she moved her hand down, until only her first finger and thumb formed a ring around the base.

Maintaining an even pressure with her finger ring, she rode him. He was fully aroused and gloriously erect inside her. Gazing into her eyes, he threw himself into the act of intercourse more enthusiastically than he had in months. In a few strokes with his erection, she came. And she came again when he did, minutes later.

She collapsed in his arms. He held her, stroking her face and hair, whispering endearments until she fell asleep. In the morning, she woke happily in their bed.

CHAPTER SIX

Don't Have Sex,
Make Love

"When Don wants to make love, he asks me, 'Do you want to have sex?'"
Julie says. "I have told him I would prefer he called it *lovemaking*, not
having sex, but he says he doesn't see the difference. I do. If he did, maybe
we'd make love instead of have sex. I'm tired of having sex. I'm turned
off to having sex. He blames it on my age, forty-eight, and wants me to
take hormones or something so I can keep up with him.

"We have had an active sex life for the twenty years we've been married, which is saying more than most couples probably can. I want more
now; and I'm not getting it. So he's getting less. He just doesn't understand what I'm talking about; and he seems to have no interest in figuring
it out yet."

Don and Julia have reached an erotic stalemate. He wants more sexual activity than he thinks she wants. In truth, she probably does want as
much activity as he does, but she wants a different kind—lovemaking, at
least sometimes. Pressuring her for more sex isn't the way for him to get
his needs met. He needs to learn how to make love to his wife.

There is nothing wrong with having sex, sharing a purely physical
erotic event with your partner. Quickies, for example, are having sex.
Indulging in the occasional quickie can make a man and woman feel
very young again. Having sex can also last a lot longer than a quickie.

Sometimes a couple wants nothing more emotional than sex play, simple release, or vigorous erotic exercise. But sex alone won't carry them into a glorious golden age together, even if their techniques and style could be used in teaching videos. People get bored, frustrated, and turned off to lovemaking when they are having sex all the time and not making love. There is a full range of erotic expression, including intensely emotional lovemaking, in a lasting, exciting relationship.

First, Clear the Emotional Air

Remember the *Seinfeld* episode about George and Susan's make-up sex? George was desperate to replenish her contraceptive supply after a fight because they were going to have make-up sex, the best sex, and he wasn't going to miss the opportunity because of a lack of contraceptive sponges. Early in relationships, couples tend to have more make-up sex than they do later, after they've developed entrenched patterns of mutual resentment.

"We never fought," says Veronica, "but we were always to some degree miffed at each other. The resentment was there, like an underground stream. We rarely made love. Rick said he just wasn't interested in sex. One day, after I had made some caustic remarks about his lack of sexual interest, he dropped the bombshell.

"He told me he found other women sexually attractive, but he wasn't attracted to me anymore. I was hurt and angry. The anger came out first. I let fly with everything I'd been holding back for years, and he did the same. We screamed at each other for what seemed like hours, but couldn't have been in reality. Part of the time I was crying.

"Then a funny thing happened. We were standing toe to toe glaring at each other, both of us breathing hard. By mutual unspoken consent, we fell into each other's arms and began kissing hungrily. We had the most passionate sex we'd had in years."

Although telling your partner you find others, not her or him, sexually attractive isn't the best way to start a fight, the sex benefits of a good emotional fight were definitely there for Veronica and Rick.

How Fighting Can Turn You On

An emotional argument involves both mind and body. When you're engaged in a spirited verbal battle with someone you love, your heart beats faster, your skin tingles, the blood seems to race through your body. That's not unlike the experience of sexual arousal, is it?

People who are afraid of their emotions try to shut them down at the first heated flush. They withdraw, which creates a sexual shutdown, too. Over the years, emotional withdrawal becomes a protective habit, one that's hard to break. Every emotion seems frightening, a threat to the hard-won personal sense of peace. A couple in emotional withdrawal may rarely or never fight, but they probably rarely or never make love either. Resist the urge to pull back from confrontation.

Six Rules for a Good Emotional Fight

Remember that a fight is verbal and emotional—not physical. And follow the rules for a good emotional fight.

- *Stay on focus.* No fair her dredging up the mistakes he made 20 years ago or him saying again how much he hates her interfering mother. This type of fight is not an opportunity to rehash old grievances.

- *Define issues.* Be clear and specific about the problems. Don't get off track.

- *Listen.* Really listen. Don't just pause until it's your turn to speak again, with your mind formulating the next sentences while your partner talks.

- *Don't interrupt.* You can be angry without being rude or bullying.

- *Don't personalize.* Stay with the issue—he doesn't pick up his clothes, she doesn't take her fast-food trash out of the car—without calling the other names like *lazy slob*.

- *Recognize his and her conflict styles.* Men and women have different conflict styles as well as intimacy styles. Respect the differences.

Also understand that aging softens some of those differences. A woman may not cry so easily and may be more direct and confrontational now than she was; a man may be more protective of vulnerable feelings she didn't know he had.

Three Ways to Make Up with Great Sex

- Make a concession or offer an apology followed by a prolonged kiss.

- Continue the verbal sparring, on a less contentious level, as you begin to undress.

- Acknowledge that you are aroused and get your partner to admit he or she is, too.

Awaken Each Other's Senses

Ben and Christine had reached a sensual dead end together by their 35th anniversary, but they didn't realize they had. Like other world-weary and jaded people, they were so accustomed to having the classic song "Is That All There Is?" whispering in their brains, they scarcely noticed the tune anymore. Discriminating consumers, skilled lovers, and intelligent, witty companions—they were everything the other could want in a partner. Weren't they?

"We didn't know we had a problem so we didn't look for help," she says. "Looking back, we know we were on autopilot for years." What kicked them into a higher gear? "We borrowed a friend's cabin in Vermont for a ski trip and got snowed in. The propane tank was running low. Ben and I spent three days conserving fuel and relying on roaring fires to keep the main room warm. We made love on chilly sheets in the bedroom one night and found the experience enormously arousing because it was such a different physical sensation.

"The next morning we made love on the floor in front of the fire, another new sensation. We went outside and played in the snow, something we hadn't done since the kids were small. There we were stuffing snow inside each other's pants and running back in the cabin to pull off our clothes and turn our naked backsides to the fire. When the snowplows finally came through and we were driving home, we agreed that we'd discovered magic.

"We'd always thought that traveling, dining out, or buying each other expensive gifts was the way to put excitement back in our marriage, and we'd been quietly disappointed when those things didn't work the way we'd hoped they would. Now we look for ways of being more sensual together, from making love on the beach at night in the Caribbean to licking honey off each other at home."

Lovemaking is much more than the sum of the technical parts. It's a sensual experience, involving the whole body, not just the genitals. Sensual people make better lovers for their partners and for themselves. If you and your lover have lost touch with your sensuality, reawaken your five senses one at a time. Through this reawakening the emotional connection between the two of you will deepen—and the sex will be better, too.

Here's a review of the five senses and their midlife status:

- *Taste.* The sense of taste serves an addition function in lovemaking: helping the lover define what part of the body is being touched. You feel a partner's genitals with your tongue when you're licking them; and, if you are a sensual person, you feel the difference between the skin texture from one part of the labia to another, from the head of the penis to the underside of the shaft. Some couples become turned off to kissing, particularly French kissing, in midlife because their partners have become less conscientious about brushing teeth and freshening breath before lovemaking. Sometimes the medications taken for minor health problems change taste or the ability to taste. Overindulgence in food, alcohol, or chronic smoking may also have changed the way one partner tastes or the other's ability to taste. Be alert to your partner's responses to the way you taste.

- *Smell.* The sense of smell is obviously an integral part of sexuality. Semen and vaginal secretions have a scent. The scent of semen in particular can be affected by chronic heavy alcohol consumption, smoking, and poor eating habits. Many men and women also use personal fragrance as a seductive tool. Hormonal changes in women can produce chemical changes in the body that affect the interaction of skin and perfume. The scent worn for a lifetime may no longer carry the same fragrance to a lover's nostrils. In some men and women, the ability to detect scent isn't as sharp as it once was, leading one or the other to wear too much perfume or light one too many scented candles.

- *Sight.* When lovers are young and/or new to each other, the sense of sight may be working overtime, compensating for the other neglected senses. The curve of her buttocks; the line of his shoulders; a profile; or a glimpse of thigh, genital, or pubic hair can arouse a lover so thoroughly that the delights of the other senses seem like the cherry on the erotic dessert. Visually delighting your partner is still possible now but requires a little thought. At just the point in life when many women eschew the sexy lingerie, they should be continually adding to their supply. Erotic wardrobe, lighting, unexpected touches such as a flower behind the ear, and other simple changes create visual excitement.

- *Touch.* The feel of a lover's skin may seem too familiar to be arousing, but that's only because the couple have allowed their senses to become dulled with familiarity. A woman's skin may actually be more sensitive to touch during perimenopause and after. And a man, as noted earlier, becomes more capable of sensual, rather than purely sexual, expression with age.

- *Sound.* The sound of a lover's voice may also seem too familiar to be arousing. Again, that need not be true. Some midlife couples have fallen into rigid communication patterns. They say the same things to each other in the same tones of voice. Their voices no longer show great animation or register seductive depths.

Five Exercises for Reawakening the Senses at Midlife
- *The sensory surprise.* Incorporate some unexpected sensory delights into your lovemaking. If she loves roses, spray the room lightly with

rose water and put fresh roses beside the bed in bud vases. Sprinkle some loose petals on the bed and use one later to massage her nipples or clitoris. Try to add a detail that will ignite each of the five senses. That's not as hard as it seems. Soft music, candlelight, and flowers are such effective romance aides because they appeal directly to the senses.

- *Practice the technique of touch focusing.* Close out everything else and concentrate solely on what you are touching. First, remove your clothing and try sitting back to back with eyes closed. How does your lover's skin feel against yours? How does the feeling change when one moves? Then feel the skin under your hands as you stroke his or her body during lovemaking. Note how the texture of the skin changes from one area to another, how varying the pressure makes touch a different experience.

- *Add the technique of touch expansion.* Introduce some unusual materials into lovemaking. Fur, silk, feathers, velvet, leather, ice, flower petals—all can be used to erotic effect on genitals and other sensitive places.

- *Play with sound.* Yes, bring music into the bedroom, but don't forget that your voice is also an instrument of sound. Move it up and down, out of the tones so familiar to your mate. Be creative in your pillow talk. Have phone sex occasionally. Sing to each other. Even if you can't carry a tune, you can elicit a giggle.

- *Expand your awareness.* Every day for at least 10 minutes pay attention to your surroundings in a new way. On a familiar street, for example, note architectural details you've missed, examine new growth on shrubs and trees. Take this heightened awareness home.

Create Erotic Trust

"I love Sharon, but she's not an easy woman," says Joe. "She's hard driving and has high standards for herself—both personally and professionally—

standards she expects me to meet, too. Our sex life has been pretty good until recently. I had some erection problems, which led to a confidence problem. She was understanding to a point.

"Our grown son teases her that her life motto should be: Deal with it. That's certainly her attitude regarding my crisis of sexual confidence. She says, 'You had a few failures. So what? Let's make love.' I've been avoiding lovemaking for the past several weeks, and she's furious with me.

"I will give Sharon credit for not being intimidated or taking my lack of erection personally. She doesn't blame herself as some women would, just me, for being a nervous Nellie."

Ask Joe if he trusts Sharon, and he'll probably say he does. With the car, the credit cards, his life maybe—but does he trust her with his sexual vulnerability? Not likely. If he did, he would be willing to risk another erectile "failure" because he'd have confidence that she wouldn't make him feel worse. Some risks can be taken only with people who are accepting.

Doesn't erotic trust naturally exist between longtime partners? Not necessarily. Frustration, discouragement, misunderstanding, and rejection, perceived or real, create distrust. Sometimes nonsexual issues erode trust. For example, a couple who have developed a pattern of saying hurtful things to each other in anger have also learned to protect their vulnerable spots, such as sexuality, from each other. They never remove all the armor. In that kind of atmosphere, neither will admit to hidden desires, secret fears. Another couple might have lost trust for a reason similar to Joe's: a partner's impatient response to a sex problem. Unable to help each other feel truly accepted, some couples may have never built erotic trust into their relationship, and by midlife the lack of passion in their lovemaking reflects that.

Acceptance doesn't mean going along with everything the other wants. You don't have to make love whenever your partner does or agree to participate in sexual activities you find unappealing. Say no without stating or implying your lover is unattractive or not desirable—or worse, perverted or sex obsessed. (And accept the answer no without being angry, resentful, judgmental.) How partners confront their sexual differences helps determine the strength of the erotic trust bond and nourishes the emotional commitment they share.

Four Steps to Building Erotic Trust

1. *Make a trust zone.* In addition to being a sensually inviting room, the bedroom a couple share should be a safe emotional place, a sanctuary from the storms outside. Many midlife couples have spoiled the sanctuary by using the bedroom to settle their differences away from the hearing of children. Agree not to balance the checkbook, argue about the bills, criticize each other, air grievances, fight about the children, or ambush each other with bad news in the bedroom. Couples can put their defenses down and share confidences, as well as lovemaking, in the trust zone.

Less than a month after establishing their trust zone, Van and Melissa, who hadn't made love in several months, began reaching out to each other in bed again. "When our daughter moved back in with us after college and his mother came to stay with us to recuperate from heart surgery, we began treating our bedroom like the command post," Melissa says. "We lay side by side every night agonizing over what we were going to do. Everything we didn't want either of them to hear was discussed in our bed. It was deadly."

2. *Have the sex talk.* How long has it been since you talked to each other about sex? Some couples have never had a frank discussion about sexuality, whereas others haven't shared information about their erotic likes and dislikes in many years. Each assumes the other knows. As their sexuality evolves, a couple needs to communicate comfortably and clearly about their needs, desires, fears, fantasies, and secret sexual wish lists. It's also helpful if they tell each other what they really like about their lovemaking in specific terms, such as, "I love the way you suck my nipples."

"We can't talk about sex in bed," says Grace. "It's too threatening. We need to be fully dressed. We take walks together at least once a week; and for us, that is the right time to talk about sex. Last week, my husband told me he wanted me to take his whole penis in my mouth sometime when I performed fellatio. I'm willing to try this. I might have felt intimidated if he'd sprung it on me while we were making love because I need to think a little about things before I do them."

3. *Establish a trust position.* Experiment with ways of holding each other to find the position where both feel closely and warmly connected, yet not pressured to perform or respond sexually. In the trust position, a man and woman become each other's calm harbor from anxiety, depression, sadness, or the frustration that follows a sexual disappointment. Some couples lie side by side, facing each other with their bodies touching from foreheads to toes. Here are some other possibilities spoon fashion, in which one partner lies with chest against the other's back; the man lying on his back with the woman's head on his shoulder; and one partner lying down, perhaps on a sofa or leaning against the pillows in bed, with the other's head in his or her lap. Although the trust position will make verbal sharing easier, talking isn't always necessary.

"When my husband and I were having some sexual difficulties last year," says Gail, "we got into the habit of holding each other in our favorite after-play position, with his chest against my back, and his arms around me, even when we had no 'after.' We didn't talk about the sex and why it wasn't working. Sometimes we didn't talk at all, and other times we talked about our feelings and our memories. We got a lot closer to each other than we had been in a long time."

4. *Schedule an emotional conference.* Make a 15-minute date for an emotional conference at the same time each week. The agenda is feelings. Each partner spends 5 minutes talking about how the other's actions have affected him or her emotionally. The actions may have occurred at any time during the relationship, all the way back to the first date. The speaker should begin by briefly describing the incident. After one speaks, the other summarizes what was said and tries to empathize. Follow a few simple rules:

- Use *I* statements. You are talking about *your* feelings, not casting blame on the other person.

- Absolutely no interruptions.

- The listener summarizes the major points, without editing, analyzing, interpreting, or judging.

- Each should have a separate agenda. The second speaker doesn't get to rebut what the first person said. Otherwise the conference degenerates into one asking, "How could you see it that way?" and the other countering, "Why don't you see it the way I do?"

What is the point of the emotional conference? It's hoped that both partners will consider how their actions affect each other and learn to listen attentively. This exercise is also a weekly reminder that no two people, even the long and happily married, view incidents and actions in exactly the same way.

Andy, 53, and Ruth, 50, patients of mine in couple counseling, had been in a relationship for 5 years when they began having weekly emotional conferences. In the early weeks, they continually interrupted each other, challenged each other's "inaccuracies," and began innocent discussions afterward that erupted into arguments. After 5 months, Andy was able to tell Ruth that he was avoiding intercourse, which she strongly favored over other forms of lovemaking, because he was afraid of not getting or maintaining a hard erection. That led him to admit he feared erectile failure would diminish him in her eyes because he'd secretly struggled with inferiority feelings all his life. In summarizing his statements, Ruth neither offered comfort nor defended her enjoyment of intercourse. She would say, for example, "I hear you say that you are avoiding intercourse because you fear failure." No editorializing.

"That conference didn't have an immediate dramatic effect on our sex life," Andy says, "but it did bring us closer. She'd never seen me as someone who felt inferior or insecure."

Master the Art of Surrender

Surrender is the opposite of *control*. In the context of erotica, the heroine often uses the word *surrender* when she allows herself to be swept away by the hero's passion. That's a very narrow view of erotic surrender. It limits the woman and leaves out the man entirely. Think of erotic surrender as the act of letting go while aroused, not ceding control to one's partner.

Most people enjoy the feeling of being in control of their lives, even though much of what happens to them is clearly beyond their control. Successful people are admired not only for the money they earn and their accomplishments but also for the amount of control they exert over their environment and the others inside it. People who practice self-discipline are also admired. In lovemaking, the man who can control his erection and ejaculation and the woman who can control her partner's arousal and her own responses are idealized. Where does surrender fit into this picture?

Surrender is an integral part of true intimacy. Letting go into full arousal is intrinsic to the higher level of sexual pleasure possible for couples after age 50. It is an art, but one you can learn through practicing the following exercises, which I prescribe for my patients:

- *Turn yourself over to your partner.* Offer to be your partner's sexual slave for a night. He or she can create a sexual script within reason. You may discover a new dimension to your sexuality this way.

- *Write a short essay titled "Why I Don't Let Go Sexually."* State all your reasons. Then describe how your life might change if you surrendered to your sexuality. Elaborate. Don't merely say, for example, "I would be embarrassed." How would the embarrassment feel? How would you and your partner handle it? Put your essay aside for a few days. Read it again and write a rebuttal.

- *Play a role opposite to the one you typically play in bed for 1 week.* If you are the passive partner, become the active one. Initiate lovemaking. Be bold and assertive in getting your needs met. If you are the active partner, be passive in all aspects of lovemaking. Don't be afraid of the new feelings these changes will generate. Give in to them.

Turn Up the Emotional Heat

"Jerry and I read some books on Tantric sex to liven things up," says Lisa. She and Jerry, both divorced and in their early 50s, have been in a monogamous relationship for 10 years, though they don't live together.

"The best ideas were the simple ones, especially keeping your eyes open during lovemaking. I'd gotten in the habit of using favorite fantasies during lovemaking, and I thought I couldn't come without them. So I closed my eyes, and had my own fantasies; I was having sex almost alone. Once I began keeping my eyes open, I didn't need the fantasies as often. I began really paying attention to Jerry, feeling and experiencing him in a new way, as well as experiencing my own arousal on a deeper level.

"The eye lock, looking deeply into one another's eyes and holding the gaze, is the most intensely intimate experience either one of us has ever had. The first time I looked into his eyes at the point of orgasm, I was blown away by the emotions I felt. The orgasm was so much more complex. He has had the same experience. Opening your eyes is the best way to connect more strongly with your partner."

Studies have shown that 90 percent of women close their eyes while kissing. Only a third of men do. During orgasm, men are still more likely to keep their eyes open than women, but the majority of both genders either close their eyes or look away from their partner at the moment of climax. Men often bury their faces in a woman's neck or a pillow. There are several reasons for this behavior. Some people may fear that open eyes will disconnect them from their own sensations. They may feel emotionally distant from their partners. Body-image issues may force them into hiding behind their own eyelids. Or they may feel awkward about exposing themselves this way. We are never so vulnerable as when we allow our sexual arousal to be seen.

Rather than diminishing erotic pleasure, keeping your eyes open during lovemaking turns up the emotional heat. Some Tantric sex positions use this concept to help lovers transcend routine lovemaking and achieve a deeper, more spiritual union—as does the Kabbalah, a book of Jewish mysticism—but don't skip this section if you balk at the word *spiritual*. Meaningful eye contact during sex intensifies the physical sensations by deepening the emotional connection between lovers. That is not an esoteric concept. It's a hot sex tip.

Try the following ways of making sex more eye-opening:

- *Open your eyes occasionally while kissing.* The visual stimulation will probably increase your arousal, as well as provide your partner useful feedback on how well his or her kissing techniques are working. Some studies have shown that men bond more intensely with women when they make eye contact during kissing.

- *Practice the eye lock.* Look deeply into each other's eyes as you are caressing each other. Hold the look. Do this more than once. You probably won't realize how little you do look into each other's eyes during lovemaking until you practice the eye lock.

- *Make frequent eye contact during oral sex.* Glance up from your partner's genitals while performing oral sex. Make eye contact. The affect may be electrifying.

- *Look into each other's eyes during intercourse.* The face-to-face intercourse positions encourage eye contact. Use the opportunities inherent in such positions. Don't look away when you feel arousal increase; that's exactly the point at which connecting will intensify the feelings.

- *Open your eyes during orgasm.* Eyes-open orgasms may feel more explosive and emotional than other orgasms; the afterglow may be more tender and prolonged. Looking into your lover's eyes at the point of orgasm is like giving an erotic gift. Even if the concentration isn't always intense, the practice is likely to generate greater feelings of closeness between a couple.

SIZZLER #6

The Love Encounter

Ben and Christy were a greatly admired couple. Successful business partners, loving parents of two fine college-age sons who'd given them little trouble as teens, physically attractive and fit individuals, they were liked, loved, and trusted by family, friends, and colleagues. After Christy discovered Ben's brief affair with a younger woman, he begged her forgiveness and ended the liaison. No harsh words were exchanged between husband and wife in public or private, and their handling of the event seemed only to enhance their standing as an über-couple.

"We have always had great sex and still do," Christy confided to a friend over lunch one day. Then she had a thought she didn't articulate: They had sex, but did they make love? She brushed the question aside, but later that night it came back to her as her erotically talented husband was exquisitely running his tongue in circles around her left nipple. Again, she closed out the intruding question and willed her body to respond.

"That was great," Ben said later, after they had satisfied each other.

"Great," Christy echoed.

Within minutes, he was asleep. She lay listening to the soft sounds of his snoring and realized she was angry at him. Not merely angry, she was furious inside. When he woke in the morning, Christy was gone. She'd packed an overnight bag, checked into a hotel, and left him a note asking for a divorce.

Ben was stunned. He and soon their family and friends were all sure she must be having an affair of her own, obviously a more serious affair than the one he'd had. What else could explain her surprising behavior? (They surely would have blamed it on menopause, if she hadn't already negotiated that passage.) For weeks, she refused to see him outside their business. Finally, she consented to have dinner with him to discuss issues surrounding the divorce he didn't want. He prevailed on her to come to the house for that meal so they would have the kind of privacy a restaurant doesn't afford.

"I'm angry at you, Ben," she said in an even voice.

"You don't sound angry," he replied, in an equally rational tone.

"I am furious." She selected a dinner roll from the basket, examined it briefly, then suddenly pitched it across the table at him. The roll bounced off his forehead.

"What!" he yelled. "What was that for?"

"For your little bimbo!" Christy shouted. She threw another roll, and then another, until the basket was empty. He let them strike his face without putting up his hands to deflect them. "How could you do it?" she asked, her voice breaking. "How could you have a fling with someone young enough to be your daughter? Didn't you imagine how I would feel when I pictured your hands all over her firm unblemished flesh?"

She began crying. He got up and walked around the table, arms open to comfort her. She pushed him away with sufficient force to cause him to lose his balance. He fell backward on his ass.

"Bastard!" she shrieked.

"You fucking bitch!" he yelled back. "You fucking perfect bitch! I have sex with someone else, and all you care about is how your skin tone compares to hers."

He got up. She stood to leave, but he grabbed her arms and held her in place. For several minutes, they screamed into each other's faces. Then he took her blouse in both hands and ripped it open. Her heaving breasts seemed to be overflowing her bra. He tore off the bra and hungrily took one breast in his mouth. She gasped and tried to pull away, but he held her firmly. He forced one thigh between her legs and rubbed rapidly back and forth. She yanked angrily at his hair, but he wouldn't take his mouth off her breast. He felt her yield.

Finally he lifted his mouth to hers. They kissed passionately and sunk to the floor together. Crying and kissing, they caressed and fondled each other. With shaking fingers, she unbuckled his pants, pulled them down, and took his penis in her mouth. He hadn't felt so hard, so powerful and strong in years.

After they made love on the floor, they moved to the bedroom where they talked and cried for hours, and then made love slowly and tenderly.

CHAPTER SEVEN

The Power of Midlife Sexual Fantasies

"I've always had a fairly active sexual fantasy life," says Wanda, 50, who's been in a relationship for 5 years with a slightly younger man she met at the baby-viewing window in a hospital maternity unit—both their daughters had given birth to sons. "I revisit old favorite fantasies some-times, particularly when masturbating. Two that never fail me are having sex on the beach with Michael Douglas—he's left Catherine Zeta-Jones for me—and some version of my assertive sex-goddess fantasy. I am wearing the highest heels and very hot clothes, maybe leather or a skin-tight short red strapless dress, and I am dominating my partner, who has to service me.

"My lover and I talk about our fantasies sometimes. He gets very aroused when I tell mine, which are usually erotic stories I've made up for him, not fantasies I've actually used during masturbation or intercourse. If I get him excited by the stories, I may use them as fantasies later, incor-porating his responses into the scenario. My fantasy life is as rich now as it's ever been, maybe richer, because we do talk about it. I'd never been with a man who liked to hear my fantasies before. He's encouraged me to be more creative with him, which is paying off for me alone too.

"One big change in my imaginary sex life since I was a young woman: I no longer have those fluffy romantic fantasies where most of the story is about pursuit and the sex at the end is 'NG,' no genitals in view. Now I picture the genitals, mine and his, and I watch them connect in full juicy color. I see a big penis, always a big penis, and every detail, including the little drops of pre-ejaculate like dew on the head."

Why Fantasies Have Such Erotic Power

Fantasies have often been compared to private movies running in the theater of our mind. Researchers believe that sexual fantasy is a nearly universal experience among both women and men. Some erotic daydreams are nothing more than fleeting thoughts, like the clips of coming attractions, whereas others are full-blown features. A man may glimpse a flash of thigh in a restaurant when a woman crosses her legs and may briefly imagine touching her. A woman may light candles in her bedroom, put on soft music, and leisurely masturbate while fantasizing to multiple orgasms. Each is having a sexual fantasy.

The tangled roots of fantasy probably lie in childhood. John Money, one of the world's leading researchers in human sexuality and the pioneer in studying the origins of sexual fantasies, says they originate before puberty, between the ages of 5 and 8, and then emerge in adolescence. The child who played at his mother's feet may become the teenager fantasizing about a cheerleader's legs and eventually the adult who proudly refers to himself as a *leg man*. Beautiful female legs will likely play a featured role in his fantasies throughout his life.

Some fantasies—like those involving less mainstream practices such as spanking, foot or other fetishes, and bondage—may have less obvious origins, but Money believes that their roots can be traced to childhood events. A little boy who gets an erection when spanked or a little girl who becomes aroused during a spanking, for example, may as an adult have spanking fantasies that he or she doesn't necessarily want to act out. The awesome power of erotic fantasies comes from these deep, twisted roots embedded in the adult psyche.

People use fantasy to aid arousal during masturbation and lovemaking. Some fantasies are soft and romantic, others are violent or sadomasochistic. Studies conducted in the past decade have shown that men's and women's fantasies are becoming more alike, with women reporting more graphic and sexually aggressive fantasies than they had in the past. Most people have favorite fantasies, those scenarios that can arouse them over and over again. Fantasies, whether violent or repetitive, are a concern only if they inhibit healthy sexual expression or the development of intimacy with a partner. Most fantasies don't.

Should you then worry about having fantasies or the nature of those fantasies? Most likely not. Recurrent violent fantasies can indicate deep-rooted emotional problems. The need to use the same fantasy every time during masturbation or lovemaking may indicate relationship issues or other problems. But for most people, no matter their age, fantasies serve many useful purposes. They enhance masturbation, create a mood conducive to lovemaking, sometimes facilitate orgasm by helping block out intrusive worries or concerns and allowing people to explore taboo activities such as sadomasochism, group sex, or affairs. Indulging in fantasy is a way of widening sexual experience without taking any risks. Fantasizing during intercourse does not mean you have a relationship problem.

At midlife, fantasies can become more beneficial. They are aids for people who don't have partners and who want to maintain their sexual vitality through masturbation. (Yes, it can be true that, if you don't use it, you'll lose it—*it* being the ability to achieve arousal and orgasm.) When arousal is a frequent problem, a man or a woman can begin fantasizing well in advance of the sexual encounter. And fantasies can make your sex life seem more interesting, too.

How does aging affect sexual fantasies?

- *You may feel less guilty about having fantasies at midlife.* Many people report having less guilt about sexual thoughts and fantasies than they once did. They may be more aware now that fantasies are a "normal" occurrence shared by most of the rest of the human race. And they may also feel less threatened by their fantasies and less confused about what they mean. A young man, for example, might fear that the occasional homosexual or group-sex fantasy indicates he is secretly gay, whereas an older man understands his fantasies aren't suppressed desires.

- *You may be more willing to share your fantasies with your partner.* As guilt diminishes, the desire to share grows. If you have an accepting partner and a strong, intimate relationship, secrets can be told. Many people are over 40 before they feel comfortable enough with themselves and their partners to share their sexual fantasies.

- *You may be more skillful at using fantasies.* With age comes sexual self-knowledge. You probably know what fantasy to use and when to use it to speed up, or even slow down, sexual responses. Freely indulging in fantasy, as noted earlier, is also a good way to prepare for a sexual encounter. At midlife, you probably know how to turn yourself on this way and don't feel guilty about doing so.

- *You may be viewing the same general category of fantasy, but the plots may be more varied.* Studies show that people in all age groups have fantasies that can be fitted into the same general categories. In a Danish study of women aged 22 to 70, age did not significantly affect the type of fantasy a woman had. Older women *slightly* favored fantasies including more foreplay and caressing, whereas younger women *slightly* favored fantasies of new experiences and partners. Similar U.S. studies show that, although fantasies vary considerably from person to person, age was not the determining factor in what types of fantasies men and women had. The fantasies within categories, however, were somewhat more varied in older people. In romantic fantasies, for example, the men and women over 40 put more detail into their romantic scenarios and chose more varied settings, perhaps reflecting travels they've taken.

"I have more control over my fantasies than I did when I was in my twenties so I enjoy them more," says Chan, 48. "I don't know about other men; but in my youth, I often felt a hostage to my own sexual thoughts. It was hard to turn them off sometimes. They got in the way. Really, they were too much of a good thing. Now I can call them up and consciously use them for my own purposes. If I am having trouble ejaculating, I can pull up a fantasy that does the trick for me—a woman masturbating or swallowing me or me ejaculating between her breasts."

Top Ten Midlife Sex Fantasies

- *Making love with someone other than one's regular partner.* This is the top fantasy for people of all ages. After 40, we still fantasize about supermodels and superheroes. In our fantasy scenarios, we very likely have not aged.

- *The forbidden partner (someone from another race, religion, or class; a relative; a friend's spouse; a much younger lover).* At midlife, the forbidden partner may likely be much younger. This fantasy lover may even be someone entirely unsuitable or inappropriate, like your best friend's son or daughter. Remember, it's a fantasy not a wish.

- *Group sex.* The fantasy of having sex with multiple partners is common to people of all ages. Some people may fantasize a group of people their own age, and others see themselves as either younger or the age they really are but with a group of much younger people.

- *The romantic fantasy.* Young women more commonly fantasize sex in idyllic surroundings than do young men. As they age, men become more romantic, less focused solely on genital sex. By midlife, men too are fantasizing about making love to their partner on a moonlit beach.

- *The spontaneous encounter.* The fantasy of sexual serendipity appeals to men and women of all ages. Midlife boomers identify it as *the zipless fuck* popularized by novelist Erica Jong in *Fear of Flying*. In that fantasy, we meet a stranger and two bodies come together in such perfect sexual union that the clothes easily fall away from our bodies, the body parts meld together beautifully, the simultaneous orgasms are shattering. No stuck zippers. No messy details.

- *Forced sex, sometimes called the rape fantasy.* Both men and women, young and old, have this fantasy, which does not indicate a true desire to be raped. They enjoy the fantasy of having another person control their responses, forcing them to enjoy sex, maybe a type of sexual activity they wouldn't really participate in. Older people, especially women, are more comfortable with the fantasy, because they know it does not represent a rape wish. In one survey, many young women reported negative feelings, including guilt, about the rape fantasy, whereas few women over 40 did.

• *Taboo sex acts, such as having sex in a public place or as some form of sadomasochistic activity.* Men and women over 40 may have more of these fantasies than they did when they were younger for two reasons: They are less likely to suppress sexual thoughts or ideas that frighten or induce guilt. And they feel more free to explore, at least in fantasy, those areas of their sexuality previously held off limits. Some men and women get a little kinkier with age.

• *Exhibitionistic or voyeuristic fantasies, in which one is having sex while being watched or watching someone else have sex.* In a common version of this fantasy, a man watches his wife make love to another man. Like the taboo fantasies, and for the same reasons, they are somewhat more common after the age of 40.

• *Homosexual encounter.* Common to both genders and all ages, the homosexual encounter is more often fantasized by the young, confusing and alarming some. By midlife, a man or woman is probably secure enough about his or her own sexual identity not to be concerned about that fantasy, which may be one reason it occurs less often.

• *Sex with a celebrity.* One study reported that people in their 20s were most likely to fantasize sex with a celebrity. Although midlife men and women do have the occasional celebrity fantasy, they may be dreaming about having sex with the president or the first lady rather than with rock stars. In fact, the same study found that 22 percent of women over 35 had fantasized about having sex with either the president or another high-ranking government figure, such as the governor or senator of their state.

Should You Share Your Fantasies?

There is no definitive answer to the question of whether to share your fantasies. Sometimes sharing fantasies ignites a couple's passions, and sometimes it douses the fire. Your fantasy may be very exciting to you, but not to your lover who considers it boring, repugnant, screamingly funny, or personally insulting. Sometimes the sharing of a fantasy robs it of its power to arouse. Once the fantasy is put out for discussion and analysis, it can be like a magic trick after the special effects have been exposed: The thrill is gone. Still, many couples take the risk of sharing and are rewarded in pleasure.

"My wife and I were sharing secrets one night, and I told her for twenty years I'd fantasized about what it would be like to have sex with her sister and her best friend," says Robert. "When I saw the stricken look on her face, I quickly added that I'd fantasized maybe a couple dozen times over twenty years, not daily obsessing. Not good enough. I was in trouble for months. She thought I wanted her sister and her best friend because they were thin more than I wanted her because she was fat, which she isn't. We didn't have sex for three weeks after my bad case of mouth diarrhea."

On the other hand, Jerry told his wife he'd occasionally had a stray fantasy about having sex with her and her best friend together, and she was aroused by the idea.

"We both agreed," Jerry says, "we'd never do it in real life, but we had a hell of a hot time in bed talking about doing it. I got my wife to say words out loud I thought I'd never hear, like, 'Now I'm taking Naomi's nipple into my mouth.' Wow!"

Five Tips for Sharing Sexual Fantasies

Before you share fantasies with your partner, keep the following tips in mind:

- *Think about how comfortable your partner will be discussing this type of sexual activity.* Some people might find violent, aggressive fantasies disturbing. Some might respond unfavorably to hearing that their partner fantasizes about group sex. There's nothing wrong with pushing each other's comfort envelopes, but doing that takes care.

- *Preface your sharing with some general discussion of fantasies, what they mean and don't mean.* You might want to read this chapter to your partner or at least summarize the main points.

- *Be reassuring about your partner's desirability.* Some fantasies may make your partner jealous. A man or woman who has aging issues, such as body-image concerns or performance anxieties, may feel threatened by hearing that you fantasize making love to someone else, particularly a friend or relative in good physical shape.

- *Let your partner know there's no pressure to act on your fantasy.* You may both decide it would be fun to try fantasy acting, but sharing shouldn't turn into coercing.

- *Remember that sharing will prompt a response.* Be prepared for your partner's reaction. The other person has the right to say, "I don't find that erotic at all." And be receptive to your partner's fantasies. You aren't the only one with a good imagination.

Should You Act Out Your Fantasies?

"My wife and I had both fantasized a threesome," Jay says, "but it was two men in her script and two women in mine. We met this couple in the Bahamas who were celebrating their silver wedding anniversary, as we were, and one drink led to another. We shared the fantasy with them, and, of course, no surprise, they'd had the same fantasy. 'Why not a foursome?' someone asked.

"We ended up in this huge bed in their suite, all of us naked, sobering up quickly, embarrassed as well as bare-assed. We made this halfhearted attempt at groping each other's partner, the women pulled off a tepid lesbian embrace and kiss, and we guys, dicks at half staff, fucked our own wives side by side in the missionary position. I think everybody faked an orgasm. We avoided that couple for the rest of our visit.

"'The next time we act out a fantasy,' my wife deadpanned as we were packing to leave, 'we'll go with the monkey story.' We found that terribly funny and still laugh about it. The fantasy sex was a dud, but trying it didn't hurt our relationship."

As for the question "To share or not to share?," there is no correct answer here either. Acting out a fantasy can add excitement to a relationship or be a passion fizzle. It can bring a couple closer together or start a fight, which, ironically, could bring them closer together anyway. In fantasy, everything is perfect and possible. In real life, zippers get stuck, feelings get hurt, and the steps of the Lincoln Memorial are hard and cold on bare skin in the middle of winter. Whether or not a couple can safely and erotically act out a fantasy depends on four factors only they can evaluate:

- *Feasibility.* Ask yourself, What price a threesome with the neighbor? Can genital contact be made and sustained while hang-gliding? Would the ASPCA file charges? A fantasy feasibility study should take each partner's physical, moral, and emotional safety into consideration.

- *Adaptability.* Acting out fantasies is like adapting a book into a film. You can't be too literal minded. In your fantasy, you are being ravished by a cruel stranger while your helpless and bound partner watches. In the bedroom version, your partner can wear a mask and behave masterfully. But some fantasies, like some books, simply don't lend themselves to adaptation.

- *The sizzle factor.* If your partner finds the fantasy disgusting, excessively amusing, or not erotic, the acting will lack passion. Both members of the troupe need to be excited by the concept. In a two-person play, there are no walk-ons.

- *The props department.* Would an arousing adaptation require more props than you can pull together from existing materials or buy, borrow, or rent? Some plays are too expensive to produce.

Choosing a Script

If you and your lover both want to try acting out a fantasy, keep in mind the four factors just discussed and have each of you write six scenarios. Be as wildly imaginative as you like within the boundaries of feasibility and adaptability. Limit the actors to two. Together, pick the one fantasy you both find the most exciting. Don't pressure your partner to try something he or she doesn't find appealing. Then adapt the scenario to reality and have fun.

Erotic Role Playing

"Acting out fantasies has allowed my wife and me to shed some inhibitions by pretending to be different people," says Ray. "We started out with the cliché scenarios. She was the maid, and I was the lord of the manor. I was Spartacus, and she was a rich, bored, and cruel Roman wife. Then we got more creative. Last week I was Henry VIII and she was Anne Boleyn. It was the night before Anne's beheading; and in our script, Henry and Anne had sex one last time. She treated his penis with great reverence, going down on it as if she were receiving a sacrament.

"Maybe we are frustrated actors. We both did amateur theater in college. This may sound crazy to some people, but we have had some of the hottest sex of our lives acting out fantasies. We are both interested in history and historical characters; and we like to imagine what some of these people were really like in bed."

Assuming the roles of historical figures won't be every couple's ideal scenario, but erotic role playing is an integral part of fantasy play. Here are the most common roles found in sex fantasies:

- *The aggressor.* One partner becomes the sex goddess or slave master, the lord or lady of the manor, or the boss. Though the scenario has been decided between the two, the aggressor appears to be in control of the action. Women are as likely as men to play the aggressor. In fact, many men fantasize about being dominated by a strong, aggressive woman.

- *The passive one.* This partner gets to be taken or used sexually by the other. Acting out passive and aggressive roles allows each partner to sample the joys of occasionally being dominant or submissive. Doctor or nurse and patient, teacher and pupil are variations of this game.

- *The stranger.* Some couples get dressed in their best clothes, go out separately, and one picks the other up at a prearranged place, preferably a classy bar. She may be sitting on the bar stool with her skirt just above her knee, legs crossed, waiting to be approached when he gets there (see page 65 for one couple's take on this fantasy).

Erotic role playing gives a couple the opportunity to explore their own undiscovered territory. Many couples have used their fantasies and role-playing games to trigger self-confrontation, which leads to growth. This can be an opportunity for forging a stronger connection to your partner, in bed and out. And some people keep their fantasies private, using them for personal exploration that enables them to be better lovers and partners in the end.

Gerald says, "I would be a less satisfying partner to my wife if I didn't have a fantasy life apart from her. There are things about me she could never understand and probably not accept. I don't believe that we must have total knowledge of each to be happy. I've seen our son and his wife go into the bathroom together. My wife and I think some things aren't meant to be shared."

He and his wife, Deanna, were both 18 and virgins when they got married. In earlier years, his fantasies often revolved around other women, those he knew or had seen in real life as well as movie stars. Elizabeth Taylor was a favorite fantasy partner. As he aged, his fantasies grew more complicated and sometimes darker.

"I wasn't satisfied with fantasizing Elizabeth Taylor in the missionary position with me anymore," he says. "I wanted her to be wearing high-heeled boots, carrying a whip, and making me grovel at her feet. I traveled a lot in my job. A kinky novel I bought in a hotel gift shop inspired some wild fantasies. And, now with the variety of sexual material available on cable TV, I have a lot of fantasies Deanna would find shocking."

On an out-of-town trip a few years ago Gerald made one of his sado-masochistic fantasies come true. He answered a dominatrix's ad and paid her to verbally abuse and lightly spank him. The experience fell far short of his expectations. Rather than feeling arousal and exhilaration or even guilt, he felt "just plain foolish."

"In reality, I didn't want to be insulted and spanked," he says. "I just wanted to indulge in the occasional kinky fantasy while masturbating. What good would it do me to share that with Deanna?"

But his private life has enriched his sex life with his partner. He has asked her to initiate sex more often, to assume the female superior position frequently, and to be vocal about her desires. In behaving in a more sexually dominant way, she didn't turn into the woman of his fantasies—something he doesn't want anyway—but his wife has become a more exciting lover for him.

"We have better sex together because of my private life," he says. "Neither one of us is the type to examine our deepest thoughts for the hidden meaning. She wouldn't thank me for laying my fantasies down on the table for her to interpret. I don't want to know about it if she fanta-sizes having sex with animals or something."

Like Gerald, some men and women find themselves entertaining sexual fantasies that would never have occurred to them when they were younger. Men especially may get kinkier as they get older, but women are not immune to the erotic allure of forbidden thoughts.

Elaine, who didn't know what the term *S&M* (sadomasochism) meant until she was past 40, says, "My husband and I admitted to each other that our fantasies had grown wilder in recent years. We attribute that to cable TV. I find myself, for example, mesmerized by women's breasts or titillated by a spanking scene. Remember, I grew up in a time when girls didn't see each other's breasts unless they had sisters around the same age; and I didn't.

"The visual images enhance our fantasies and give us something to talk about, though neither of us wants to act out what we call our *dirty-mind movies*. I have discovered that, if I'm not in the mood for sex, I can put an X-rated tape in the bedroom VCR during foreplay and get warmed up. After a few minutes, I don't need to see the screen. I'm running my own film."

These couples use fantasy to enhance their sex lives—without sharing or acting out. If you don't want to have the full-blown fantasy discussion, use your sexy scenarios in your own way to generate excitement. Keeping a fantasy private is not the same thing as withholding information a partner may be entitled to have.

Seven Steps for Connecting Fantasy to Reality

One of the common themes running through the sex questions people ask is: How can I get my partner to do what I want? What if you want to encourage a reluctant partner to participate in your fantasy life in some way? The young may stumble over the issues surrounding this central question more than the rest of us, but everyone eventually faces this situation. If the desire is perceived to be outside the bounds of normal, the issue takes on greater power and it becomes harder to ask your partner to indulge the fantasy. The following tips will help you decide if you should turn your fantasies into real life:

- Be clear about what you want. Do you want to share fantasies—in other words, do you want to play "I'll tell you mine, if you tell me yours?" Do you want your partner merely to listen or to give feedback? Or do you want to act out—or at least talk out during lovemaking—your fantasies?

- Differentiate between the elements of fantasy that could be made real and those that should probably not be. If your fantasies run toward heavy S&M, for example, it's unlikely that you really want to act them out. You may want to talk through them during lovemaking or adapt them in softer ways to real sexplay. Make the difference clear to your partner or you may risk scaring or offending him or her.

- First, introduce your desire as a subject rather than a request. Maybe you haven't ever discussed bondage, spanking, making love in the pool, or playacting with your partner. Bring up the subject, gauge the reaction, and move carefully from there.

- Anticipate the difficulties. Your partner may feel jealous, threatened, repulsed, or amused by your innermost erotic thoughts. Be prepared for that. Don't overreact. In other areas of life, we can stand to hear, "What a silly idea!" or "I'm not interested in that at all!" When sexuality is on the line, many people get defensive.

- Remember that telling doesn't necessarily lead to action. Your partner will probably need to mull over your erotic thoughts before making a decision about participating actively in them. It may seem as if you had waited a long time for this great fantasy moment, but you should remember: It's news to your partner. And news takes time to digest.

- Be receptive to change. After studying your fantasies, your partner may want to edit them. Be open to the possibilities suggested. Compromise is part of lovemaking as well as of life.

- Remember what fantasies are—and aren't. Look on them as an arousal tool in your erotic kit. Maybe they don't, and never will, work for your partner. They have to work only for *you*. Don't read too much meaning either into having fantasies—or having them rejected.

Overcoming a Negative Fantasy Experience

Remember Robert, whose wife refused to have sex with him for 3 weeks after he shared his fantasy about having sex with her sister and her best friend? Here's my prescription for avoiding that outcome:

- *Prevention.* Sometimes a shared fantasy simply fails to excite the other or causes unintentional hurt. In some cases, however, lovers share fantasies with malice aforethought. They flaunt their fantasies to wound their lovers or at the least to get a reaction. Bad idea. You might receive momentary satisfaction, but you'll pay a long-term erotic price for that fleeting moment of venomous glory.

- *Develop a thicker skin.* Granted, it doesn't feel good to hear that your beloved craves the neighbor. You can retreat behind wounded pride or take a more mature view of human sexuality. Your partner's fantasies will not always include you, even if you're Jane Seymour or Brad Pitt. Develop a stronger sense of your erotic self, one that does not depend entirely on your partner's desire.

• *Don't withdraw.* What about your partner's fantasies is so disturbing? Talk about it. Insist he or she listen without being defensive.

• *Appreciate your lover's honesty.* He or she deserves credit for taking an emotional risk. Sharing something as intimate as one's sexual fantasies takes some courage. Whether you can appreciate or accept those fantasies, you can admire the honesty.

• *Get perspective.* Remember that fantasies are only *thoughts*, not actions, not wishes. Focus on how your lover acts toward you sexually and how your actions affect his or her responses. If you've acted out a fantasy and found the experience disappointing, put it behind you. Some thoughts are better enjoyed in the head than in the bed.

SIZZLER #7

My Secret Sin

Wanda closed her eyes and slipped into the cool waters of a blue lagoon. Floating on her back, she felt the gentle waves lapping at her breasts and penetrating her labia like liquid fingers. The gardenias pinned behind each ear gave off a delicious scent, filling her nostrils. She was alone and intensely happy. Her lover, a Hawaiian bodybuilder, would soon be joining her in paradise. Meanwhile...her hand drifted to her genitals.

With her orgasm, the lagoon, gardenias, and expected lover fell away. Wanda was alone on her bed in a comfortable suburban home. Her children were away at college, her husband off on a business trip. And, like in the fantasy, Wanda was alone but intensely happy.

My fantasies are my own business, she thought. She didn't add: *As long as I use them only when I'm masturbating.* But she might have. Wanda felt guilty about having fantasies during lovemaking with her husband. She feared becoming dependent on them. Did the fantasies mean she didn't love him? That she wasn't happy in her marriage? Because she was afraid they meant exactly that, she banished them from her mind. Surely they were the dirty thoughts she'd been warned about many years ago in her Catholic girls' high school.

Wanda separated her private sex, masturbation, from the sex she shared with her husband, Anthony. Then one day he turned her sex life upside down. Anthony told Wanda that he had fantasies too.

"I did something naughty while I was out of town," he said. She raised her eyebrows and smiled at him encouragingly, expecting him to confess he'd put an expensive purchase on one of their credit cards or had consumed a series of high-fat, high-cholesterol meals. "I rented one of those X-rated movies on the hotel TV."

"Will it show up on your bill?" she asked. "Will your boss find out?"

"It will show up only as a pay-per-view charge," he said, laughing at her. "My boss won't question an in-room movie charge, honey. It's not as if I threw a party in my room."

"Oh," she said. Suddenly the significance of what he had done struck her. "An X-rated movie. Aren't those things disgusting?"

And didn't his renting one mean he was dissatisfied with her in bed?

"You would have liked it," he said. "It was told from a woman's point of view. She was masturbating to a fantasy of sex with a man of a different race, and suddenly he appeared, like a genie out of a bottle."

Wanda blushed scarlet. He knew. Her husband must have guessed.

"Wanda?" he asked. Anthony hadn't known before, but he knew now. "You have a secret life?" Tears sprang to her eyes. Laughing, he grabbed her to him in a big embrace. "My darling wife, we all have fantasies. There's nothing wrong with that."

He begged her to share her fantasies with him, but she wasn't ready for that. Maybe she never would be. He agreed not to push her for details. Their conversation did, however, have a big affect on their sex life, perhaps unbeknownst to him. A week later, while they were making love, she let her mind run free.

As Anthony's tongue circled her clitoris, she put her arms over her head and grasped the bars of their antique brass bed. She imagined her wrists were chained to them. A captive sex slave, she was being deliciously tormented by her master. Ownership wasn't enough for him. He wanted more than her grudging compliance. He wanted her pleasure.

"If I can make you come, I will know I truly own you," he'd whispered in her ear as he chained her to the huge bed in his luxurious suite.

"Never," she'd said, writhing, as he twisted her nipples cruelly between his fingers.

"Never," she repeated more weakly as he lovingly lashed her genitals with his tongue. "Oh, no," she gasped. Groaning and writhing, she tried at first to pull away from his mouth, but she couldn't. He held her thighs firmly apart. In the morning, she would have bruises where his fingers had been.

When she could hold out no longer, he abruptly took his mouth away.

"Oh, please," she begged. "Please."

"Call me master," he insisted, and she did.

The fantasy dissolved in a series of rippling orgasms. When at last they were finished, she looked into Anthony's eyes. For several minutes, he'd truly been her master, and he seemed to know it.

CHAPTER EIGHT

Getting in Sync with Your Partner Again

"Sometimes I feel overwhelmed by Kevin's need for physical affection and attention," says Belinda. Both in their mid-50s, Kevin and Belinda have been married for 30 years. They have two teenage children, two busy careers, a large suburban house, the requisite dog and cat, cars, gym memberships, friends, and extended families. "In bed at night he wants to hold me and be held. He craves cuddling and intimate chats. Often I'd rather read a book on my own side of the bed, with him reading a book on his side, or have him downstairs puttering in the den like he used to do.

"The sex is still good. I'm not complaining about the sex. I just wish he didn't need so much attention from me when we aren't having sex. Last week after we'd made love one night, I wanted to get up, go pour myself a glass of wine, sit alone in the living room and sift through a pile of magazines I hadn't had time to read. He wanted afterplay.

"Ten years ago, the situation was reversed. I wanted more affection, more cuddling, more time talking about feelings. He had limited tolerance for all that. I had to learn how to cope with the differences between us. Now he comes to me brimming with emotion and expects me to be delighted with his soulful outpouring. I'm not, but I try not to show it. Will we ever be in sync?"

When a couple is out of sync, one partner wants a more intimate relationship, while the other wants more time for self. When men and women are young, she is typically the partner who wants more intimacy. Kissing, caressing, embracing, and cuddling may be more satisfying to her than intercourse. At midlife, as she develops a need for self-fulfillment that makes intimacy less important to her, she also has increased sexual self-confidence and finds greater satisfaction in intercourse. Orgasm, more easily achieved, may take on a new significance in her erotic life. And now, inspired by his changing physiology, *he* wants more tenderness in their lovemaking, more shared confidences in their afterplay. Intimacy has become more meaningful and important to him. Early in the relationship, she may have complained he doesn't have enough "we" and too much "I." Now she is reveling in her "I" time, while he is craving more "we."

This sexual role-swapping is common, if perplexing, to the couple who finds themselves suddenly in opposite emotional positions. A recent study found 61 percent of women under 35 named "love" their primary reason for having sex. Only 38 percent of women aged 36 to 57 said that. For men, the results were reversed. Only 31 percent of the younger men cited "love" as the primary reason for making love, but more than half the older men did. Another study found that women over 40 placed a higher priority on erotic pleasures such as swimming in the nude and watching X-rated videos than other women *or* men in all age groups.

There are, of course, other contributing reasons for a couple being out of sync. They may be in different developmental phases, with one, for example, thriving in the workplace while the other is floundering. One may have a better relationship with teen or adult children than the other does. Or one may be in the emotional throes of dealing with ill or disabled parents, whereas the other's parents are in good health. In some couples, one has significant aging issues while the other seems to move easily into a new life stage. What's common to all these situations? One partner needs more comfort and safety from the marriage, and the other, in a personal cycle of growth and stability, needs less.

Accept Being Out of Sync

In every long-term relationship, the partners will almost surely experience some out-of-sync time. Balancing one partner's greater need for intimacy against the other's desire for self-fulfillment is an ongoing process. Here are some hints for doing that:

- *Don't expect the relationship to meet all your needs.* Sometimes everyone has to provide his or her own comfort and solace in the face of disappointment, sadness, or frustration. People find that comfort in many different ways, including long walks with the family dog, hobbies, and sports. Some people turn to religion. Friends and relatives can also provide support. An intimate partner is more than a source of succor and not the only person whose companionship can make your burdens seem lighter.

- *Acknowledge your own (or your partner's) inner strength.* Most people are not as fragile as they think they are during emotionally needy times. Recall how you have handled difficult situations or crises in the past. You are strong and resilient. (Or, your partner is strong and resilient; stop worrying so much about his or her temporary need for attention.)

- *Realize that being out of sync with your partner is normal, not a problem.* Couples who expect to be soul mates and on the same wavelength for life have unrealistic expectations. Long-term intimate partners may connect intensely or feel like two very familiar ships passing in the night. Both synchrony and time spent out of sync are necessary for healthy interaction.

- *Use the out-of-sync time for personal growth.* This is a positive, useful time for both partners, not a traumatic event. Out-of-sync periods encourage couples to expand their individual coping skills and increase their ability to comfort themselves and develop personal hobbies and interests. Sometimes friendships and other family relationships are strengthened.

How Being Out of Sync Affects Sex

"Molly and I went through a period a few years back where we weren't connecting sexually or otherwise," says Dan. "I was stagnating in my middle-management job, and she was very happy with her work as a school librarian. In addition, she'd gone back to college part time to work on her master's degree. Every day to her was filled with excitement; and every day to me was another day at the same old grind. I hated my job and simultaneously was terrified of losing it one day to corporate downsizing. And I resented her, because my income made it possible for her to do what she wanted to do. Thanks to me, she had it all.

"I wish I could say I manfully resolved my issues through solitary soul searching, but I didn't. I punished her by withdrawing sexually just at the point when she wanted sex more often. She was the initiator, and I was the one with the headache. One evening she stood in front of the television set wearing high heels and a black satin nightgown, and I craned my neck around her to see the set. We had a big blowup that night after I'd rejected her. It cleared the air, and we began to talk. She hadn't realized how stifled and trapped I felt in my job. It was my fault she hadn't because I'd never told her. We agreed that we had to work toward equity in the marriage, something that wasn't in our initial agreement when we got married. At twenty-two, I thought I'd always want to be 'the man,' carrying the family's weight. Now I'm back in school, too, taking courses to prepare me for a switch to self-employment. We alternate semesters because we can't afford the cost of both of us going at once, and we can't leave our young teenagers on their own that much either.

"Our relationship has definitely improved. Sexually, it's never been better. We are making love more often now than we were ten years ago when the kids were preschoolers. Last summer when they were at camp, we made love in the pool. It was fantastic."

Being out of sync may affect a couple's sex life in one of the following ways.

A Decline in Lovemaking

Like Dan, many men and women who perceive themselves as being the partner shortchanged in life or in the relationship react by withdrawing sexually. That may be a subconscious desire to punish the more positive partner who wants to make love more often or more fully. It may also be the direct result of mild depression, and with depression comes a decline in libido.

HOW TO HANDLE: Meeting him at the door dressed only in plastic wrap isn't likely to solve the problem. Nor is coming home with a dozen roses. If the unhappy partner doesn't or can't initiate a dialogue, the other one has to do so. Start talking, but not about sex. Don't say, "Why don't you want to make love anymore?" Ask about what's going on in the rest of his or her life.

An Affair

One or both partners may have an affair. The one who wants more sex in the relationship feels cheated and justified in looking elsewhere. The other partner feels misunderstood, used, and unloved by his or her mate and thus also justified in looking elsewhere. When couples are out of sync with each other, they can often convince themselves that having an affair is warranted. (For more on affairs and how they affect a marriage, see Chapter 15.)

HOW TO HANDLE: If you're thinking about having an affair, weigh the risks carefully. When people get involved in highly charged emotional affairs, they almost always experience pain and conflict. Even a casual affair can be damaging to a relationship.

What if your partner is having an affair? First, try not to say anything you really don't mean, like threatening to walk out. That only puts you in a weaker position. Sometimes a brief separation helps. On the other hand, it may culminate in only an illusory resolution: The straying mate's apology is accepted by the aggrieved partner, but neither examines the underlying causes for the affair.

If both partners want to heal the relationship, the affair will most certainly have to be ended. Counseling is useful in helping couples deal with feelings of guilt, anger, and resentment and helping them establish communication and, eventually, trust again.

Arguments About How Often and How to Make Love

Typically, the partner who is feeling less emotionally needy wants to make love more often or in more creative and inventive ways than the other does. The average out-of-sync couple tries to resolve the differences through argument. It doesn't work. The partner who wants less sex may be depressed or despondent and is probably experiencing a decline in libido that is not likely to be elevated by a logical case for more sex.

HOW TO HANDLE: Stop arguing. Be more attentive to your partner when you do make love. Don't pressure by being overly seductive. Be more subtle when you do attempt to seduce or initiate, more gentle and generous when you decline. If you're the less interested partner, don't automatically say no. Instead, say maybe, and maybe you'll change your mind. If you're the more interested partner, remind yourself that your partner isn't rejecting you. His or her current lack of interest in sex is an attitude subject to change.

Hotter Sex

A woman's midlife sexual awakening can be the spark that ignites a smoldering sexual fire in a longtime relationship. If a man is not caught up in his midlife issues, he may be responsive to her taking the sexual lead now. He wants more intimacy; and to most men, that does include more sex. Her increased interest in lovemaking may flatter and arouse him. And her increased responsiveness may free him from concerns about pleasing her in bed or "giving" her sufficient orgasms.

HOW TO MAKE IT HAPPEN: Each partner can take some cues from the other's previous sexual behavior in a role-swapping situation. She once appealed primarily to his genitals when she wanted to make love. By wearing erotic clothing, setting a seductive mood, and touching him in certain ways, she let him know what she wanted. Now he can approach her in the same way.

Although 20 years ago, *he* seduced *her* with romance, now he could use a little romance. Many couples think romance, like foreplay, is what men do for women to get them into bed. Even women who are savvy enough to understand their man's increased need for erotic touch fail to appreciate his corresponding desire to be treated in a romantic way. At midlife, he will at least fully appreciate the romantic gestures—flower- and scent-filled bedroom, candlelight dinners, and other little touches he noted only in passing as he headed straight for the genital connection when he was younger.

"Woo him," advises Jeannette, 52, who has been married for 32 years to Daniel. "Men reach a point in their lives when they are tired of being in charge of the love and romance department. Send him flowers. Compliment his appearance. Touch him with pride when you're out in public. Curl up next to him on the sofa, massage his neck, and ask how his day went. Listen to him attentively. After twenty or thirty years, women stop listening. Reach him through his heart and soul, and his penis will follow.

"When our lovemaking began to decline a few years ago, I pestered Daniel about it. Then I remembered a similar period in our marriage when the kids were toddlers, ages one and three; and I was too tired and stressed for sex. He brought me back to erotic life by wooing me. So I pitched some woo, and it worked beautifully."

The Relationship-Synchrony Quiz

Each partner should take the following quiz separately; compare answers when you're both finished. This isn't meant to be a test; it's merely a tool for helping you recognize how in sync you are.

1. Do you look forward to rejoining your partner at the end of the day?

2. What aspect of your life gives you more pleasure or stimulation: relationship, work, children, hobbies, or other?

3. Describe the five aspects of your relationship that are most pleasing. Now list the five least pleasing.

4. Is your sex life satisfactory? If not, what would make it better?

5. Have there been recent occasions when you wanted to show affection to your partner but didn't? Why not? Give the full details, including your feelings.

6. Recall three instances in the past month when either you have annoyed your mate or vice versa. Give the full details, including your feelings.

7. What was the reason for your latest quarrel? How was it resolved?

8. Name five enjoyable activities you've done together and five you've done alone in the past month. Which did you enjoy more? Explain.

9. Would you prefer more time alone? Or more time with your mate?

10. Was there a period in your marriage when you were more accommodating to your mate's request or desires than you are now? And vice versa?

How to Use Your Responses

- *Look for patterns.* Do the two sets of responses indicate the relationship is a greater source of satisfaction for one than the other? Is there a repetition of resentment, feelings of loneliness, anger, or hurt?

- *Empathize with your partner's responses.* Empathy doesn't require agreement with the other's viewpoint. The most refined form of feeling-oriented communication, empathy is an effort to understand the other's beliefs, practices, and feeling without necessarily sharing or agreeing with them.

- *Don't play blame and counterblame.* Assigning blame to a partner for being out of sync with you is counterproductive. Some couples make blame a major part of their relationship. Resist that trap. Just accept that each of you is currently in a different place.

- *See where compromises and exchanges can be made.* Could one partner get more time alone by giving the other a greater role in choosing shared activities? Is it possible for each to be more accommodating of the other without relinquishing autonomy?

- *Negotiate compromises.* Make an appointment with each other for a compromise-exchange discussion. Each partner should state specifically what he or she would like and should avoid vague generalities. For example, "I would like greater closeness" is too broad, but "I would like to eat dinner with you four nights a week" is specific. Don't try to negotiate feelings. And be patient. Compromise takes time.

Common Midlife Situations That Get in the Way of Sex

The following sections introduce typical midlife situations can have an affect on sexuality. In each situation, there is often an out-of-sync element that adds to a couple's problems.

Raising Teenage Children

Research has shown that the most stressful time for a marriage is when the children are teenagers. For parents confronting their own midlife issues *and* raising teenagers, as many people are today, the level of difficulty climbs in geometric proportions. To be the midlife parents of a 15-year-old is to live on the horns of a major life-stage dilemma, complicated in many cases by the lack of synchrony between the partners. A sudden and precipitous decline in lovemaking often occurs in these marriages. If the relationship was close, warm, and intimate, it will survive a sexual drought or two. The partners will find their way back to each other.

The obstacles to sex in this situation are created by adult attitudes and fears as much as by the stresses of raising teenagers. A midlife father may contrast himself to his teenage son, bursting with sexuality, the constant reminder of his own (perceived) dwindling ability. Some men have affairs, probably with a younger lover, out of the need to prove they aren't over the hill sexually.

The midlife mother of a teenage daughter has her own issues. Coping with wrinkles, gray hair, and sagging breasts, she is reminded of her own (perceived) fading looks every time her daughter walks past her. Compounding the problem, her husband, this girl's father, may be so uncomfortable with his daughter's emergence into womanhood that he is suppressing all sexual feelings. He avoids his daughter and his wife, leaving them feeling rejected and confused. Overwhelmed by the youth in front of them, parents in these situations may let themselves go physically and withdraw sexually.

Sometimes power issues between father and son put the mother in a difficult position. He is so busy trying to prove he's still in charge that he antagonizes everyone, including his wife. Either one parent or both may regress and behave like teenagers themselves. They are rebelling against their own perception of how they are expected to be. In all these scenarios, one parent may likely be experiencing more difficulty with raising teenagers than the other, creating an out-of-sync element.

Caring for Aging Parents

The term *middle age* may have been adopted because it accurately describes where people are at this point in their lives: caught between the needs of their maturing children and their aging parents. Both are demanding, leaving the midlife adults in the center struggling to meet everyone's needs simultaneously. Aging parents are also a reminder of one's own coming decline.

The death of a parent makes almost everyone more conscious of mortality; some become more aware of their blessings, others of their discontents in the face of time running out. After losing a parent, some of us may want more from our relationships, including more and better sex. With a critical or authoritarian parent no longer looking over the shoulder, a man or woman orphaned at midlife can feel the pressure to change and improve, even if that means getting a divorce or having an affair. Old issues, such as premature ejaculation, routine sex, infrequent sex, or orgasmic difficulties may loom as problems that can no longer be tolerated.

The out-of-sync element comes into play when a partner understandably doesn't have the same life-changing response to the death of his or her parent-in-law.

Fear of Declining Sexuality and Other Age Issues

Fear of erectile dysfunction is a major issue for many men. If they have one experience of erectile dysfunction, they fear it is the beginning of the end of their sexuality—in other words, they catastrophize. Some men become quietly frantic, either withdrawing from sexual expression or behaving in a hypersexual way with other, probably younger, women. Other men seek medical help for what is really a minor psychological problem: fear of aging, fear of loss, and fear of death, all displaced onto the penis. Often all they need to do is confess their fears to their partners, thus building intimacy and making it possible for both to bring transition to a higher form of lovemaking.

Menopause can be a woman's excuse for shutting down sexually. Religious views encourage some women to stop being sexual when procreation is no longer possible. If a man buys into the menopause myth about her declining interest in sex, she may interpret his caution as disinterest and may retreat. It's easy for a couple to get out of sync when one is unhappily immersed in aging issues and the other is handling them more easily.

Living in an Empty Nest

When the kids leave home, a couple may have the hottest sex they've had in years. After decades of being careful not to alarm the children, they can have sex in the afternoon, make noise during lovemaking, walk around the house naked. With greater privacy, more time for intimate conversation, and less accountability to other family members, partners in a good relationship may find their sexuality blooming.

But the masquerade is over for those couples whose relationship revolved around the kids. These couples generally fall into one of the following three types of sexually challenged relationships:

- *Conflict-related couple.* These folks live to fight. Conflict is so much a part of their lifestyle that their grown children, other family members, and friends can't think of them any other way except trading verbal blows.

- *Devitalized couple.* The partners in this relationship were in love once, but they've now grown apart. A low-energy couple, they seem apathetic rather than conflict ridden. Passive but congenial, they probably consider themselves happy.

- *Convenience couple.* These couples are similar to the devitalized couple with one exception: The spark was never present in their relationship. Their emphasis is not on the marriage but on other things, such as money and property, civic and social involvements, family and friends, and careers and hobbies.

When the partners in these relationships are out of sync, they have a much harder time connecting than other out-of-sync couples.

Health Problems

The effect of diabetes, high blood pressure, heart problems, and other chronic illnesses on sexuality is discussed at length in Chapter 14. When one partner is suffering from a debilitating illness, the other, no matter how sympathetic, is probably not as needful of emotional comfort within the relationship. This particular out-of-sync situation can be more difficult than some others.

Anti-Sex Myths

By age 60, a man isn't deemed sexual in our society unless he's wealthy, well-preserved, and sporting a beautiful young woman on his arm. A woman that age has to be Catherine Deneuve or Helen Mirren to be considered a sexual being. The ideas of beauty and sexuality in our society are not as sophisticated as they are in European societies, where style, experience, and character hold their own with fresh skin and tight bodies.

In the United States, adult children are uncomfortable imagining their parents as people who have sexual needs. They want Mom and Pop to be stereotypical aging parents, soft pot-bellied grandparents. The job description excludes sex appeal. An older couple can become seriously out of sync if one accepts society's sexual limits on aging and the other doesn't.

Retirement

Some couples now retire at age 50. If they share interests and leisure activities, they can have fun together and will probably find their sex lives improving. When a man retires and his wife doesn't, there may be a power shift in the marriage and a change in attitude about his role; this may contribute to erectile dysfunction. Some men become depressed and anxious after retirement, which can lead to erectile problems. In general, men and women who were happily sexual throughout their lives have an easier time understanding and accepting their changing sexuality, are more imaginative in bed, and can enjoy the satisfactions of age without being tormented by the sexual ambitions of youth.

Various studies reveal that sexual desire continues in the majority of men and women throughout their 70s and beyond. The psychoanalyst Eric Erickson, a pioneer of research on sexuality throughout the life cycle, found that older people experience a more generalized sexuality as opposed to specific sexuality—in other words, they may become more sensuous while having intercourse less often. Again, a couple becomes out of sync when one makes this transition with relative ease while the other one is having trouble adjusting.

How to Reconnect in Bed

"Jeff made a lot of money in a high-profile, high-pressure corporate job, so much money that he could afford to retire on his fiftieth birthday without us having to give up any of our lifestyle," says Diane, an artist who has a studio at home. "I was a little concerned about his retiring, because I was so used to his being gone, working twelve-hour days, traveling for days, even weeks at a time. We had separate lives, and suddenly we were going to put them together. I was afraid he'd get bored playing golf and would drive me nuts looking for attention. Surprisingly, he was fine. He became involved in volunteer projects, began doing a little consulting work, and by the time he'd been 'retired' six months he was so busy and happy in his new life, I felt left behind.

"He was more interested in lovemaking than he'd been since we were first married. I was always pushing him off, telling him I was too busy with my work or too tired. One afternoon he came out to my studio with a picnic basket, including a bottle of chilled champagne and two glasses. I started crying and couldn't stop. He insisted I make an appointment with my doctor."

After her internist could find no physical reason for Diane's mild depression and lack of libido, she recommended counseling. In therapy, Diane quickly came to terms with her problem: She felt old because her husband was retired. And old people didn't have sex.

"My mother was sixty-five and my father was sixty-nine when he retired," she says. "When Jeff retired, I was suddenly catapulted into old age. I hadn't realized how many negative attitudes I had about aging until then. It took me a while to be comfortable with Jeff's increased sex drive and my own suppressed sexual feelings, but now I am. We celebrated the first anniversary of his retirement by taking a romantic cruise. This may sound like a cliché, but we had the best sex of our lives."

Five Steps for Getting in Sexual Sync

Become More Verbally Intimate

If you want more affection, a certain type of caress, more oral sex, more frequent lovemaking—*ask*. Many people find it difficult to ask for what they want sexually because they believe their longtime partners should know. They don't always. Would you like to add a degree of wildness to your lovemaking? Talk about your fantasies and secret wishes. The more verbal you can be about your erotic desires, the more likely you are of realizing them.

Learn How to Say No

It is possible to say no to sex or a certain sex act without rejecting your partner or feeling guilty. Hearing an unqualified and unexplained negative response can feel like being hit with a weapon. The recipient is wounded; the refuser is guilt ridden or angry at being "made" to feel guilty. Explain your refusal even if you aren't quite sure of the reasons yourself. "I don't know why I'm not in the mood for lovemaking, but I'm not," is preferable to simply saying no.

Some people say no in nonverbal ways, like his repeatedly being unable to get an erection or her being unable to reach orgasm in encounter after encounter. These are hurtful and damaging ways of denying a partner.

Respond to a Partner's Emotional Needs

Take care of the often unexpressed feelings; and the sex will follow. The best way to a man's (or woman's) heart may not necessarily be the stomach, but the best way to his or her genitals certainly may be the heart. You probably can't use reason to bring an out-of-sync (and sexually detached) partner around to a more positive way of thinking, but you can help him or her feel the way back to erotic life. What are your partner's emotional needs? And what can you do to help meet them?

Check Your Attitudes

Do your attitudes need to be readjusted? Review Chapter 1 and reassess your thoughts on sex.

Mix Up Your Lovemaking Styles

There are four basic lovemaking styles. Too many couples at midlife have fallen into a rut, making love in one, perhaps two different styles. When they are out of sync in other areas of their lives, lovers especially need to vary their lovemaking styles. The change may jolt them out of their individual spaces and help them reconnect.

QUICKIES: Quickies are brief episodes of sex centered around intercourse. Sometimes there is an aura of stealth surrounding the encounter. A couple may have a quickie in the bathroom while the children are watching television in the family room. They may snatch the erotic time from the middle of a busy workday in a *nooner*, while his visiting mother is on the phone making plans with other family members, or in a semipublic place such as their own backyard at twilight. The urgency and excitement inherent in the brief sexual encounter make it a stimulating and pleasurable experience for both partners, whether orgasm is achieved or not.

Most relationships don't have enough quickies. Lovemaking need not always be a production. Sometimes the needs of the higher-sexed partner can be met through an occasional quickie. At midlife, a man may be capable of having an erection, sustaining it through intercourse, yet not needing or wanting to ejaculate. His partner, on the other hand, may be able to have an orgasm more easily than she ever did. She may come to the quickie aroused from fantasy or minimal foreplay and be ready for release. For them, an occasional quickie can give her what she wants and needs, while making him feel like a great lover.

Comments: A 52-year-old woman says, "Fast and frantic sex is energizing. About once a week we have a quickie in the shower in the morning before work. If one of us doesn't want to come, that's fine. We're more charged for lovemaking the next time around."

GARDEN-VARIETY LOVEMAKING: In garden-variety lovemaking, the partners employ trusted methods of arousing each other, use their favorite positions, and typically continue lovemaking until both reach orgasm. The encounter may last 15 to 30 minutes and almost always takes place in the bedroom at the same time of night or perhaps early morning. This style is comfortable, predictable, and emotionally safe. During times of stress and anxiety, couples find solace in their familiar sexual pattern.

If this is the only way a couple have been making love for a while, however, they need a change. Sometimes making love a different way, like a change of scenery, can bring people closer together. If nothing else, it will probably open up communication. To do something different, you have to communicate.

Comments: A 49-year-old man says, "We have a basic lovemaking pattern that is like an oasis for me when I need it. Our sex life has always been active, creative, and inventive. But the old standby—foreplay, oral sex, her orgasm, missionary position, my orgasm—is my shelter, my church, my rock. If I've had a performance problem, if we've had some relationship problems, if she hasn't come the last few times we've made love, this is the way we need to do it to get back to our sexual selves."

THE LONG ROMANTIC ENCOUNTER: Lovemaking at a leisurely pace with great attention to seduction and loveplay may last 45 to 60 minutes or longer. Like a special dinner, it is likely the end result of some advance planning. Perhaps one or both partners staged a romantic scene. Preliminaries may include a shared bubble bath or shower, an erotic massage, a candlelight dinner at home or in a restaurant, or the donning of special clothing.

Couples tend to plan these long romantic encounters more often early in their relationships. At midlife, they may have fallen out of the habit. If you add one long romantic encounter to your lovemaking agenda every month, you'll be surprised at the benefits reaped, including a richer enjoyment of the other sexual styles. One such session can sustain intimacy for days or weeks.

Comments: A 51-year-old woman says, "When our youngest left the nest last year, we made a list of things we were going to do for ourselves that we had stopped doing while raising the kids. Romantic dinners topped the list. After our first candlelight dinner we had a wonderful lovemaking session. Now we plan one every three or four weeks. We take turns planning and shopping and then do the cooking together. The dinners inevitably end in long lovemaking sessions. We block out the whole evening for just us. We turn the phone off and let the answering machine pick up. It's heaven."

THE SEXUAL ADVENTURE: Some people have never or rarely engaged in adventurous sex. This style adds elements of play and risk to the encounter. A couple may try an unusual position, use sex toys, share or act out their fantasies, watch erotic films together, or add props or elements such as food or ice to their lovemaking. Where does the risk come in? The adventure may be wildly erotic or embarrassingly funny. An idea that sounded arousing may in execution be merely silly.

The sexual adventure adds *variety* to lovemaking. Without an occasional trip down a less familiar erotic lane, the average couple will find it hard to reach a level of high energy, excitement, and passion in their other lovemaking styles after years of being together. And being playful in bed will help you feel young.

Comments: A 50-year-old man says, "My first wife never wanted to do anything out of the ordinary in bed. Oral sex made her a little uncomfortable. Without some changes in the patterns, sex gets boring. My second wife understands that. She likes to play. We've been together fifteen years now, and I still find her exciting. I know there isn't anything I can't say to her about sex. We've done some crazy things, like pulling over to a rest stop area on an interstate to have a quickie in the car. We have a box of sex toys and costumes under the bed."

How to Use Afterplay to Improve Your Relationship

For the out-of-sync couple, afterplay may be their best opportunity for reconnecting. During that period of cuddling, caressing, and sharing intimate thoughts after lovemaking, men and women are more vulnerable to each other than they are at other times. Tender and affectionate afterplay will probably make them feel in sync again, at least temporarily. No, the other problems and issues won't go away, but the lingering feelings of caring and understanding will make them seem less insurmountable.

Here are some tips for making the most of afterplay:

- If there has been a sexual problem, don't address it now. Afterplay is not time for a sexual postmortem. Don't obsess on what went wrong. Use this time of warm acceptance to make each other feel better. Don't allow your nonsexual problems into the bed while you're cuddling either.

- It's okay to express sexual thoughts and feelings. If you haven't told your lover how much you enjoy certain touches, you can do so now. Inject a note of playfulness into the conversation by suggesting something lighthearted and fun you want to do together.

- Spend at least 5 minutes on afterplay; 15 minutes is better.

- Say "I love you." The words have a special meaning in tender moments and can be balm to a sore ego.

SIZZLER #8

Making Time for Love

When the sex was over, he let go of her reluctantly. Gloria was satisfied with weekly lovemaking, but David wanted more. More sex; more caressing, kissing, cuddling, and afterplay; more affection; and more time spent alone with his wife. When he retired at age 55, he looked forward to sharing long walks in the woods and on the beach, preparing gourmet meals together, making love in the hot tub. He had romantic plans. She, on the other hand, had a job she loved.

At 7 years his junior, Gloria had taken a dozen years out of her work life to be a full-time mother. At 48, she was finally coming into her own professionally. She had friends of her own, new interests, and less time for David than she'd ever had. Often she gently pushed him away when he was being affectionate with her. When he suggested things they could do together, she countered with, "That would be lovely, darling, but you don't need me tagging along to enjoy yourself."

The waitress at the coffee shop where he sometimes had a late breakfast alone was beginning to look good to him. He flirted with her and wondered what it would be like to have an affair. Some mornings he took the thought further. What would it be like to leave Gloria and start over again with someone new, a woman more interested in him? But the waitress rebuffed him, and he felt dejected.

Predictably, he took his frustration out on Gloria, the real target of his resentment. He accused her of being "selfish, so absorbed in her own life" that she didn't have time for him anymore. That made her angry, and she said, "You're the selfish one. I arranged my life to suit the needs of you and the boys for years. Now it's my turn, and you're jealous. Nobody said you had to retire. You could find part-time or consulting work. You could volunteer. Take up a hobby. You could get a life!"

Her words stung. But after he stopped smarting, he realized she'd scored some points. In a few weeks' time, he'd begun laying the groundwork for a part-time consulting career, signed up for a French class, and joined a poker group. He still wanted more sex. How to persuade Gloria?

David saw his wife as a woman in near perpetual motion. To seduce her, he'd have to slow her down. "What could I do to make your life easier today?" he asked her casually one morning as she was hurrying to get dressed. Surprised, she was at a momentary loss for words and finally suggested he could pick up her suits at the dry cleaner. He did, and she was grateful enough to hug and kiss him warmly that night. The precedent was set. He, who had more time, handled the bigger share of household chores, particularly running errands. Their evening meals became more leisurely.

One soft, late-spring evening, after enjoying a dinner that he'd prepared, they took their coffee onto the deck. The air smelled of lilac and freshly mowed lawns. She inhaled deeply and sighed happily. He lifted her feet into his lap and began to massage them, one foot at a time, beginning with the toes and working up to the ankles. When he was finished, she wiggled her toes in his lap, prodding his semierect penis.

"Don't cut me off at the ankles," she teased.

He kneaded and massaged her calves, then worked his way up her thighs. He felt her flesh growing warmer beneath the thin cotton fabric of her slacks.

"I'm warm," she said. "Would you take off my pants?"

He took off her pants, kneeled before her, and pressed his face against the hot cotton triangle of cloth covering her pubis. She moaned, then giggled. Reading her mind, he whispered, "It's almost dark." Their deck was relatively private anyway. Through his fingers pressing lightly into her flesh, he felt her acquiesce. With one hand, he pushed the cotton aside and began stroking her labia with his tongue. When her juices were flowing, he raised his face. She kissed him with more passion than she had in years.

Wordlessly, they tore off clothes until they were both naked below the waist. His penis stood firm and proud. She opened her legs and beckoned to him with her hands. He sat on her chair, his legs astride her, and she guided him inside her. They kept their eyes open while they made urgent love. He felt her orgasm as intensely as he felt his own.

CHAPTER NINE

Stretching Your Sexual Boundaries

"Before my fiftieth birthday, I realized I was living in a series of connecting boxes," says Thomas. "Every area of my life was circumscribed by somewhat arbitrary rules. I wanted to be that kid who colored outside the lines again. It's easy to see how many men, and women, too, go off the tracks at midlife. They need to shake something up, so they shake everything up. I didn't want to do that. I didn't want an affair, a divorce, a new career, but I really wanted, needed something to change.

"Sex is where I put my initial focus for change. We weren't having as much sex as I wanted. Our lovemaking routines, though satisfying, weren't exciting. When I tentatively broached the subject to my wife, June, one night, she surprised me by saying how much she'd been thinking the same things.

"'We should be getting more out of life now, not less,'" she said. "That became our rallying cry. Together we began coloring outside the lines. It started with sex. For several years she'd been having fantasies about trying anal sex and had been too embarrassed to tell me. We went to a sex emporium to buy anal condoms, special lubricant, and a book on the subject. Just being in there got us so excited, we were groping each other in the car in the parking lot afterward.

"When we got home, we read the book together, getting more and more aroused. I performed cunnilingus on her to bring her close to orgasm. She lay across my lap moaning and writhing in pleasure while I gently played with her anus, inserting first one well-lubricated finger, then two. By the time she was in position and I had the head of my penis pressed against her anal opening, she was more than ready. It was an awesome, powerful, life-changing experience. We were both astounded at how profoundly moving and passionate anal sex was for us.

"After that day, we were closer than we'd ever been; and I felt freer than I'd felt in years."

Measuring Your Sexual Boundaries

What are sexual boundaries? Those erotic lines you and your partner have become afraid, embarrassed, or too lethargic to cross. For some couples, the boundaries are the limited times of sexual activity, for example, only at night or in the morning, only on the weekends or no more than twice a month. Some couples use only one or two lovemaking styles. Others don't participate in oral sex or share their fantasies or make love outside the bedroom. They have sex in the same way every time as if lovemaking were a Thanksgiving Day menu, not subject to change. And many couples have sex only when both are in the mood, the mood being specifically erotic. Sad, angry, silly, and mournful are not sexy moods. A significant number of couples have sex only a few times a year or not at all, perhaps because their boundaries kept shrinking until there was no remaining space for sexual expression.

As Thomas and June once did, many midlife couples contain their sexuality within a set of boundaries that didn't exist for them in their youth. They didn't get together one day a decade ago and say, "Let's put some limits on our sex life." The boundaries developed over time, a product of repetitive routine lovemaking, maybe some unsatisfactory encounters, and the failure to communicate to each other about their changing needs and desires. Other factors, many of them covered in previous chapters, also play a role in the establishment of sexual limits. They include those familiar villains negative attitudes, repressed anger and resentment, and untreated depression and anxiety, among others.

The Sexual-Boundaries Quiz

How are your boundaries drawn? Think back over the past year. Honestly evaluate how your sex life has been defined by the following criteria.

FREQUENCY

1. Did you have sex more often during some weeks or months than others? Or do you maintain a steady rate of sexual activity, a rate that may be lower than one or both would actually prefer?

2. Does that rate represent a precipitous drop-off over lovemaking of previous years?

MOOD

3. Are you sticklers for making love only when both are in the mood? Or can you adapt your mood to one or another style of lovemaking?

4. Have you recently tumbled into bed on a gale of laughter or been carried there on a flood of tears?

TYPE OF SEXUAL ACTIVITY

5. Do you always have intercourse when you make love?

6. Is the pattern of loveplay culminating in intercourse predictable?

7. Do you sometimes make love without intercourse, without desiring orgasm?

8. Is lack of variety one of your sex-life complaints?

LOCATION OF SEXUAL ACTIVITY

9. Do you always make love in the bedroom? Or have you experimented with lovemaking in other rooms of the house or outdoors?

10. How long has it been since you planned a weekend getaway or vacation mainly to make love in a different setting?

Your answers indicate where you've been drawing the sexual lines. Moving outside those lines, stretching your boundaries, may feel uncomfortable initially, but the rewards are certainly worth a little discomfort. If you thought you were too firmly entrenched in that rut to get out of it, you wouldn't be reading this book.

How to Have More Sex

"My wife delighted in finding statistics proving we were not having as much sex as the average couple in their fifties," Harry says. "I had lost almost all interest in sex. All my excuses—tired, busy, stressed—seemed like the real thing to me. When she pressured me to have sex or explain why I didn't want to have sex, we ended up in an argument.

"Maureen tried every seductive trick to get me interested again. Finally she said, 'I'm not ready to take a vow of celibacy. If you aren't interested in sex anymore, you have two choices. We can get a divorce, or we can stay married and I will take lovers, discreetly, of course.' I wrote her comments off to female histrionics.

"I didn't believe she meant it until I saw her go into action at a party one night. She had a younger man hanging all over her. Watching them together, I saw her through his eyes. She is still a beautiful woman who has kept herself in excellent shape and has a charismatic personality. I saw the exchange of business cards, and I had no doubt she meant to schedule an intimate lunch with him. It was a blow to the solar plexus. I took her home and made passionate love to her. For the next few weeks, we were very emotional together, alternately fighting and making love and crying because we realized how close we had come to losing each other.

"I feel like a man who walked away from a bad accident with only a few scratches. Did I learn something? You bet. My wife is a fascinating woman who had really grown into being her own person right under my nose. I hadn't been putting any energy into our relationship, and now I am."

Desire is the erotic urge preceding arousal. Low sexual desire is the number one sex problem in America today, especially among people at midlife, and few of them will have the same eye-opening experience or the same response to it that Harry had. Many men and women don't feel the urge to make love, they blame their low libido on fatigue, stress, the demands of jobs, growing children, aging parents, and lack of time. If one partner would like to make love more often, he or she may stop initiating lovemaking after several rejections. Although there is no normal rate of lovemaking frequency, no standard that must be met, most couples of any age have a normal rate of frequency for themselves. When they are feeling good about themselves and connected to their partners, they typically want to make love on average a certain number of times per week or month. One partner's loss of desire may be confusing, disappointing, and hurtful to the other who has maintained the same or an increased level of sexual interest.

Frequency is a problem when:

- One partner feels continually frustrated by the other's lack of desire

- Both partners have lost desire, feel disconnected from each other, and are unhappy about having infrequent sex

- The couple fights about how often or when to have sex

Some people have naturally low sex drives. In their youth, they were less interested in sex than other people their age; and at midlife, they may have only occasional desire. Obviously, this isn't a problem if they're not in a relationship or married to someone with a similar low sex drive. Disparate sex drives often do create tension in a couple. If the woman suddenly blossoms sexually at midlife, the unexpected disparity can be more troubling to both partners than it would be if it had existed throughout the marriage.

The reasons for low desire are complicated. Almost everyone goes through at least one phase of low desire in their lifetime, typically such ebbs occur at crisis points, such as major illness, some kind of loss, or following the birth of a child. These phases are usually temporary. Some medications suppress desire (see Chapter 13) and, particularly at midlife, excessive smoking, drinking, and eating can have the same dampening effect on libido. In some people, low desire is a function of low hormone levels (see Chapter 11). When inhibited desire is a chronic condition that cannot be explained by physical factors, the causes are often rooted in unresolved relationship issues. Sometimes, like Harry and Maureen, a couple has grown apart because one or both neglected the relationship. Passion doesn't thrive inside a marriage of convenience or a financial and parenting partnership.

Ten Steps for Increasing Desire

There are many good reasons for wanting to make love more often. Sex is not only a way of sharing pleasure but is also one of the primary means a couple has of building, maintaining, and reinforcing emotional intimacy. When a man and woman are satisfied with their sex life together, their bond seems stronger.

- *Start building sexual bridges to each other.* Touch more frequently. When frequency becomes an issue, some couples stop touching each other altogether. They may fear a hug, a held hand, or a caress could be misconstrued as a sexual signal.

- *Set aside nonsexual time for each other.* Spend more time together. Do all or most of your evenings out involve friends, business events, family functions, or civic affairs? Get to know each other as interesting people again.

- *Agree not to make frequency a control issue.* The partner who wants more sex will agree not to be overly seductive or demanding. The partner who isn't interested in sex very often will take the responsibility for letting the other know when he or she is feeling desirous.

- *Don't expect your partner to gratify all your sexual desires.* Masturbate. Fantasize. Indulge your sensuous nature.

- *Don't expect your partner to be responsible for turning you on.* If your libido is low, encourage and nurture your sexual fantasies. Read and watch erotica. Masturbate, but not to orgasm.

Give yourself more sensuous treats, such as clothing that feels good against your skin.

- *Separate sex and romance.* Have you stopped being romantic because you're afraid a romantic gesture will be construed as a sexual invitation? Romance can but doesn't have to be a prelude to sex. It can be an end in itself.

- *Speak freely.* Frequency is in your minds whether you discuss it or not—and may, in fact, become a bigger stumbling block if you don't voice your concerns. Without blaming each other, have a conversation about desire. Be specific about how often you feel desire, what it feels like to you, what seems to instigate those feelings.

- *Examine your issues.* Now might be a good time to review some of the material covered in earlier chapters. Do you have unexpressed resentment toward your partner? Unresolved anger? A low level of desire could also reflect a lack of optimism, enthusiasm, or passion in your life in general.

- *Make a nondemand sex date with your partner.* You can be sexual without having intercourse or achieving orgasm. It may be enough to hold and stroke each other. Or perhaps the partner with less desire would enjoy bringing the other to orgasm.

- *Move straight to arousal.* You don't have to feel desire to experience arousal. A man who thinks he has no interest in lovemaking can get an erection when stimulated by his partner. Being aroused does not mean you have to complete a sex act. Like romance, it can be an end in itself.

How to Put the Sex Back in a Sexless Marriage

Catherine and Ben are an enviable couple. In their early 50s, both are attractive, physically fit, and successful in their respective careers—advertising and computer sales. Their handsome teenage son has caused minimal family strife, and both sets of their parents are in good health even though they're in their 70s and 80s. Not caught, as are many of their contemporaries, in the classic midlife stressful situations, they look like a couple who probably enjoys a good sex life.

"We haven't had sex in over a year," Catherine says. "People we know would be shocked by that. Our friends think we're a sexy couple. My women friends envy me because Ben always treats me with such courtesy, tenderness, and chivalry in public. We have genuine feelings for each other. There are no big issues, no looming problems between us. I would like to make love more often. Ben puts so much of his energy into sales that he's depleted by the time he gets to bed."

Does Catherine really believe that two healthy, fit, attractive, and sexy people who have genuine feelings for each other haven't had sex in a year because his energy is depleted by his work?

When pressed, Ben admits there are "a few issues, one being Catherine's shopping habits. If I am feeling aroused at night, all I have to do is look around the master suite or, God forbid, open one of the doors to her two walk-in closets to lose my erection. We'll never be able to retire, but maybe we'll open a clothing museum."

When couples stop having sex altogether, the reason is frequently blocked anger. Short bursts of anger can clear the air and ignite passion because that anger is recognized and acknowledged. Long-term anger, unacknowledged and unresolved, builds up and blocks sexual expression. The sex problem won't be resolved until the anger problem is.

If you and your partner are not having sex try one or more of the following tips:

- *Acknowledge the problem.* At midlife, if a man abstains from sex for long periods of time, he will likely have trouble with arousal when he does try to make love again. A woman may also have difficulties with arousal and orgasm under the same circumstances. Someone has to say, "We haven't made love in months (or years). There's something wrong."

- *Make schedule adjustments so you can spend intimate time together.* A couple who isn't making love needs to open a dialogue about the issues surrounding their sexual shutdown. Often they plan their lives carefully so they are too busy to talk in anything other than brief updates. See the hints given in previous chapters for opening intimate dialogues.

• *Incorporate as many of the steps for increasing desire into your life as possible.* Do what you can. Holding hands while walking together could be the beginning of a bridge back to each other.

• *Consider counseling.* You and your partner may both need a little help to define and resolve the underlying emotional or relationship issues causing the problem. That can often be accomplished in a surprisingly short time.

You *can* put the sex back in a sexless marriage, but the sooner you begin, the better.

How to Get in the Mood for Love

"Carrie used to tell me over the phone, 'I'm not in the mood for sex, don't come over,'" says John of his companion of 20 years. "I sometimes teased her by responding, 'So what's the mood for sex? I can have sex with you in any mood.' Often I could cajole her out of her not-in-the-mood-for-sex mood and get her to invite me to spend the night."

John and Carrie have an unusual relationship. Neither has ever been married or lived with another person after shedding their college roommates. An archaeologist based at a Midwestern university, he has spent as long as 2 years at a time in Egypt, many time zones away from St. Louis, where Carrie is a professor of anthropology. Yet they have maintained a "close and monogamous relationship" by both accounts.

"We need more privacy than most people," he says. "Being a solitary person has made me more observant, not less, of people's moods. I can read Carrie's moods and flatter myself that I respond in a productive way most of the time."

When they met, Carrie says, she "suffered from having read too many romantic poets in my girlhood. I was given to exaggerated fits of grand passion or periods of sweet tenderness with my lovers. When I was feeling otherwise inclined, I told the lovers no. I had never laughed in bed before John. What a revelation. I remember having a tremendous orgasm and looking dead into his eyes when he *laughed*! 'Whatever do you find amusing?' I asked after I'd caught my breath. He said, 'I just feel happy and you have such big, serious eyes.' "

Whatever mood you're in, you can be in the mood for love. Life is full of moods. One day you feel good, the next bad, and between those two poles are compressed all the joys of love and the anguish of loss. Practically any mood can lend itself to lovemaking. Think of eating. How many of us eat only when we're hungry? Few, indeed. We eat when we're sad, joyful, frustrated, resentful, anxious, or for no reason at all except a meal is being served. Food comforts us.

Why not consider sexual contact in the same way? Reach out for your lover when you need comfort or feel giddy. Take the mood, whatever it may be, and direct its energy into some form of lovemaking. You may be surprised at the effect this has on your erotic creativity.

Exploring Alternative Forms of Loveplay

Close to the top of most sex wish lists is the word *variety*. What does it mean? Almost anything that takes a couple out of the same-time, same-place, same-way mode of lovemaking. Implementing some of the suggestions already offered in this book will add variety to your sex life. A move as simple as turning on the lights can create change. Like spices in cooking, some people respond to a hint and others need a large dollop before they experience a new sensation.

In the next sections, I'll explore some less-conventional forms of loveplay.

Heterosexual Anal Sex

Anal intercourse takes place when the penis is inserted into the anus rather than the vagina. This has to be practiced with full consent and special care, including the use of anal condoms and copious amounts of a water-soluble lubricant such as Astrolube or K-Y jelly. Unlike the vagina, the rectum does not produce lubrication. An oil or petroleum jelly product can cause condom breakage. The practice should be limited to monogamous couples because it is a high-risk activity for HIV transmission. Why use condoms then? To prevent bacteria present in the rectum from entering the man's urinary-tract system through his urethra.

According to various studies, approximately 40 percent of heterosexual couples have tried anal sex at least once. The anus, like the vagina, has sensitive nerve endings. Some women become highly aroused both by the sensations and the psychological connotations of anal penetration. Men are excited by the tightness of the anal opening, the forbidden nature of anal love, and the idea that a woman would surrender herself to them in this fashion.

Anal intercourse requires mutual trust, good communication skills, and patience on the man's part. Follow these steps:

1. He should make sure his partner is very aroused (and well lubricated) before he approaches her anus.

2. The woman should concentrate on relaxing the anal muscles, not tensing them, and should expect some initial discomfort.

3. Entry should be effected carefully and with her cooperation, followed by short, shallow thrusts.

4. Once movement is established, he won't be able to thrust as vigorously as he would during vaginal intercourse without risking damaging delicate tissues.

5. The experience will probably be pleasurable for both as long as he is prepared to move slowly, follow her lead on depth of penetration, and stop at any time she requests.

Comments: A 48-year-old married woman says, "As a young woman I was intrigued by sexual variations. I read about anal sex, bondage, and spanking and wanted to try those things. I found some old magazines in the attic of the first house we bought. Now I know the beautiful brunette in the bondage layouts was Bettie Page, the fifties cult model. Then I only knew I was excited by the pictures. I fantasized about a man tying me over a vault and fucking my ass. Just saying those naughty words in my head turned me on. Twenty years later I told my husband about the pictures, my fantasies, my desire for experimentation. It blew him away. We had anal sex that night. It hurt a little more than I thought it would, but only at first. I felt like I had completely surrendered to him, giving him something more precious than my virginity had been. Why did it take me so long to get over my modesty and tell him what I wanted?"

Bondage

Bondage is erotic restraint, the sensual experience of safe captivity. Light bondage, or *tie and tease*, may be the most common sex game couples play. One partner ties the other, either lightly binding wrists together or binding wrists and sometimes ankles to the bedposts. The bound partner is then "helpless" and must submit to the other's sexual ministrations. The object of the game is intensifying pleasure through delaying gratification. The one in charge teases the other to the brink of orgasm, pulls back, and teases again.

Follow these steps:

1. Using silk scarves or ties or Velcro restraints (purchased in a sex toy catalog or store), loosely bind your partner's wrists and/or ankles. If he or she is comfortable with it, add a blindfold.

2. Check the bindings to make sure they are not constricting blood flow.

3. Kiss, caress, stroke, and fondle your partner's body, avoiding the genitals.

4. Using the oral techniques outlined on pages 53–58 and the manual techniques detailed on pages 58–61, stimulate your partner to a level of high arousal.

5. Abruptly stop genital stimulation.

6. Again kiss, caress, stroke, and fondle his or her body, avoiding the genitals.

7. Repeat the stop-and-start method of genital stimulation until your partner begs for an orgasm.

8. Remember, even light bondage can lead to muscle cramps. You don't want to sustain the experience so long your partner is begging for a muscle massage, not an orgasm.

Comments: A 54-year-old man says, "My wife and I love to play tie and tease occasionally. Both the dominant and submissive roles in this game have their own joys. To be in charge of the other's pleasure, the withholder and dispenser of the orgasm, is a potent experience. Seeing your bound partner panting, sweating, and writhing is a real turn-on. She likes to leave on a silk teddy or camisole and panties. After a while, they're plastered to her body. Very erotic. But I also enjoy being bound and tormented. The sense of being controlled is freeing. I don't have to perform. She has to make me come. We didn't start playing sex games until later in our marriage, after the kids were gone away to school, and it's brought us closer together. At a family reunion, she whispered in my ear, 'What would they think if they knew what I did to you last night?' "

Spanking

Erotic spanking is the administering of blows to the buttocks for the purposes of arousal. In less politically correct times than our own, spanking was regarded as a form of lighthearted sex play between partners. The *Kama Sutra* offers detailed instructions on administering the four kinds of blows to produce the eight kinds of sounds. On television in the 1950s, Ricky spanked Lucy. Their bedroom set was required by network censors to hold twin beds, not a double, but spanking was permissible. In the movies from the '30s through the '50s, Spencer Tracy spanked Katharine Hepburn, and Cary Grant spanked many women and these are just a few examples. Today spanking is a taboo activity; but an astonishing array of magazines, books, and newsletters devoted to the practice are available in this country. A good number of people are at least fantasizing about breaking the taboo.

Spanking as foreplay is typically a part of an erotic role-playing scenario in which the naughty girl or boy is disciplined by an authority figure. The hand is most commonly used, but spanking implements can range from a kitchen spatula to a specially purchased lightweight whip.

If you and/or your partner have administered the occasional light slap during intercourse to favorable response, you might enjoy an occasional spanking game. Follow these steps:

1. Agree on the terms beforehand. How many slaps? With a hand or what instrument? How hard?

2. Make sure your partner is fully aroused before the hand meets the ass.

3. Start with a very light touch. Gentle slaps bring blood to the surface, minimizing bruising.

4. Carefully monitor your partner's response.

5. Have a safe word, which when spoken by the spankee means "stop right now." Saying, "Oh, no, don't spank me," may be part of the script. Make the safe word something like *peanut butter*; don't use the word *no*.

Comments: A 50-year-old man says, "My partner and I take turns spanking each other occasionally. We had never thought about adding this to our repertoire of sexual tricks until we saw a video that included some spanking. She said, 'I can't believe how much this is arousing me.' I lied and said it didn't arouse me. She put her hand around my erection and said, 'Oh, no not much,' then with the other hand slapped my ass. What a feeling! Delivering the slap and receiving it are both strong sexual sensations. A well-timed blow can make my erection hard again if it's beginning to wane during intercourse."

Light S&M

More theater than pain, light S&M (sadomasochism) games are erotic power exchanges between consenting partners. They sometimes involve costumes and props and nearly always include role playing. One partner plays the dominant character and the other the submissive in an erotic drama. The dominant controls the action by administering light doses of physical pain and/or verbal abuse and making the submissive person do his or her sexual bidding. The submissive partner is really in charge, however, because it is understood between the players that the game doesn't go any further than the submissive one desires.

The word *sadomasochism* is derived from combining *sadist*, "one who enjoys inflicting pain and/or humiliation" with *masochist*, "one who enjoys receiving pain and/or humiliation." People who take the behavior to the extremes are a small minority. For them, the exchange of pain has almost or entirely replaced sexual activity. They refer to S&M as a lifestyle because it defines how they live their lives. The vast majority of people who dabble in S&M, however, use it as an occasional form of erotic play to intensify arousal and orgasm. Couples who infrequently engage in S&M are generally switch players, alternating the dominant and the submissive roles. Here are some tips, if you want to give it a try:

- *Don't underestimate the importance of costumes and props.* Certain items of clothing, types of fabric or other material, and special accouterments have S&M connotations. Visit a sex-toy shop or browse a catalog for ideas. Generally, they include tight-fitting leather or rubber garments, the color black, bustiers, corsets, garter belts, stockings, very high heels on pumps or boots, masks, nipple clamps, bondage gear, and spanking implements.

- *Work from a script.* You don't have to write down the dialogue, but you must have the plot worked out before beginning. Talk about what you want to do—in detail—with your partner.

- *Set limits and stick to them.* A velvet-covered whip can sting. So can words. Be clear about how far is too far to go, both verbally and physically.

- *Use a safe word.* The submissive partner should be able to stop the game at any time by saying the safe word. Do not use the word *no*; it may be confusing.

- *Remember that a little goes a long way.* Your fantasies may involve giving or receiving a level of rough treatment that would be a turn-off in real life.

- *Arouse your partner.* Be sure your partner is aroused before you administer pain, and be sure he or she continues to be aroused by the action.

- *Take turns.* Switch roles the next time you play.

Comments: A 45-year-old woman says, "Playing with S&M brings emotions to the surface for us. I'm not sure it would be a good idea for couples who have hidden anger. One might lose it while dominating the other. But for us it's been a healthy way to express latent feelings of dominance and submission. We take turns being the master or the slave. The last time he was master he ordered me to crawl across the floor on all fours and suck his dick. I haven't been so aroused performing fellatio in a long time. I really wouldn't want to be sexually enslaved, but it's fun to pretend for a little while. It's just as much fun to play mistress when it's my turn to make him serve me."

Exhibitionism/Voyeurism

An exhibitionist has sex in public places. The average couple can get their own illicit thrill by making love in a semipublic place, such as their hot tub on the deck or by making out in the car in the parking lot at the mall. Voyeurs become aroused by watching other people have sex. Again, the concept can be adapted for home play. A couple can, for example, make videos of themselves having sex and watch them together.

True exhibitionists and voyeurs take big risks to get what they need for arousal because they can't be sexually excited in a variety of different ways like most people. Their focus is very narrow. Erotic dabblers have a wide range of arousal choices, and they don't put themselves and their partners in dangerous or illegal situations. Keep the following facts in mind:

- The thrill comes from the *possibility* of discovery, not the likelihood of it. Making love in your own swimming pool on a summer night imparts an erotic edge because the neighbors might see or hear. But it's still *your* pool. If you make love in a public pool after hours, have bail money in the car.

- If you take nude photographs of each other, keep compromising photos and videos under lock and key, and don't store them on viewing devices, such as the Internet, digital phones, and so on.

- Employ the tricks of the trade. Use soft lighting for your erotic photography. Shoot his penis from "up and under," as they do in the business. In other words, have the camera slightly beneath his erection, the lens tilted upward. Mist her labia with water for that dewy look.

- Adapt your fantasies for reality. Making love in Central Park could get you arrested. How about on the living room floor behind the palm tree with the drapes open?

Comments: A 58-year-old man says, "At fifty-four, my wife still has beautiful breasts. She's full and voluptuous like Elizabeth Taylor. I like to take her out wearing low-cut gowns, almost cut to the nipple line. She looks magnificent, like a goddess. Men of all ages, and women, too, admire her. I get very aroused by that, and so does she. Sometimes we can't wait to get home. Our daughter, who wants her to start dressing 'her age,' disapproves of her exhibitionism. We pay the girl no mind on this issue."

How common is kinky sex? Anywhere from 10 to 30 percent of people have experimented with some form of kink (excluding anal sex, a separate category) at least once in their lives. Americans have probably gotten kinkier in the past decade for several reasons: the prevalence of media imagery celebrating bondage and S&M images; the availability of sex information and erotica about kinky practices; the increased level of social tolerance for sexual variations, especially among more educated people; and the aging of the baby boom generation. As people grow older, they are more comfortable with expressing long-held desires and more likely to need variety to maintain their sex lives in a satisfactory way.

Ten Places to Have Sex Out of Bed

Location is another factor that defines sexual boundaries. If you never make love anywhere except a bed, you are missing opportunities for variety. Try some of the following ideas:

- *Shower.* Great for oral sex. The water gently trickling over the head and shoulders of the partner kneeling at the other's genitals adds to the pleasure.

- *Living room.* You can have sex in a chair, on the sofa, on the floor, and maybe on the coffee table. A fireplace in winter adds ambiance, but candlelight works, too.

- *Kitchen and dining room.* Try the floor, table, or counters. If he is tall, she can sit on the counter while he stands. The association with food can make sex more interesting, especially if the table hasn't been cleared.

- *Garage.* Have you ever made love sitting on a parked riding mower? Look around the garage for other ideas. Improvise.

- *Deck.* An obvious choice for warm nights, even cold ones under a down comforter.

- *Pool.* Another obvious choice.

- *Other bathrooms, not your own.* There is nothing like a quickie in a friend's bathroom or public restroom to energize a relationship plagued by routine sex.

- *Car.* Not for teenagers only.

- *The great outdoors.* Every couple should make love on the beach or the lawn at least once in their lives.

Phone Sex

If you haven't looked at a sex magazine—or girlie magazine as they were known when we were younger—in recent years, you would probably be more surprised at the pages of phone-sex ads than at the nude layouts. Men have always been aroused by sex talk that's so graphic it creates strong visual images. The phone-sex industry was developed to fill an unmet need.

If either you or your partner travel on business—or even if you don't—phone sex is a way to generate exotic enthusiasm for the coming reunion. Here's how to play the game:

- Warm up by leaving erotic messages on his or her voice mail—assuming no one else has access to the messages, of course.

- Don't feel guilty about talking dirty. Nice girls were raised to avoid saying bad words. That's what makes it so exciting when they come out of her mouth for only his ears. The voice can be arousing, too, just like mouth, lips, tongues, hands, and genitals.

- Learn some new words. Erotic novels are filled with euphemisms for the genitals and their interactions. The steamier romance novels are another good source of inspiration.

- Practice. If the words don't come easy to you, say them out loud when you're alone. Get used to the feel of naughty words in your mouth. Like learning a foreign language, dirty talk takes some practice.

- Rent movies you consider erotic—and listen to them. Yep, close your eyes so you won't be distracted by the visual content of the film. You'll be surprised at how much the words, tone of voice, and inflection contribute to the experience.

- Read erotica out loud to each other. You may find it easier to be creative on your own after reading other scripts. Choose novels with a lot of dialogue.

- Choose a scenario that you know will be particularly arousing to your partner. Phone-sex operators say that anal sex, oral sex, and female-domination scenarios are the most popular with their callers. Remember to be specific. The heat of phone sex is in the details.

- Add sound effects. Heavy breathing, panting, and soft moans add a sense of reality to the experience.

- Expand the game. When you're more comfortable with phone sex, create scenarios out of your own unexpressed desires and hidden fantasies.

- Make a ruling about whether masturbating to orgasm will be permitted. Why wouldn't it be? If you're going to see each other within a day or two, you may want to save the orgasms for then. A certain level of mental excitation can be sustained if phone sex doesn't end in orgasm.

SIZZLER #9

The Bonds of Love

Ian suggested the game as a joke. Marta, his partner of 10 years, had become more dynamic and forceful after age 50, while he had grown more patient and easygoing. She saw aging as time running out, whereas he saw it as time slowing down. He often told her that she "had a habit of cutting off his sentences before the verb," especially if she thought she knew what he was going to say. She did, she conceded, frequently interrupt him while he was talking; but, she countered, she did know what he was going to say on those occasions because he said the same things over and over again.

"I should tie you to the chair and put a gag in your mouth when I need you to listen," he teased.

"Would you waste an opportunity like that by talking?" she countered.

Their eyes met, and each recognized a devilish glint in the other's gaze. They began teasing each other more readily. The mock threat of binding and gagging was invoked when one expressed an opinion contrary to the other's—or when Ian retold an oft-told story. Erotic tension, which had been largely absent from their relationship for years, bubbled beneath the surface again.

"Would you like to play a game?" Ian asked Marta. She was seated at her dressing table, fresh from a bubble bath, a gray cashmere robe loosely belted around her waist. He put his hands on her shoulders; and she set down the jar of face cream she was holding in her hand. "I think about this game every time I see you sitting in that chair now."

Wordlessly, she nodded her head. He had her complete attention for a change.

"Don't move," he said gently, but firmly.

While she waited, heart beating fast, he took four silk ties from one of the racks in his closet. Their eyes met in the mirror when he returned to the bathroom, ties in hand. He hadn't seen that eager yet shy expression on her face since their earliest days together. He smiled.

"Spread your legs," he said, "and put your hands behind your back."

She complied. He fastened her ankles to the chair legs with two ties and secured her wrists with another. She was breathing heavily, her breasts rising and falling seductively inside her robe. Holding her face in his hands, he kissed her, gently at first, teasing her lips with playful licks of his tongue, before thrusting it forcefully into her mouth. She surrendered to the kiss, and he pulled away. He wrapped the fourth tie around her mouth, gagging her.

"You're my captive audience," he said.

Eyes flashing mischievously, she squirmed in the chair. He pulled open the robe, exposing her breasts and her pussy. She arched her back and twisted her torso, throwing herself into the game.

"Are you ready to listen?" he teased. She shook her head from side to side, a negative. "Oh, you're going to be feisty? I'll have to do something to make you more receptive to my words."

He took her breasts in his hands and massaged them. An urgent sigh formed in the back of her throat. She arched her body forward to let him know she wanted a stronger touch. He got the message. As his hands moved down her body, her gyrations increased. When he inserted two fingers into her vagina, she rocked the chair back and forth, riding him.

"Do you want me to lick your pussy?" he asked.

She nodded a vigorous yes. He brought her to the brink of orgasm with the skillful use of fingers and tongue, then abruptly stopped. She squealed in protest.

"You have to do something for me before I give you an orgasm," he said. "Will you do it?"

She nodded that she would, and he removed her gag. As she sucked in big gulps of air, he unzipped his pants to expose his erection. He put his hands on the sides of her head as he had when he'd kissed her and guided her toward his penis. The position wasn't comfortable for her, he knew, and in this situation, that added to his pleasure. She fellated him to orgasm.

Marta looked beautiful to him, with traces of semen around her lips and sweat on her brow. He knelt before her and licked and sucked. She didn't have to tell him not to stop after her first orgasm; he knew.

CHAPTER TEN

The Unlimited Potential of Midlife Orgasm

"Everything I thought I knew about orgasms after forty was wrong," says Mark, 51, a practicing internist in Maryland. "I remember an older man, a colleague I admired, telling me when I was in my late twenties that I should enjoy my orgasms while I still had 'real' ones. He said after forty the male orgasm was a pale shadow of its former glory. That's not true at all.

"The mature orgasm is richer, more varied in depth and intensity than the youthful orgasm. When you're young, you want to ejaculate purely for the release. Every orgasm feels pretty much the same. There is a physical urgency in the last stage of arousal that you may not feel, at least all the time, in maturity. But the orgasm now is more deeply and diversely felt. Beginning in the genitals, it radiates out into other parts of the body. Sometimes I feel it in my elbows and my toes.

"If I were explaining this to a younger man, here is what I would say: 'In your twenties you drink more wine; by age fifty you drink less, but the wine is better, and your ability to appreciate it has grown a hundredfold. At my age, son, you know a good bottle of wine.'"

The Midlife Orgasm

In both men and women, an orgasm is a series of rhythmic contractions triggered by intense physical and psychological stimulation and typically lasts 3 to 20 seconds, with intervals of less than a second between the first three to six contractions. Some women experience spasms for a minute or longer. The contractions are centered in the genitals and the rectal sphincter. At midlife, men especially may experience fewer contractions. Women may have the same number of contractions into their 60s or early 70s. This diminishing of the number of spasms was once thought to signal a decline in the quality of the orgasmic experience. If an orgasm were only the release of sexual tension and primarily a genital event, perhaps losing a spasm or two over the years would qualify as a diminishment.

But an orgasm is more than the sum of its contractions, especially at this point in your life. The orgasmic potential of midlife men and women has been underestimated by doctors, therapists, and laypeople. The sexologist Herbert Otto studied a group of people over 40 who were able to experience a fuller range and depth of orgasmic sensations than they'd ever known through the use of "shaping and developing" techniques. Why might you want richer, fuller, deeper orgasms? The reasons include the following:

- *Better health.* Some health benefits of orgasm have been documented by researchers. Orgasm promotes cardiovascular conditioning, imparts a healthy glow to the skin, and improves overall body tone. Recent studies have shown that breast-cancer survivors who experience orgasm—through lovemaking or masturbation—recover more quickly than those who do not. In addition, orgasm triggers the release of chemicals in the brain that can help relieve headaches and other minor aches and pains.

- *Psychological benefits.* There are real psychological benefits associated with orgasm. In 1940 famed physician Wilhelm Reich in his groundbreaking book *The Function of the Orgasm* broadened the definition of orgasm beyond the genitals. He was the first sexologist to say that a person's emotional health was related to his or her capacity to experience orgasm. Reich thought orgasm was a whole-body event, a belief he shared with the Eastern sexologists and one that was largely ignored by Western authorities on the subject until recently.

• *Intimacy.* Orgasm during lovemaking builds intimacy; it has relationship-bonding power. After orgasm, men and women often feel closer to their partners, a feeling that has in part a physical basis. The chemical oxytocin is released in the brain on orgasm and has been called the *cuddling hormone* because it inspires feelings of attachment. Women, it is not surprising, produce much larger amounts of oxytocin than men do—until midlife, when the percentages are more nearly equal.

The Orgasm Quiz

The following quiz will help you develop more awareness of your orgasmic experiences. The first step in increasing orgasmic potential is understanding where you are now. This is not a test in the sense that there are no right or wrong answers.

1. List all the ways you are orgasmic, including via oral sex, masturbation, manual stimulation by your partner, and intercourse.

2. Do you experience orgasm differently depending on the way it was achieved? Can you explain the differences?

3. How frequently do you reach orgasm during lovemaking?

4. Have you ever had or do you sometimes or often have multiple orgasms?

5. Have you ever experienced an extragenital orgasm or an orgasm achieved with stimulation to areas other than the genitals?

6. Have you ever felt an orgasm in parts of your body other than the genitals?

7. Be as specific as possible in describing exactly what kinds of stimulation, including pressure and amount, bring you to orgasm.

8. How do your emotions and your feelings toward your partner affect your orgasms?

9. How does your partner's orgasm affect yours?

10. Do you have a particularly sensitive body part (aside from the genitals) that, when stimulated at the same time your genitals are being stimulated, affects orgasm?

Use your answers to the quiz questions to help you develop a better awareness of how you reach orgasm, of the feelings of orgasms achieved using different methods of stimulation, and of how much you may have been limiting orgasmic potential by attitudes and behaviors.

Orgasm is a blend of physical, psychological, and emotional factors. In youth, the physical element often takes precedence over the others, especially for men. As people mature, the psychological and emotional elements take on greater importance, again especially for men. At any age, the orgasmic experience varies, depending on many physical, emotional, and psychological factors such as the type of sexual activity and the closeness felt toward the partner.

How to Build New Pathways to Orgasm

Even if you are not interested in pursuing extended, multiple, extragenital, spontaneous, and/or full-body orgasms, you can experience orgasm more fully and deeply than you do now. What could stop you? Two things: thinking you can't, and using exactly the same approach to masturbation and lovemaking as you've been using for years. It's time for a sexual shakeup.

Masturbate
Orgasms attained through masturbation feel different from those reached during lovemaking with a partner, but masturbation encourages greater

sexual self-awareness. With no emotional distractions, you can assess how a certain method works. To gain knowledge about your sexual responses, practice the techniques described in this chapter during masturbation and then transfer them to lovemaking. Allow sufficient time for self-pleasuring. Create a sensuous and comfortable environment by using soft lighting, music, scents, candles, or other accessories you save for special lovemaking times. If you don't own a vibrator, buy one.

Most important, alter your solo style. Don't fall back on the trusted habit to bring you to orgasm after a trying just a few minutes of being adventurous. Many people are more comfortable about trying something new with a partner after they've experimented privately on their own bodies.

Focus on Parts Other Than Genitals
Devote a masturbation or lovemaking session almost exclusively to one area of your body that brings you intense pleasure when fondled, but hasn't led to orgasm. This may be a woman's breasts, a man's nipples, a hot-spot area, the inner thighs, or some other place. See how much more sensitive the area becomes when you use different techniques for stroking and massaging and continue stimulating it past the point at which you would have shifted to genital stimulation.

But don't make orgasm a goal. If you reach an irresistible level of arousal and want to have an orgasm via clitoral or penile stimulation, fine. Does the orgasm feel stronger or deeper than usual? In other masturbation or lovemaking sessions, focus on different areas.

Focus on the Genitals
Now focus your erotic attention exclusively on the genitals during a single masturbation or lovemaking session. Without being distracted by touches or caresses to other body areas, you can see exactly how using different techniques influence arousal and intensify orgasm. But, again, orgasm need not be a goal. If you don't feel like having an orgasm, don't worry about it.

Add Special Effects
During a masturbation- or lovemaking-focus session, add a vibrator and other sex toy, if desired. Continue stimulating the same area but alternate

the manual (or oral) stimulation with the vibrator. How do the sensations change? Does orgasm happen more quickly? Feel different?

Create Fusion

When most people are close to orgasm, they continue stimulating the genitals in a certain way, usually faster and harder, in highly focused movements. They may kiss their partners at the same time, but other than the kiss, which is more an intense mouth lock, they connect only at key genital points. Typically during intercourse, the man maneuvers so that the head of his penis receives the greatest friction, and the woman tries to angle her body to receive clitoral friction, which she may or may not augment with her own hand or his.

Using techniques that worked during single-area focus sessions, stimulate your own (and your partner's) other hot spots, breasts, nipples, or inner thighs simultaneously with the primary genital friction. An orgasm achieved from stimulation to more than one site is called a *fusion orgasm*. Many people experience it as more intense and widespread than an orgasm reached via stimulation of the primary genital areas.

Keep an Orgasm Diary

At first you may find it difficult and perhaps rather foolish to keep an orgasm diary. Try anyway. What you record in your diary will help further expand and develop your orgasmic potential. During the afterglow, write down everything you can remember about your orgasm in the following categories:

- *Body sensations.* How many orgasmic contractions did you feel? Where were they located? What were the different feelings in various parts of the body? Did you feel waves of warmth in other body areas? Tingling sensations in certain parts? Describe where, how, and how intensely you felt the physical sensations of orgasm.

- *Emotions.* What were your feelings as you reached orgasm?

- *Images.* Did you see colors or images at orgasm? Were you involved in a fantasy that culminated in orgasm? Did a scrap of a fantasy or remembered real-life scenario come into your mind at orgasm?

Comments: A couple in their early 50s who were initially reluctant to employ these methods for learning new pathways to orgasm eventually did so because "We were in such a rut that orgasm didn't feel that good anymore."

After 6 months, she says, "I am more orgasmic than I have ever been. The orgasms are more varied. Sometimes I have light, fluttering orgasms that seem to skip across my clitoris and send delicious chills up my spine. And other times I have these deep shuddering emotional orgasms that defy description. One night I cried as I came."

And he says, "When I was young, I felt orgasm throughout my penis, into the base, and the surrounding area including the anus. A few years ago I noticed the orgasmic sensations were more limited to the head and first third of the penis, with the other parts feeling minimal tingling. Now I feel orgasm throughout the entire genital area and beyond. Orgasm is often a very intensely emotional experience for me now, too."

Extending Your Orgasm Time

For young men, orgasm is an almost certainty; whereas for young women, it may be a sometime event. At midlife, women get more sometimes and men don't always find orgasm inevitable. Both are ideally suited now to experience extended orgasms, something a man probably can't master in youth and a woman might not have the confidence to try.

A strong pubococcygeal (PC) muscle is required to extend an orgasm beyond its minimal seconds. One way to develop this muscle is via Kegel exercises (page 81). If you haven't been practicing them, start now. Once the PC muscle is strong, use it to extend your orgasm.

- The man pumps his penis in time with the contractions by squeezing his PC muscle.

- The woman squeezes her vaginal walls in time with her contractions.

- Both the man and the woman should begin squeezing with the first contraction.

Repeated use of the method gradually extends orgasms and, for many people, makes the initial contractions more intense.

Comments: A couple who gave themselves face-lifts for their 50th birthdays, which were 6 weeks apart, also began doing Kegel exercises when they were recovering from surgery.

He says, "It was the only workout I could do for a while, so I thought why not. My expectations were minimal, and I was really surprised by the results. Using the PC technique for extending orgasms has worked very well for me. I have more contractions and feel them more strongly."

She says: "I have a physically fit vagina for the first time in my life. Any woman who thinks that doesn't have an effect on the quality of orgasms doesn't have a fit vagina. It's a huge difference. Yes, I can make my orgasms last longer and feel stronger. The contractions continue gently subsiding for several minutes afterward. It's like having earthquake aftershocks going off in my vagina."

Multiple Orgasms at Midlife

Multiple orgasms occur when a woman (or a man, which is less likely) has a second, third, or more orgasms without completely returning to the resolution phase. In other words, a level of excitation is maintained between orgasms; the woman or man is not starting the climb over again from a low point on the arousal scale. Probably all women are capable of having multiple orgasms, although it is estimated that fewer than 50 percent ever do. Far fewer men do, and whether all can or not depends on one's perspective on sexuality.

At midlife women are more likely to have multiple orgasms than at any other time. As previously noted, her erotic responses are more rapid, her level of confidence higher, and her sexual self-awareness greater. For many women, regular orgasms or multiple orgasms begin to happen now because older women have finally gotten over their embarrassment about needing manual clitoral stimulation during intercourse to achieve orgasm. Once they feel free to touch themselves or ask for touch, they become more orgasmic.

There are several types of multiple orgasms:

- *Compounded singles.* Each orgasm is distinct and separated by a partial return to the resolution phase.

- *Sequential multiples.* Orgasms occur 2 to 10 minutes apart with minimal reduction in arousal between them.

- *Serial multiples.* Numerous orgasms are separated by mere seconds or minutes at most with no diminishment of arousal. Some women experience this as one long orgasm with spasms of varying intensity.

How Women Can Have Multiple Orgasms

Mental attitude is key to multiple orgasms. First, if you haven't discarded the idea that lovemaking ends with a man's ejaculation, do so now. His orgasm isn't the signal for the end of lovemaking. Next, a woman must be focused on her own pleasure to achieve multiple orgasms. Shut out intrusive thoughts. You deserve pleasure, and now you are going to take it. Finally, start on warm. Prepare for the possibility of multiples by fantasizing about sex before the encounter, caressing your own genitals in the bath or shower before lovemaking, and having a glass of wine, if that helps you relax.

ALTERNATING STIMULI

- Ask your partner to give you the first orgasm via cunnilingus. Oral sex more fully arouses the female genitalia, making orgasm during intercourse more likely.

- After the first orgasm, he should manually stroke her to another orgasm, if possible.

- If she does not reach orgasm easily by manual stimulation, revert to oral.

- After a second orgasm, he should immediately enter her, with either of them continuing manual stimulation at the same time. Some women report that intercourse at that point seems to spread the sensations of orgasm throughout the body.

- Maintain a pattern of varied stimulation as long as desired.

Comments: A 52-year-old woman who recently experienced multiple orgasms for the first time says, "Alternating stimuli, with the first orgasm via cunnilingus, works for me. The other methods don't. In fact, I like two oral orgasms. After that, if I'm in the right mental place, I can fly. I feel myself soaring into a level of pleasure I'd never reached any other way."

MANUAL CONTACT: Women who aren't comfortable touching themselves during lovemaking are less likely to experience multiples because they have to depend on their partners to know exactly where and how to apply the stimulation that would take them from one peak to the next. Even the best lovers can't always get it right.

• Stroke yourself during cunnilingus or intercourse.

• Vary the stimulation to the clitoral area.

• When you feel orgasm approaching, move the stimulus from the clitoris to the area surrounding it to spread the orgasm.

Comments: A 54-year-old woman says, "I can have multiple orgasms in a variety of ways. I'm one of the lucky women. Manual stimulation is the surest way for me to get there. From masturbating, I know exactly when, where, and how to touch myself to bring on the spasms. My husband of twenty-nine years is an excellent lover, but he can't pinpoint the site and pressure changes I need to take me from one orgasm to another as fast as I can. Besides, he loves it when I touch myself."

REPEATED DIRECT STIMULI: Although some women are more likely to have multiple orgasms using alternating stimuli, others have a better chance of doing so if their partner and they repeatedly stimulate the clitoral area in the same way. A few women need constant, concerted stimulation at the focal point to have multiple orgasms. Many women, however, find the clitoris too sensitive to sustain this pattern of stimulation.

Comments: A 50-year-old woman says, "I can keep having orgasms if I or my partner continue stimulating the clitoris throughout and beyond the first orgasm. Sometimes the clitoral area gets so sensitive, I think I can't bear the touch. If I don't pull away, the acute sensitivity passes. I move into a place where I sometimes feel like I could come forever."

THE FLAME: Some women can have multiple orgasms only during cunnilingus. This technique, after using the strokes listed on page 57, often works. The directions are for him.

- Pretend the tip of your tongue is a candle flame.

- In your mind's eye, see the flame flickering in the wind.

- Move your tongue rapidly around the sides of her clitoris, above and below it, as the candle flame moves.

Comments: A 53-year-old woman says, "This is nirvana. I don't know where my husband learned it. He said from a book. Wherever he picked it up, I'm glad he did. After the second or third orgasm this way, my whole body feels like it's convulsing. I'd never had multiples until he pulled this little trick out of his bag."

G-SPOT MULTIPLES: Some women can have multiples only when they have clitoral stimulation at the same time as vaginal stimulation in the area of the G spot. Here's how a man can make this happen for her:

- Using the come-hither gesture with a finger or two (see page 62 for specifics), a man stimulates the G-spot area as he performs cunnilingus.

- During intercourse in a position she considers favorable for G-spot stimulation, he strokes her clitoris.

Comments: A 51-year-old woman says, "This works for me, especially in the rear-entry position where I get the best G-spot stimulation. One reason the position works is that I stimulate my own clitoris. I still like to have the first orgasm via cunnilingus, then switch to rear-entry intercourse and manual clitoral stimulation."

How Men Can Have Multiple Orgasms

The refractory period—the time after ejaculation before a man can have another erection—does increase with age. As little as minutes in young and virile men, the refractory period can last days in a man in his 70s or older. By midlife, the refractory period may be as much as 24 hours. How are multiple orgasms possible under those circumstances?

According to many Western authorities, male orgasm and ejaculation are the same thing; and multiple orgasms are rare in men. According to Eastern belief, male orgasm, like female, is a psychosexual event that, unlike female orgasm, typically includes ejaculation, but not always. In other words, orgasm, the pleasurable sensations of the rhythmic contractions, and ejaculation, the release of semen, are separate events. Those who subscribe to this view of male sexuality say men *can* experience multiple orgasms and are far more likely to do so at midlife when they have greater control of the ejaculatory process and are able to differentiate between orgasm and ejaculation.

Stan Dale, who has a doctorate in human sexuality from the Institute for Advanced Study of Sexuality in San Francisco, is often credited with popularizing the concept of male multiple orgasms through his workshops and the national media attention they garnered. Dale discovered his own multiple-orgasm capability at midlife and quite by accident. He says he discovered the difference between ejaculation and orgasm when he was required to ejaculate into a small jar for the obligatory sperm-count test a month after having undergone a vasectomy. After 15 minutes of "the most unsensuous masturbation" of his life, he produced the required sample. As he was walking back to the nurse's station, he thought to himself, *That was a nonorgasmic ejaculation.*

The discovery led him to the study of Eastern erotic arts. The following techniques are adapted from his studies.

THREE-FINGER DRAW: Practiced in China for 5,000 years, the three-finger draw is a simple and, according to Taoist practitioners, *effective* method for inducing multiple orgasms in men. Similar to the perineum massage (see page 61) the three-finger draw uses three curved fingers to apply pressure to one spot on the perineum, rather than the whole area, at the moment of ejaculatory inevitability.

- Locate the pressure point in the middle of the perineum, the area between the anus and the scrotum.
- Use three slightly curved fingers to apply pressure, not too light and not too hard, to that point as soon as you feel ejaculation is imminent.
- Repeat as often as necessary until you can experience a nonejaculatory orgasm.

Comments: A 47-year-old man says, "I recommend practicing during masturbation because it's not easy to find the right spot. After you find the spot, don't expect a miracle. This takes time and patience. After much practice, I have made it work. Was it worth the trouble? Oh, yes. Sometimes I have multiple orgasms and sometimes a single orgasm without ejaculation. Either way, I am ready for lovemaking again sooner than I am after I ejaculate. My wife loves it."

THE BIG DRAW: The big draw technique requires a strong PC muscle—just like a number of other techniques.

- When you feel ejaculation is imminent, stop thrusting.
- Pull back to approximately 1 inch of penetration, but do not withdraw entirely.
- Flex the PC muscle and hold to a count of nine. Alternately, flex the PC muscle nine times in rapid succession instead of holding the count.
- Resume thrusting with shallow strokes.
- Repeat as often as necessary until you experience a nonejaculatory orgasm.

Comments: A 54-year-old man says, "Mastering the art of orgasm without ejaculation separates the men from the boys. It took me several months to develop my PC muscle and make the big draw work for me, but it was time well invested. I feel erotically powerful now. I can come without ejaculating; I can come and come again and again. I am at the top of my sexual game at a point in my life when I had anticipated being on the slippery slope downward."

THE ART OF BRINKMANSHIP: Some men train themselves to experience orgasm without ejaculation fairly easily using the art of brinkmanship: pulling back at the last possible second before ejaculation.

- Practice while masturbating.

- Continue stimulation to the point of imminent orgasm.

- Then stop. Don't resume stimulation until your arousal level has declined.

- Repeat as often as possible. With practice, you should be able to experience the contractions of orgasmic release without ejaculating.

Comments: A 50-year-old man says, "When I was young, we called this coitus interruptus, and it was something you did to avoid ejaculating inside a girl so as not to make her pregnant. As a callow youth, I had so little control that I was coming by the time I sensed I was about to come. The message doesn't make it to the brain in time for the body to react. As a mature man, I have exquisite control, and I have learned to use this technique to prolong, increase, and multiply my orgasms. I really believe any man can do it, and the only thing stopping most men is ignorance."

THE VALLEY ORGASM: According to the Taoist master Mantak Chia, who teaches workshops on sexuality, the *peak orgasm*, or male orgasm with ejaculation, is "one fleeting moment of intense, even excruciating pleasure, then nothing." On the other hand, the *valley orgasm*, without ejaculation, is "a continual rolling expansion of the orgasm, a greatly heightened ecstasy." To the men who experience them, the valley orgasm feels like a rolling series of orgasms without ejaculation. Here are some tips for having a valley orgasm:

- First, make love using the nine-shallow, one-deep thrusting method described on page 76.

- Stop thrusting when you feel you are near orgasm.

- Use the big draw—or the five-finger draw if you aren't yet the master of your PC muscle—to delay ejaculation.

- Hold your partner in a close, comfortable embrace.

- Continue shallow thrusting.

- Each time you feel ejaculation is imminent, use the big draw.

- You will experience the sensations of orgasm, though more diffuse, without ejaculation.

Comments: A 48-year-old man says, "My wife got me involved in Tantric and Taoist sexual practices and teachings. At first, I was skeptical, but I went along to make her happy. Gradually, I realized our sex life was improving. It took me a while to master the art of having an orgasm without ejaculating; but once I did, I was in love with the concept. The valley orgasm isn't going to happen every time or even very often for a man, but when it does, it is incredible. I feel like a born-again lover."

How to Have an Extragenital Orgasm

An orgasm achieved with no genital contact is an extragenital orgasm. Fewer than 10 percent of women—and even fewer men—can reach orgasm simply from kissing passionately or by having their breasts or nipples kissed or sucked, their thighs caressed or licked, or their ears or neck nuzzled. How can it be done? Women and men who experience extragenital orgasms are able to excite themselves through erotic thoughts and fantasies to the point at which any form of physical stimulation sends them over the edge into orgasm. In men, the phenomenon most frequently occurs during a wet dream, or a nocturnal orgasm and ejaculation caused by an erotic dream. Anywhere from 10 to 20 percent of women have also had a sleep orgasm, the female equivalent of the wet dream.

Here's how to have an extragenital orgasm:

- Have a more traditional orgasm first. Some women can experience an extragenital orgasm after they've had an orgasm through clitoral or vaginal stimulation. Fewer men can experience this after having had a traditional orgasm.

- Either caress or have your partner caress your genitals until you are on the verge of another orgasm.

- Switch the stimulation to a nongenital area such as breasts or thighs.

- Alternate from genital to nongenital stimuli until you are so close to orgasm that a simple touch like running a finger down the inner thigh could induce it.

Comments: A 44-year-old woman says, "I rarely have a nongenital orgasm, but when it happens it's always at the end of a prolonged and intense lovemaking session that produced multiple orgasms. The first one occurred shortly after my fortieth birthday, what a gift! There's an element of serendipity in these occasions. Much depends on how I am feeling physically, mentally, and emotionally, and how closely I am relating to my husband. When it does happen, it happens during afterplay. My husband will be holding and caressing me, perhaps massaging my breasts, and unexpectedly I am coming again."

How to Have a Spontaneous Orgasm

The ultimate no-hands solitary sex experience, a spontaneous orgasm occurs with *no* physical stimulation at all. According to limited research on the subject, a few women actually can think themselves to orgasm. For her book *Women Who Love Sex*, Gina Ogden not only interviewed women who claimed to have this experience but measured their physical responses in a clinical setting and proved their claims had merit. How do such woman do it?

- First, relax. Take a bubble bath, have a glass of wine, put on some music, and/or light candles.

- Create a lush, passionate, and emotional sexual fantasy. Really move into it.

- Breathe. Lying on your back, knees bent, feet spaced well apart, start with deep breaths. Pull your breath into your body so deeply you can feel your diaphragm expanding and can imagine air going all the way down to your genitals. When you breathe out, pull that air all the way out, again imagining you are drawing it up through your genitals into your body.

• Pant. After a dozen or so deep breaths, pant. Breath rapidly from your belly with your mouth open.

• Now use the *fire-breathing* technique. Begin with relaxing shallow breaths. Then breathe deeply. Inhale through the nose, exhale through the mouth. Make the breathing continuous or circular. Imagine a circle of fire beginning first as a small circle, nose through mouth, then expanding to include chest, belly, and finally genitals. Feel the erotic heat moving in a circle throughout your body as you breathe.

• Flex the PC muscle either alone or in combination with the breathing. Coordinate your flexing with your deep breathing. Switch to panting, then back to deep breathing, finally to fire breathing—all the while flexing and relaxing the PC muscle.

• If you don't have an orgasm this way, don't despair. Most people won't. But use the technique during masturbation or intercourse and see how much stronger your orgasm is.

Comments: A 52-year-old woman says, "I am easily orgasmic, multiply orgasmic, capable of extended and whole body orgasms, but I couldn't make this one quite work. I could get to the point where just touching my clitoris a few times brought me to orgasm. However, I recommend the exercise, simply because it leads to an incredibly intense orgasm when you finally give up and touch yourself."

How to Have the Ultimate Orgasm: A Full-Body Orgasm

Sexual ecstasy, or high sex as it is known in some Tantric circles, is a way of making love that expands arousal and orgasm beyond the genitals and extends the time of orgasmic response—giving lovers both extended and whole-body orgasms. A whole-body—or total-body—orgasm is an orgasm that seems to be felt throughout the entire body. Many people experience this kind of orgasm only when they are feeling a strong emotional connection to their partners. Some can have a whole-body orgasm when they are feeling particularly sensual, sexual, or both. For most, the experience is a complex blend of emotional, sensual, and sexual elements.

The whole-body orgasm is more possible in midlife than in youth. Here are some exercises that will increase your chances of experiencing one:

- Practice the techniques for extending your orgasm until you are able to do so.

- Practice the techniques for spontaneous orgasm until you are able to become aroused almost to the point of orgasm through fantasy and breathing alone.

- Practice the techniques for multiple orgasms until you are able either to have them or to continue a state of arousal past orgasm.

- Combine the skills you've mastered in a lovemaking session with your partner when you are feeling very emotionally connected.

- If you do not experience a whole-body orgasm, you will almost undoubtedly have a wonderful time together.

Comments: A 53-year-old woman says, "My husband and I sometimes experience whole-body orgasms, I more often then he. We have taken workshops in Tantra and put the principles to work in our lives as a whole, not just our sex lives. A whole-body orgasm occurs for me when I'm really in tune with my body and his, with my soul and his, and when I am rested and in a good emotional space. It feels like the orgasm will blow off the top of my head and push out the ends of my toes at the same time."

The Simultaneous Orgasm

The point of this chapter is to encourage you to expand your orgasmic potential, not to tell you to set orgasm goals or measure your performance against those of the people quoted here. The exercises are all worth doing, whether they result in extended, whole-body, extragenital, or multiple orgasms—or not. They will improve the quality and perhaps the quantity of the orgasms you're having now. And that, in turn, will give you physical, psychological, and emotional benefits as well as help strengthen the intimacy bond with your partner.

Some couples still believe that the ultimate expression of sexual intimacy is the simultaneous orgasm. In films and novels that were popular when men and women over 50 were forming their sexual ideas and ideals, the lovers almost always appeared to come at the same time. Their ecstasy at the same moment left little room for alternative interpretations. Women—the consumers of more romantic fiction—particularly believed mutual climaxes were better than separate but equal ones.

In fact, the simultaneous orgasm is more serendipitous than typical. The belief that they should climax when their partners did led some women to fake an orgasm at the propitious moment, then feel secretly angry and dissatisfied afterward. In real life, men, especially when younger, reach orgasm before women do, and women are far more capable of multiple orgasms than are men. Modern lovers have adjusted the mythology to their own reality. Often the man performs cunnilingus or manual stimulation on his partner to bring her to orgasm before initiating intercourse.

Clearly, simultaneous orgasm can't, and shouldn't, be the ideal. Some couples like to experience it occasionally because they enjoy the special intimacy that coming together brings to lovemaking. A mature couple has a much better chance of making the following technique work than does a younger couple does because the response cycles of men and women over 50 are more closely matched. With a little attention to timing and advance planning, you can make this technique work.

The Technique

1. Time your response cycles so that you know approximately how long it takes for each partner to reach orgasm during your most typical lovemaking pattern.

2. Assuming it takes her longer than it does him, let him stimulate her alone until she reaches the point where she is the same

distance away from climax as he will be when stimulation begins for him.

3. Assuming it takes him longer than it does her, let her stimulate him alone, using a stop-and-start pattern of stimulation until he is approximately the same distance from orgasm as she will be when he begins stimulating her.

4. Communicate with each other. If one of you is moving faster toward climax than anticipated, say, "Slow down."

Is One Orgasm Better Than Another?

Perhaps because we are such a competitive society, men and women too frequently want to know if they are having the best possible orgasms via a particular method or at a certain point in their lives. Cultural theories about orgasm have added to confusion. Most of us are old enough to remember when the clitoral orgasm was considered inferior to the vaginal orgasm for women. That thinking was seriously challenged by the work of William Masters and Virginia Johnson in the 1960s. The clitoral theory was challenged again by the G-spot proponents in the 1970s, who maintained that the female orgasm achieved through vaginal (G-spot) stimulation was deeper and more intense than the clitoral orgasm.

When we were young, we thought the youthful orgasm was better than anything our elders might be experiencing. And now that we are the older generation, we think we have once again discovered erotic bliss of the sort another age group can't comprehend. Well, some of us do. Others pine for the golden days of their youth when the penises were hard as blue steel and the orgasms flowed like jug wine at parties.

There really is no best orgasm. Whether the orgasm seems to originate in one place or another makes no difference in measurable responses. A woman may not be able to have an orgasm via intercourse alone or, if she does, only by delaying penetration until she is on the brink of climax. A man may not be able to have an orgasm every time he makes love now. However and whenever they occur, orgasms are joyous events. And so is lovemaking without them.

SIZZLER #10

Come Again

Elaine was amused and a little puzzled when she discovered her husband, George, immersed in a book with a distinctly New Age title and cover illustration. Was this a harbinger of midlife crisis? Curious, she picked up the book to see what was inside as soon as he was out of the room.

"Tantra?" she asked when he returned with a fresh cup of coffee. "Isn't that some kind of Eastern religion?"

"More like sacred sexuality," George said. He took the book from her hand, flipped a few pages, and read out loud an excerpt from a chapter on orgasms. Looking up from his page, he noted how closely she was paying attention. He grinned. "Shall I read further?"

"Oh, please," she said, patting the sofa cushion beside her. "And get comfortable while you do."

Like many Western readers of Eastern philosophy, George and Elaine paged past the sections pertaining to spiritual development and went straight for the sex advice. He, she was surprised to discover, had purchased the book because he wanted to improve the quality of his orgasms. The nagging feeling that they once were, and could be again, better kept him from fully enjoying lovemaking in what they both jokingly referred to as their golden years.

"*My* orgasms are better than they were when I was young," she retorted. "I don't know what's wrong with yours."

"Maybe they are," he said. "But wouldn't you like them to be still better?"

Heads touching, they read. The language wasn't erotic, yet they were both aroused. Could they use the techniques described to prolong George's arousal phase and delay his orgasm? Could Elaine have multiple orgasms on a frequent basis?

"What have we got to lose?" George asked; and Elaine acknowledged they had nothing to lose and much to gain.

They began "orgasm training" as they laughingly called it. That training consisted of Kegels and other physical and breathing exercises—activities they did both separately and together. When they were able to influence their orgasms by using their newly strengthened musculature and breath control, they added some new techniques. Soon Elaine was having multiple orgasms whenever she wanted them. More surprising, George experienced his first set of multiples, too. When it happened, they were both delighted.

Elaine particularly enjoyed one part of the training: helping him delay orgasm. That prolonged lovemaking, turning sex into a leisurely experience that made her feel wanton and pampered. She had to be closely attuned to his arousal level to help him prolong the intensity he craved by varying or abruptly stopping stimuli during intercourse, and she grew deft at gently squeezing the head of his penis to stop ejaculation.

She played with his penis as she'd done when they were young lovers, but with greater assurance. Together they could control this magical organ in new and wonderful ways. Frequently, they made love with the caveat that George could not come. Elaine could have as many orgasms as she wanted. After a session or two of nonorgasmic lovemaking, he was desirous of release; and even she could feel his ejaculation was stronger inside her than it had been for decades.

"I want to come," he told her on a rainy Sunday afternoon. They were lying in bed, reading. She allowed him to arouse and satisfy her, before she said, "No, you can't come today. I think you should wait another day or two." He was exasperated, but she remained firm. "As your orgasm coach," she said, "I think it's time to push your training up a notch."

A few days later he initiated sex. "I'm coming this time," he said, and she replied, "We'll see." Concentrating more on his pleasure than her own, she repeatedly brought him to the brink of orgasm, then helped him hold back until he couldn't restrain himself.

She felt him inside her, his penis throbbing in the familiar rhythm, with each jolt more intense. But he did not ejaculate. Gasping, he told her, "I came, but I didn't come!" He pulled his penis from her vagina. It was slick with her juices—none of his own—and still erect. She guided him back inside. Within seconds, he was coming again. He experienced several orgasms before finally ejaculating explosively.

"Thanks, coach," he whispered when he could talk.

CHAPTER ELEVEN

Sex and Hormones

"After I developed the first symptoms of menopause, hot flashes and night sweats, I was inundated with advice from family and friends on whether or not to ask my doctor for hormone-replacement therapy," says Jill, 52. "Everyone had a position, and they sent me books, newspaper, and magazine articles backing their position. I was in a quandary. Finally, my husband suggested I talk to my doctor, a woman I trust, and ask her *advice*, rather than asking her for medication. He rather gently added: 'Tell her you aren't interested in making love anymore, and see if she thinks there is a hormonal link.'

"My doctor said there very well could be a hormonal link to my lack of interest in lovemaking, but it could also be caused by other factors, including relationship issues, my own attitudes about aging, any number of things. As for the hormones, she said she never just writes a prescription for them. She orders blood tests. If the blood tests show the estrogen is very low and there are no medical reasons for not doing so, she puts the patient on hormone-replacement therapy (HRT) and monitors the progress. She gave me reading material to take home.

"The tests showed my estrogen level was very low. I went on HRT. The hot flashes, night sweats, and low libido disappeared. I'm not saying that HRT is a sexual panacea, but it was what I needed. Women should make informed choices, based on their own research and their medical doctor's opinion, and not be influenced by others."

How Hormones Affect Sexuality

Controversy surrounds testosterone replacement for both men and women and especially hormone replacement (estrogen or a combination of estrogen/progesterone) for women. This chapter examines the effects of hormones only on sexuality. I present the options but do not endorse one particular approach. To make an informed decision about taking hormones, you need to consult your health-care providers and take into consideration the most up-to-date research on side effects and benefits. An article you read 2 years ago may not be supported by the newest data.

It is generally wise to question any medical authority who takes an extreme position, saying either hormones should *never* be prescribed or that they are *always* the answer. It's also smart not to trust a doctor or therapist who sees you in only one dimension, in physical or in psychological terms. Especially at midlife, the answers to our questions are found in multiple areas, and hormones are just one part of the physical component. Consult with a health-care provider who knows your medical history and is willing to follow your progress as you age.

Estrogen and testosterone are the principal hormones that directly affect sexual desire and performance. As we age, we experience a decline in the levels of these sex hormones. In men, the decline of testosterone is a very gradual process. Beginning in young adulthood, a man's testosterone levels begin to fall gradually, dropping to about a third to a half of their peak by the age of 80. In women, menopause, at an average age of 51, precipitates a dramatic decline in the levels of estrogen and progesterone. Menopause has far less affect on the production of testosterone, which is present in small amounts in women.

Although estrogen and testosterone are the best-known hormones driving female sexuality, lesser-known hormones may also play significant roles. A 2003 American Association of Retired Persons (AARP) article by Melissa Gotthardt quotes Irwin Goldstein: "Estrogen imbalance isn't even half the problem. There are 10 sex steroids in all, and only three are estrogens; the other seven are androgens, which most people think of as the male sex hormones. We're finding that three out of four women who see us for lack of desire have serious androgen shortages."

Research on the relationship between androgens and female sexuality is relatively new and has provided conflicting results. Some of the androgens produce serious side effects in women, and the effects of others are not fully understood. Studies are ongoing, and recommendations for these and/or other steroids are controversial. The rest of this chapter, therefore, focuses on estrogen, progesterone, and testosterone.

Hormones for Women

ESTROGEN: When a woman's estrogen levels drop, the growth of new cells in the vagina decreases, resulting in thinner vaginal walls. As a consequence, intercourse can cause irritation and even tears in the tissue. In addition, the vagina may become less elastic, and the vaginal lips lose some of their firmness, which may contribute to discomfort or self-consciousness during lovemaking. Furthermore, because estrogen promotes vaginal lubrication, decreased hormone levels lead to vaginal dryness, making intercourse painful.

Estrogen promotes blood flow through the arteries; thus declining estrogen levels means decreased blood flow to the vagina. As a result, the vagina in older women doesn't become as engorged with blood as it did when they were younger. This may decrease vaginal sensitivity and may lessen the pleasure of intercourse.

Low estrogen levels can also cause a change in touch perception in some women. Nerve endings may be affected, and so it may take longer for a woman to become aroused or to reach orgasm.

Only about 30 percent of women report a significant decline in libido associated with menopause and lower estrogen levels. For these women, HRT can be a valid treatment, assuming there are no other health issues to prevent them from taking hormones.

PROGESTERONE: In combination with estrogen, progesterone regulates the menstrual cycle. It prevents cells of the uterine lining from growing in a disorderly fashion, causing them to slough off at a certain point in the menstrual cycle. Although some forms of hormone-replacement therapy (HRT) include both estrogen and progesterone, progesterone alone has little if any effect on sexuality.

Testosterone

Many women find their interest in sex actually increases after menopause. The reason? The decrease in estrogen increases the ratio of testosterone to female hormones, which can lead to a stronger sex drive. On the other hand, some women find that their sex drive is unchanged by menopause.

Hormones in Men

TESTOSTERONE: In boys, the surge of testosterone at puberty causes the development of typical adult male characteristics such as face and body hair and a muscular physique. The hormone is also responsible for the maturation of the male genitals, including the quality of the erection and erectile endurance. Throughout life, testosterone fuels the sex drive, or libido. Although testosterone levels decline with age, for most men in good health, hormone levels remain adequate for sexual functioning well into old age.

Conquering Common Hormone-Related Sex Problems in Women

"When my wife's interest in lovemaking declined at menopause," says Curt, 54, "it never occurred to me that there might be a hormonal reason for it. I thought she was going through a psychological crisis about aging. To me, menopause was a woman's midlife crisis. For her part, she was too embarrassed to talk to her doctor about the problems we were having in bed, though she knew they had a physical basis, and I didn't.

"She had been avoiding sex because intercourse, even with a lubricant, was painful. After her doctor put her on HRT for other reasons, our sex life improved. She told me then she'd been suffering pain, but the pain was gone. I insisted she mention it to the doctor because I was concerned the pain would come back. The doctor said her vagina had been showing signs of atrophy, which was corrected by HRT.

"We were lucky. This is how people give up on sex. They are too embarrassed to talk openly to each other or even to their doctors about their problems. So the woman suffers in silence until she withdraws sexually, which the man accepts as the nature of life."

Although many women experience an increase in libido and find it easier to reach orgasm, some report sex problems associated with hormone loss. According to one survey, 14 percent of women reported fewer orgasms after menopause and 16 percent had some pain or discomfort during intercourse. In another report, about a third of women over 65 found intercourse painful because of changes that have occurred in size, firmness, and lubrication of the vagina.

If you suspect that decreased estrogen levels are affecting your sex life, make an appointment with your doctor. Ask for a pelvic examination and blood tests to determine your estrogen levels. If your doctor diagnoses hormone deficiency, you can ask him or her if HRT is the correct solution for your situation.

The following sections describe common problems associated with hormone loss and offer some solutions. Be sure to ask your doctor before using hormone products.

Vaginal Dryness

Some women have almost no diminishment of lubricating ability, especially if they are thoroughly aroused, whereas others have significant problems with dryness. Vaginal dryness is a signal a woman and her partner can easily misread. Because they are accustomed to measuring her arousal level by the amount of her secretions, they may equate dryness with lack of desire. A simple misunderstanding can cause both of them to pull back from initiating sexual contact.

HOW TO HANDLE

• *Lubricate.* Use a water-soluble lubricant such as K-Y jelly. Replens is a lubricant that can be used daily, not just in preparation for intercourse, to nourish and maintain the vaginal area. Often this is the only treatment necessary.

- *Have more sex.* More frequent sexual activity helps regulate estrogen levels and promote greater production of estrogen, even in menopausal women.

- *Change your diet.* Add more soy products (see "A Note About Soy" on page 188), and avoid substances that dry your membranes (including the vagina), such as antihistamines, diuretics, alcohol, and caffeine. Drink eight glasses of water a day.

- *Use an estrogen cream.* Natural, plant-based estrogen creams, such as OstaDerm V, can be found in many health food stores. These creams can be used in conjunction with a natural progesterone cream. Transdermal estrogen formulas, which contain a small dose of estrogen, can be prescribed by your doctor.

- *Use estriol.* Estriol is a type of natural estrogen, which, when applied topically, stimulates estrogen receptors in the vagina, increasing lubrication and plumping up tissues. The effects on the rest of the body are minimal. Studies suggest that this therapy may also help ward off urinary tract infections and improve incontinence. Topical estriol is available as suppositories, tablets, or cream and requires a prescription; it is currently available only from a compounding pharmacy (one that will create customized drugs).

Comments: "Vaginal dryness made me feel old," says Kate, 52. "It was like the wrinkles on my forehead. It got to me. I knew the problem could be solved with K-Y jelly, and I knew younger women often need to use lubrication, too. Logic didn't help. I had never needed additional lubrication, and now suddenly I did, and I felt old.

"My doctor suggested Replens, a lubricant I could use on a regular basis, not as a preparation for intercourse. That made all the difference for me. If I could consider it an addition to my beauty routine, like alpha-hydroxy lotions and sunscreen, I could live with it. Pulling out a tube before intercourse was too humiliating. We all have to do it our own way, don't we?"

A Note About Soy

Before taking any soy product be sure to read the label. Recent research suggests a link between some soy products and some forms of cancer. Avoid soy products that have been heavily processed because studies indicate that the effects of processing may contribute to some cancers and that the soy itself is safe. Research on soy products is still under way, and no firm conclusions have been reached. For more guidance, talk with your physician.

Vaginal Atrophy

Vaginal atrophy is the term used to describe the aging vagina that has shrunk in size, has lost its elasticity and firmness, and has thinning walls. Typically, there is some narrowing of the vaginal opening and shortening of the vaginal canal. One woman who suffered from atrophy before taking corrective measures (which in her case included masturbation with a dildo, natural estrogen creams, and lubricants) described it as "feeling shriveled and dried up."

HOW TO HANDLE

- *Enjoy more frequent sexual activity.* The best prevention of vaginal atrophy is an active sex life. If you haven't been sexually active for a while, you can restore the vagina by following the suggestions in this chapter.

- *Masturbate.* If you don't have a partner or aren't having regular relations with your partner, use a penis-shaped vibrator or dildo (available in sex-toy shops or through mail-order catalogs) to get your vagina back into shape.

- *Do Kegel exercises.* Kegels strengthen and tone the vaginal muscles (see page 81 for instructions). Doctors recommend them for use after childbirth because of their restorative powers.

- *Use an estrogen cream.* In addition to promoting vaginal lubrication, these creams can thicken tissues.

- *Try vitamin E.* Some evidence indicates that vitamin E (topical or oral) may be beneficial in reducing the symptoms of vaginal atrophy.

- *Eat more soy products.* Soybeans contain phytoestrogens (compounds that act like weak estrogens in some parts of the body), which have been shown to rebuild and moisturize thinning vaginal walls. Soy flour, soy milk, tofu, and many other soy products can be found in most health food stores. Be sure to read "A Note About Soy" on page 188.

Comments: A 60-year-old woman says, "I went for five years without a sex partner after my husband died. I had been on HRT for five years when my doctor decided it was no longer necessary. She gave me dietary recommendations and advised the regular use of estrogen creams and lubricants as well as the continued practice of Kegels. On my own, I figured out that masturbating with a vibrator to simulate intercourse would help. When I met a man and became sexually active with him, I had no problems. If I hadn't kept my vagina in shape, I would have had. I know other women in my age group who've been through similar dry spells and experienced pain, even bleeding, during intercourse because they hadn't kept in shape."

Loss of Sensation

Some women don't respond to genital touch in the same way as a result of low estrogen, which causes diminished blood flow to the area. Often there is only a small degree of change in sensation. A woman can compensate for that by asking her partner for a firmer or more extended touch. Women who experience significant loss of sensation should consult a doctor for advice.

HOW TO HANDLE: If this is your only sex problem caused by low estrogen levels, consider changing your lovemaking style to include more vigorous thrusting or more active foreplay.

Comments: A 50-year-old woman says, "I realized I wasn't responding to touch in quite the same way about the same time I began having some of the minor symptoms of menopause. I didn't connect the touch issue with the other stuff. I thought my husband didn't excite me as much as he once did because we'd been together so long. With my doctor's approval, I wanted to try handling my hormone situation naturally. It didn't quite work for me, and she put me on HRT, with the proviso that we would evaluate every six months whether I would stay on or go off. Almost immediately I felt the difference. We were making love, and I realized I experienced his touch in the same way I once had. I was more quickly aroused, and my orgasms came more easily. Women need to hear about the sex benefits of boosting estrogen. We get a lot of the other information, but not this."

Loss of Libido

There can be many reasons for loss of libido. Low estrogen is one of them. If you're suddenly less interested or completely disinterested in lovemaking, have your estrogen levels checked before you assume the cause is rooted in your relationship with your partner. Your libido may be a temporary casualty of hormonal imbalance, nothing more.

HOW TO HANDLE: If tests indicate that your estrogen levels are low, read the suggestions for vaginal dryness and atrophy. If your estrogen levels are normal, examine your attitudes about aging, your lifestyle, and your relationship and read the suggestions given earlier in the book.

Comments: A 50-year-old woman says, "I did experience the classic hormone-related loss of libido. My husband and I had the classic response: We blamed the marriage, not hormone loss. We went to see a marriage counselor, who never said a word about physical causes. He didn't suggest we have medical evaluations as a prelude to therapy. Ironically, an article on HRT that I read in a magazine in his waiting room alerted us to the possibility there might be a simple physical cause for my lack of interest in sex. I made an appointment with my doctor. Tests showed my estrogen level was way low. I went on HRT, and my interest in sex returned. Now I tell everyone: Don't trust a therapist who doesn't want a medical evaluation before she or he starts taking your marriage apart."

Evaluating Hormone-Replacement Therapy for Women

The reports about HRT can be confusing, the literature is sometimes equivocal, and comments from women vary. Some women have found HRT to be very helpful, others have steered clear on the advice of their physicians, and still others have been prescribed supplementation on a short-term basis.

What to do? It's not an easy question to answer, especially for women who are feeling the drop in their libido or have other health concerns and are also concerned about a recent report by the National Heart, Lung, and Blood Institute. The institute released the results of its Women's Health Initiative (WHI), a well-respected and well-conducted study of the long-term effects of HRT.

Researchers concluded that hormone replacement, over the long term—especially beyond 5 years—raises the risk for breast cancer, heart disease, and stroke, although this increased risk was relatively low. Earlier reports, based on less rigorous studies concluded just the opposite: that HRT might actually protect against heart disease. Further confusing the issue, the WHI research found that hormone-replacement therapy helped lower the risk of hip fractures and was associated with a lower incidence of some types of cancer. However, WHI researchers stressed that, over the long term, the risks outweighed the benefits of HRT.

Note that the WHI study focused on women who were taking both estrogen and progesterone. Studies are under way to assess the benefits and risks of taking estrogen only.

The question remains: What to do? A definitive answer is somewhat elusive. Some doctors are comfortable with short-term (less than 5 years) HRT, whereas others believe that menopause is not a disease that needs a medical cure. Another group stresses the importance of determining the issues of concern for each woman and then considering non-HRT solutions first. There is a general consensus that women with a history of heart disease and breast cancer avoid HRT and the American Heart

Association concurs, noting that HRT should not be used solely to prevent heart disease.

Remember, too, that HRT comes in a variety of forms and combinations. Prominent complementary physicians Jonathan Wright and Julian Whitaker, for example, are proponents of bioidentical estrogen and progesterone, which are made up to be in sync with the natural hormones found in the body. These supplements act in the same way as the body's own hormones. Such physicians are part of a group of practitioners who believe that the closer medicines come to being natural, the more likely the body will accept them and the less risk there will be.

Adversaries of the approach point out that bioidentical hormones have never been studied in large clinical trials. Proponents don't disagree; however, they note that scores of small studies and thousands of cases of careful clinical observation demonstrate the safety and efficacy of these drugs.

The Sex Benefits

The HRT debate is generally focused on the health issues, but HRT offers real and important sex benefits. If you do not want or cannot take HRT, you are not out of luck; many of these benefits can be gained through other means, as discussed in this chapter.

- For some women, cessation of hot flashes and night sweats is a sex benefit. These women may have been avoiding sexual contact because they couldn't predict when a hot flash would make them feel uncomfortable and unattractive.

- With HRT, the vagina becomes more elastic, the walls thicken, and natural lubrication returns, making intercourse more comfortable.

- Blood flow to the genitals during arousal is increased, creating stronger sensations during lovemaking.

- Nerve endings become more sensitive, restoring the familiar sense of touch in the genital area.

Comments: "There is an active school of thought now telling us that menopause is a natural event and shouldn't be medicalized," says Noreen, 51, an obstetrics and gynecology (OB-GYN) nurse who is on HRT. "These are the same people who said childbirth is a natural event and shouldn't be medicalized. I have assisted women in giving birth for more than 25 years. I've watched women go through agonizing labors for hours on end without so much as a painkiller because they thought they had to give birth naturally, and I've assisted other women who turned to pharmaceutical help as needed. When it was over, there was a healthy mother and a healthy infant; when something did go wrong, painkillers were not the cause of it. Why did one mother have to endure so much pain to get there? Why is it women are the gender who are supposed to endure every suffering naturally? Who tells men not to take a painkiller when they're in pain? Who would dare tell men to suffer the irritations and miseries of menopause without help if they went through the kind of sudden testosterone withdrawal that we go through in estrogen withdrawal? HRT makes it possible for me to enjoy life, enjoy sex more than I have in a long time. And by the way, when I gave birth, I had a little help from some drugs."

And from Carolyn, also 51: "My doctor told me that not all women need HRT. A lot depends on whether you have slightly low or very low estrogen levels, your bone density, and your lifestyle. I had slightly low estrogen levels. That had no noticeable effect on my sexuality. I was able to use natural supplements combined with weight-training exercises to bring up my estrogen level. If I'd needed HRT, I would have taken it, and I think women who need it for sexual functioning should consider that as important as other needs. But if all you require is a slight boost, why do it with drugs when you can do it naturally?"

The Mitigating Factors
Your doctor may advise against estrogen replacement if you have certain risk factors. Be sure to tell your doctor if you have experienced any abnormal or unexplained vaginal bleeding. Other important factors are a history of liver disease, sickle-cell anemia, embolism, heart attack, stroke, breast or uterine cancer, and/or fibroid tumors. If you are a heavy smoker, let your doctor know.

The Side Effects

Some women on HRT experience side effects, most of which are caused by a vitamin B deficiency. Consider supplementation if you experience fatigue, depression, or mood swings.

If you note a loss of libido after starting HRT, talk to your doctor so you can rule out any medical problems. Then look for any underlying emotional or psychological reasons for lack of interest in sex. If necessary, consider seeing a psychologist. Typically, a woman's sexuality is more sensitive to psychological factors than is most men's. Consequently, intrapersonal factors such as depression, anxiety, and low self-regard will push sexual activity lower on the priority list. In like manner, interpersonal factors such as relationship conflicts, lack of intimacy, trust issues, and the other sources of dissatisfaction will also dampen libido. For all of these issues, talking it out with a professional who specializes in relationship and sexual concerns is a wise consideration.

The Bottom Line

One outcome of the WHI research is that the first and best option for many women is to use menopause as an opportunity to get and stay healthy the natural way, via good nutrition, exercise, weight management, and avoidance of smoking. Women who have solid medical reasons (as assessed by a physician) to start HRT, should keep in mind the results of the WHI study and work with their doctor to end therapy within 5 years. When in doubt, seek a second opinion. All older woman should have regular checkups, including breast examinations.

Weighing the Alternatives to HRT

You likely consider your doctor as the best source of information for alternatives targeted to specific medical conditions such as bone density. But it is also wise to consult with your physician about sexual issues. Before heading off to the health food store to stock up on herbs, do some research and check with your doctor. Some herbal remedies have serious side effects when taken in large doses or in combination with some medications, alcohol, or certain foods. Some herbs should not be taken if you have specific medical conditions, and some people have allergies or sensitivities to particular natural remedies.

Unlike drugs, herbal and other natural remedies aren't controlled by the U.S. Food and Drug Administration (FDA). Not all manufacturers are reputable or produce products with consistent benefits.

Be sure to read the labels; not all menopausal remedies provide sex benefits. Chasteberry, for example, is said to *reduce* libido. The following products *may* be helpful in relieving hot flashes, vaginal dryness and atrophy, and decreased libido:

- *Black cohosh*. Available in capsules, tablets, drops, and powders, black cohosh has been available under a reliable brand name Remifemin in Europe for decades and in the United States since 1996. Remifemin (40 milligrams a day) has been approved for the relief of menopausal symptoms by Germany's Commission E (a government agency). The effects of this herb have been supported by more clinical research than any other natural therapy for menopause. Compounds in black cohosh help reduce hot flashes, night sweats, mood swings, and other common symptoms. In one double-blind study, significant improvements were noted within 4 weeks of starting the herb, and, after 6 months, a majority of women reported a 70 percent reduction in physical and emotional symptoms.

- *Korean ginseng*. An effective stimulant, Korean ginseng (*Panax ginseng*), one of the 11 species of ginseng is reputed to improve sexual functioning during menopause by boosting energy and an overall sense of well-being, thus stimulating libido. The research on ginseng has been conducted primarily in Europe and is very promising. For example, in one controlled study of women, Korean ginseng root improved symptoms of fatigue, insomnia, and depression. Isolated reports have also shown Korean ginseng to have estrogen-like activity in women. Ginseng is an ingredient in some natural menopause remedies. The chief side effects, which occur in a small percentage of people, are restlessness and sleep disruption. Therapeutic dosages of ginseng start at around 500 milligrams of root per day.

- *Licorice root*. Because it contains high levels of phytoestrogens, licorice root would seem to be nature's own HRT. Unfortunately, regular use of the herb can have dangerous side effects, such as raising blood pressure and lowering potassium in some people. Don't use it without consulting a doctor who is knowledgeable about herbs.

Many people who shop in health food stores are under the false impression that natural is always safer and better than prescribed drugs. That's not necessarily true. As mentioned, most natural and herbal products aren't regulated by the FDA; thus you must be cautious when buying and ingesting them. Some of these products cost more and have worse side effects than does estrogen. Again, read the labels, buy known and trusted brands, do your research, and inform your doctor if you decide to take an alternative drug.

Testosterone-Replacement Therapy

For Women

"I just didn't feel sexy anymore," says Carole, 53, describing the state of her libido only a year ago. "I had sailed through menopause without problems. My marriage was in good shape, no problems at work, no problems with the kids, my parents, or his family. I'd stopped having sexual fantasies and wouldn't have thought about sex at all if it weren't for my husband who was still thinking about it. Medical tests turned up no reason for me to feel the way I did.

"My doctor said, 'There's a controversial new treatment. I'd like to try it on you. Have you heard about testosterone-replacement therapy for women?' I had visions of me growing a beard, talking in a low growl, and losing my breasts. She laughed. I thought, What have I got to lose? I didn't tell my husband exactly what it was. I just said, 'a little hormone.' No point in scaring him.

"That little pill put my sex drive back in gear. I couldn't believe the difference it made in my life, almost overnight. It's rejuvenated our marriage. We're planning a second honeymoon. My husband couldn't be more delighted, though he still doesn't know my little hormone is the same one fueling him."

Sexual desire is only partly biologically driven, of course, but testosterone, sometimes called the "hormone of desire," is the primary biological component fueling the sexual engines of both men and women. In women, it is produced in the ovaries and adrenal glands and in trace amounts in the uterus. The woman's total testosterone production is less than one twentieth of the average man's of the same age. For most women, the slight decrease in testosterone production accompanying menopause does not create a libido problem. In fact, as noted earlier, some women report stronger sex drives after menopause, when the ratio of testosterone to estrogen increases. But for a significant minority of women like Carole, a low testosterone level seems to be the cause of libido loss.

British studies have shown that the addition of testosterone to estrogen-replacement therapy is more effective than using estrogen alone to boost libido, particularly in women who have undergone a total hysterectomy, including removal of the ovaries. Before you rush out to obtain a prescription, you should know that testosterone is not a libido wonder drug for women who have lost interest in sex because of psychological, emotional, or relationship issues. In fact, British studies have shown that 50 percent of women who take testosterone report no increase in sexual desire. Studies in the in the United States have been equivocal: Some have shown a boost in libido compared to a placebo, and others have failed to show any significant effects. What's more, in December 2005, the FDA expressed concerns about the long-term safety of using a testosterone patch.

Will testosterone therapy increase your sex drive? If you can trace loss of libido to the beginning of menopause, then the answer is maybe—but remember that the safety of such a treatment has to be established. Women who receive testosterone supplementation are generally tested to see if their estrogen levels are within the normal range. It is difficult to interpret testosterone levels in women because normal levels seem to vary widely from woman to woman; what's high in one woman may be normal for another. Testosterone is not usually given to women who are not on HRT; and in light of the FDA studies, it is not the sex hormone of choice. Most doctors will recommend estrogen replacement instead. If you are interested in trying testosterone, try to determine exactly when you began to notice a loss in libido and talk to your doctor.

WHAT TO EXPECT

- Your cholesterol levels will be checked before beginning therapy and then will be monitored regularly during treatment. Testosterone can decrease the levels of high-density lipoprotein (HDL; the good cholesterol).

- The hormone may be given as a pill, injection, or patch or as small pellets that are implanted under your skin. Generally, patch users report fewer side effects and better results.

- You will be asked to keep your doctor informed of any change in your libido. If the hormone works, you can probably continue indefinitely.

- You may experience a few unpleasant side effects, such as oily skin, acne, unwanted facial hair, and—in rare cases—a lowering of the voice.

- You may enjoy the unexpected bonus of increased clitoral sensitivity.

For Men

"My testosterone level was in the low-normal range; and my sex drive was below normal," says Ted, 56. "My doctor prescribed testosterone replacement with the warning that it might not have much effect. It did. The additional hormone in my system was like a libido jump-start, all I needed to get me going. Once I regained interest in sex, I started making love to my wife more often. The sex got better, and my interest grew.

"My wife and I are back in sexual sync now. We both give a lot of credit to testosterone replacement. If you need a little push, get the push. Don't be proud."

Testosterone, produced in the testes, plays a major role in a man's desire, arousal, and ability to get an erection and ejaculate. Production begins declining at midlife, but many other factors influence sexual response and performance. For example, how a man feels about his partner, emotional and psychological issues, variety, frequency, and the lovemaking skills (both his and his partner's) can all affect desire. Furthermore, arousal and performance may be affected by medications, medical conditions (such as blocked blood vessels or nerve damage) and lifestyle choices (such as smoking and drinking). Testosterone is an important part of male sexuality, but not the whole story.

Can testosterone replacement reverse the effects of flagging libido, erection disorders, even erectile dysfunction? The answer is sometimes. Testosterone-replacement therapy is not the solution to all erection problems, especially for men who have normal hormone levels before undergoing therapy. Supplementation is generally prescribed only for men older than 60 and only when low testosterone levels have been documented.

WHAT TO EXPECT
- The hormone may be given in conjunction with other erection-improving medications.

- The hormone is given as a pill, tablet, injection, or patch. The injection lasts from 2 to 4 weeks, and can sometimes be self-administered.

- You should notice improvement in your erection within 2 weeks and an increase in desire even sooner. Some men experience minimal to no benefit.

- Increased libido does not necessarily lead to improved sexual performance or increased pleasure.

- Side effects include water retention, high blood pressure, headache, and—less often—an enlarged prostate.

Both men and women should view HRT as one of the options available for increasing desire and improving sexual performance and satisfaction. Neither a panacea nor a medical evil, hormones provide sexual benefits for some patients. Be an informed consumer, and tell your doctor about any changes you experience.

Younger Love

One lovely spring morning Emily realized she had metamorphosed into a woman of a certain age. Clamping a wide-brimmed straw hat onto her head, she walked out into her garden where the daffodils and tulips were in bloom. She took deep breaths of the soft, fresh air. In her mind's eye, she could see herself as she moved, walked, and breathed. Not long ago she would have envisioned a younger, more buoyant version of herself. The hat would have symbolized romance, the tulips possibility.

The new Emily was matronly, one of the older characters in a Jane Austen novel. She had been feeling older than her 52 years for many months. And now she looked older, too.

"Emily!" her husband, Alex, called from the house. "I'm leaving now. See you tonight!"

See you tonight. Raising her arm to wave at him, she remembered when those words conjured erotic visions. She sat on a garden chair and surveyed her domain. The tender young leaves on the rosebushes taunted her. They were yellow roses, once her favorite flower. How long had it been since she'd brought bouquets of roses into the bedroom or sprinkled rose petals on the bed, in anticipation of Alex's making love to her?

Sighing, she made a mental list of the day's obligations. First, she had a doctor's appointment—routine checkup. And from there, she would off to the supermarket.

Fast-forward 4 weeks. Emily, straw hat at a rakish angle, dashed into a compounding pharmacy to pick up a refill of bioidentical hormones. She engaged in mildly flirtatious banter with the pharmacist, who'd been a classmate of hers in high school. Afterward, she ran a series of errands, arriving home in time to clip the first yellow roses in anticipation of the evening ahead.

Alex came into the kitchen as she was arranging the flowers in vases, one for the dining-room table, another for the night table on her side of the bed.

He nuzzled her neck. Her heart beat faster. She turned in his arms and lightly brushed his lips with hers.

"We're having your favorite dinner," she said huskily.

"As long as I'm having my favorite dessert," he responded, "anything is my favorite dinner."

They had cocktails on the patio. She kicked off her shoes, reached across the space between them with her leg, and ran her foot up and down his inner thigh. He captured her foot in his hands and held it against his crotch as he massaged her instep. Sighing, she closed her eyes and leaned her head back. The breeze lifted the ends of her hair, and she felt her nipples harden.

Their foreplay continued over a candlelight dinner. While feeding her a spoon of lobster bisque, he spilled a drop on her neck. He licked it off. Later, as she served him chicken and rice, she grazed his back with her breasts. By the time they walked hand in hand to the bedroom, both were glassy-eyed with desire.

Slowly, they helped each other undress in between embraces and kisses. By the light of two dozen votive candles, they lay down together, with the scent of yellow roses wafting over them. He took her in his arms, and she thrilled to his touch.

In a full-body embrace, they kissed deeply until she felt his penis stir against her. She reached down, took it in her hand, and held it firmly. He responded by putting his hand to her genitals. She was wet already.

"Oh, Emily," he whispered.

Her desire ignited his. Eagerly his tongue explored her mouth as his fingers sought out her clitoris. As her breathing grew harder, so did his. She moved her body against his hand. Everything fell away. The room, the bed, the reality of their lives all disappeared until there was nothing but Alex doing wonderful things to her body and the scent of roses in her nostrils.

Guiding her hips, he pulled her over on top of him. She mounted him easily. Her wet swollen vagina embraced him. They made love the way they had in their youth.

Emily was no longer a woman of a certain age. She was young again.

CHAPTER TWELVE

Overcoming Erectile Dysfunction

"I thought I was becoming impotent two years into my second marriage," says Alan, 56. "I panicked. Four years after I lost my first wife to cancer, I married Dee. In the early days of our relationship, I had erections and enjoyed the lovemaking tremendously. Then sometimes I wouldn't be able to get an erection or sustain it through intercourse. Dee was very understanding. She said I was pressuring myself to be a great lover for her and I should relax. I didn't tell her how frightened I was about becoming impotent, but I made an appointment with a therapist.

"We talked through my performance problems. He said I was applying very strict standards to measuring my erections. True, I wasn't getting many spontaneous erections, but that, he said, was a natural change accompanying aging. I needed stimulation to get erect, and, of course, I'd been embarrassed to ask Dee to stimulate me to erection. I thought I had to be erect when I approached her. And I wasn't really 'losing' an erection during intercourse either. Sometimes I don't need to have an orgasm. I can sustain intercourse for quite a while, long enough to satisfy Dee. Then my erection subsides.

"Once I understood what was happening, I stopped worrying. I ask Dee to get me hard; and she's very enthusiastic about doing that. If I hadn't talked to a therapist, I might have worried myself into becoming impotent."

By the time they are 40 years old, 90 percent of men have experienced at least one erectile failure. This is a normal occurrence, but many men panic at the first sign of erectile problems. Now they are likely to run to a urologist and ask for one of the highly publicized erectile dysfunction (ED) pills, which they may not need and may not find effective. Being in a new marriage at midlife might have intensified Alan's responses to his perceived erotic failures. He could have been experiencing some guilt about having a second lease on his sex life after his first wife's tragic death. On the other hand, the very newness of his relationship with Dee probably inspired a level of sexual performance he wasn't able to sustain. Isn't that true of new lovers at any age? These circumstances, combined with his lack of knowledge about the sexual aging process, set him up for performance problems. That might have led his wife to blame herself for his lack of interest in making love and caused her to withdraw from attempts to initiate sex. If he hadn't received good advice and reassurance from someone he trusted, Alan might have indeed worried himself into erectile dysfunction.

What Erectile Dysfunction Is—And Isn't

Erectile dysfunction is the chronic or ongoing failure to get or sustain an erection. A man at any age can fail to achieve a desired erection or lose an erection during lovemaking. In youth, the situation is embarrassing and sometimes confusing. Most men, however, know that the occasional erectile problem is typically linked to fatigue, overconsumption of food or drink, or a relationship issue. At midlife, a man may read a lot more into a bout of ED. He may see his future in a single failed erection. How he and his partner handle this situation can determine how frequent they will be.

As discussed earlier, men over 50 experience natural and common changes in their sexual response. The following normal situations do not indicate ED:

- You need direct penile stimulation to have an erection, and you no longer get an erection just from thinking about sex or seeing your partner in an alluring pose.

- It takes you longer to achieve erection.

- You require more time to achieve ejaculation, and you do not need to ejaculate every time you have intercourse. After a period of intercourse, your erection subsides, and after ejaculation, your erection subsides more quickly than when you were younger.

- Your erection isn't as hard as it was when you were a teenager.

- You need more time to recover between ejaculations.

Such changes are gradual, and you shouldn't be frightened by them. Changing response patterns enable a man to be a better lover than he was because he is now responding at a pace more similar to his partner's. Lack of knowledge and refusal to accept the aging process as an erotic opportunity can prevent men from seizing the sexual moment. Anxiety also plays a major role in creating an ED dynamic. If a man misinterprets his responses and becomes anxious about his potency, he will be tense and fearful about lovemaking and convey those negative attitudes to his partner.

Some men do experience erection difficulties that are more serious than the normal changes associated with aging. Psychological factors, ranging from performance and stress issues to intimacy conflicts, can contribute to erection disorders. Physical problems, such as diabetes, vascular disease, and urological and neurological conditions, can also cause ED. Heavy smokers and drinkers may suffer extensive damage to the small blood vessels—including those in the penis—which leads to ED.

For some men, ED stems from a combination of physical and psychological factors. They need to address the issue on several fronts with the help of a therapist and physician. A simple prescription drug isn't likely to solve their problem.

The Sexual-Response Assessment

If you have concerns about your erections, ask yourself the following questions. Before you begin treatment it is important to determine the origin of your condition: Is it physical, psychological, or a combination of the two?

Do you have an erection at least once a week when you wake up in the morning?

The answer to this question is important because it indicates whether your problem is psychological or physical. In an investigation conducted at the University of Chicago's Sexual Dysfunction Clinic, 32 men who said they were suffering with ED were asked about morning erections. They were also given a thorough urologic examination, including specialized tests designed to evaluate erection disorders. Of the men whose exams indicated psychogenic (psychologically based) ED, 86 percent reported having morning erections. In contrast, 100 percent of men who were found to have an organic (physical) basis for ED did not have morning erections.

If you frequently have morning erections, be sure to tell your doctor; your problem is most likely psychogenic in nature and may respond to counseling or psychotherapy. Men who don't have morning (or nocturnal) erections very often or at all and those whose erections are very soft—more like a swelling than an erection—may have a physical impairment to erection. These men may respond to any of a variety of medical therapies.

Are you able to get an erection firm enough for intercourse under some circumstances—for example, during masturbation or with a different partner?

Your answer to this question distinguishes between situational and global erection disorders. A man with a *situational disorder* can get an erection in some circumstances but not in others—for example with one partner but not another, or during masturbation but not with their spouse. If you are able to stimulate yourself to erection, you are capable of having an erection with your partner. Erection difficulties in these cases are likely to be psychogenic in origin. Physical conditions generally do not discriminate, leading to a *global disorder*: you are likely unable to get an erection in any situation.

Did something in particular happen in your life that seems to have triggered your erection difficulties?

If your erection difficulties started at the same time you began a new job, moved, retired, or lost a loved one, your problem is likely to be caused by stress. Sometimes when ED persists for several months after the triggering event, you can be caught in a self-perpetuating cycle of erectile failure: Stress leads to erection failure, the episode of ED creates anxiety, and this leads to another failure. Anxiety and the anticipation of failure interfere with sexual responsiveness.

Do you get a firm erection but usually lose it when you attempt to penetrate for intercourse?

If you are getting sufficient stimulation, that loss of firmness may signal a slowly developing physical problem. Poor diet, sedentary lifestyle, heavy smoking or drinking, and other behaviors may be catching up with you. But the abrupt loss of a firm erection on penetration may also indicate a psychological conflict. If this happens frequently, have a urological examination to eliminate any physical cause before you begin looking at personal and relationship issues. Gradually losing your erection after several minutes of intercourse is not a cause for concern. You may be tired, or you may need to vary your sexual routine.

Can you feel mentally aroused even if you have trouble with erections?

Almost every man has had some period in his life when he didn't feel his normal desire for sex. In most cases, this is temporary, and desire soon returns. When loss of desire persists, look for an underlying physical or psychological cause. If you suddenly realize that you have lost all interest in sex or that your frequency has dropped dramatically, there may well be something wrong.

These questions can help you evaluate your situation and determine if the problem is more physical or psychological. They can also be used as talking points to open a discussion with your partner. Your erection problems affect her, too. If you are experiencing minor, typical age-related difficulties, you can make some lifestyle and other changes that may lead to stronger erections and fewer episodes of erectile failure.

Seven Ways of Preventing Erectile Dysfunction

You can probably improve the quality of your erections, extend their longevity, and minimize the possibilities of losing an erection during lovemaking by adopting the following suggestions:

- *Eat a low-fat diet and exercise regularly.* Diet and exercise have an effect on your libido and your ability to have an erection. See Chapter 13, for details.

- *If you smoke, stop.* Smoking causes much of the vascular damage in the penis that results in ED. Long-term heavy smokers have a far greater probability of becoming impotent than do nonsmokers. One recent study found that men who smoked a pack a day for 20 years had a 60 percent greater chance of having a diminished erection capacity than did nonsmokers.

- *Expand your definition of sex.* As mentioned frequently in this book, there is more to making love than having intercourse—especially at midlife. Lovers over 50 won't move onto a higher sexual plane if they don't grasp this message. A man is also more likely to have erection difficulties if his lovemaking style is intercourse driven. The pressure to perform will be greater for him than for a man who enjoys satisfying his partner in a variety of ways.

- *Have frequent sexual contact.* The more you make love, the more you will be able to make love. Erectile tissue becomes less supple with age. Without frequent erections, there is no regular flow of blood into the penis. After several months or a year of not having an erection, a man may have difficulty in achieving one.

- *Don't make ejaculation the goal of lovemaking.* Once you take the pressure to ejaculate out of lovemaking, you will probably have more frequent erections, sustain them longer, and enjoy the experience much more.

- *Share information with your partner.* Explain your changing sexual-response pattern to your partner. If intercourse has always ended in ejaculation until recently, she may think she has failed to excite you sufficiently. Let her know that your sexual patterns now more closely resemble hers. She has been able to enjoy intercourse without needing to reach an orgasm every time.

- *Don't take medications you don't need.* Some prescription drugs have a negative effect on a man's ability to have an erection. When your doctor prescribes a drug, ask about its sexual side effects; sometimes there is an alternative drug that won't affect your sex life. Another way to avoid medications is to make lifestyle changes (usually pertaining to diet and exercise) that render medications unnecessary or that will lower your dosage. Be sure to ask your doctor about alternatives to any prescription.

"Don't take your erections or your potency for granted is the message men need to hear around their fortieth birthday," says Gene who recently turned 50. He began to have some erectile difficulties about a decade ago. "I wasn't getting hard enough often enough and I wasn't staying hard enough," he says succinctly. "I knew that some change was inevitable, but I was experiencing too much change. I had the sexual responses of a man twenty years my senior.

"At about the same time I developed erection problems, my doctor told me I had mild hypertension. He said I had two choices: Go on medication or lose twenty pounds, start exercising regularly, make some dietary changes, and stop smoking. Initially I took the easy way out. I went for the pills. The erection situation got a little worse. My wife was unhappy, and so was I.

"One night we had a big argument that ended with her crying and accusing me of cheating her out of a sex life. She said my potbelly wasn't attractive. That hurt. She also said she was worried about me. Would I cut my life short the same way I'd cut our sex life short? The next day I ordered a treadmill. It wasn't easy to make all the changes I had to make, and I backpedaled a few times in the early months. But I lost the weight, quit smoking, and generally cleaned up my act.

"The erection situation improved a great deal. I'll never get as rock hard as I did when I was twenty, but, on the other hand, I have better erections at fifty than I was getting at forty. I've also learned how to be a better lover. When I look at some of my friends who are overweight, smoking, and popping pills for hypertension, I know they aren't getting erections. I'd like to talk to them about it, but that's not the kind of thing men do."

A healthier lifestyle will most likely lead to healthier erections, but any man can expect to lose an erection during lovemaking on occasion. If he doesn't let that bother him, he'll likely get it back. The worst thing you can do about a subsiding erection is to focus on it.

Four Steps to Restoring Sexual Function

- *If you lose your erection, let it go.* "The first few times I lost an erection during intercourse, I grabbed my penis and started working it, desperately trying to get hard again," says James, 51. "It didn't happen. My wife commiserated with me. Sex was over. Then I tried something different. When I felt my erection going, I pulled out before she could notice or respond, and began performing cunnilingus on her. That has become my pattern now for handling the unexpected soft spots. Usually I get hard again. Even if I don't, I have satisfied her, which makes me feel good."

- *Concentrate on pleasing your partner.* James's approach, performing cunnilingus when his erection falters, is a good one. When a man forgets his own perceived "problem" and concentrates on giving his partner pleasure, he relieves his performance anxiety. And he creates a win-win situation. Maybe he will get his erection back, but even if he doesn't, he will feel good about himself as a lover.

- *Use a partial erection to good advantage.* Paul, 56, says: "When I feel my erection subsiding during intercourse, I pull out, take my penis in hand and get creative. Grasping my member firmly, I stimulate my wife's clitoris with the head, brushing it back and forth, often bringing her to orgasm this way. Sometimes I use the head of my penis to stroke her inner thighs or her nipples. Often I get really hard this way. We both enjoy penis play." Some men can also have intercourse with a partial erection by holding the base of the penis firmly as they thrust. You don't need a full erection to make love with your penis. Experiment with ways of stimulating your partner with the erection you have.

• *Don't blame your partner.* When experiencing hurt pride after an erectile failure, a man might lash out at his partner, accusing her of failing to arouse him sufficiently. Don't do that. Not only will you hurt her and invite a defensive assault but you'll only feel worse about yourself later. Once a couple has started a cycle of blaming, it's hard to break free and move to a place of acceptance and understanding. Let down the barriers and share your fears and concerns with her, without blaming her or yourself. Some men find it more difficult to talk about their erection problems than about their emotions. For them, a savvy and understanding woman can make the difference between a frustrating sexual future and a transition into another, less erection-based kind of lovemaking.

How a Woman Can Help

If your partner is experiencing ED, whether physical or emotional in origin, you can respond in a way that will increase his chances of regaining or obtaining an erection. Here are some tips:

• *If he loses an erection during lovemaking, let it go.* Unless he requests or indicates by his behavior that he wants you to perform fellatio or manually stimulate his penis to try to bring the erection back—don't. Focusing on his limp penis probably won't help and may hurt by intensifying his performance anxiety. Hold him. Kiss and stroke him, but ignore his penis. You don't have to prove your desirability by bringing his penis back to erotic life.

- *Ask for oral sex or manual stimulation.* Such a request will take the focus off his penis and give him the opportunity to feel like a good lover. Be responsive to his ministrations. A woman's arousal is very arousing to a man. It's possible that he'll regain his erection by losing himself in your excitement.

- *Don't be solicitous.* Show your understanding by not fussing over him. If he's feeling inadequate, don't tell him his lack of erection isn't important. A man who has been sexually humiliated doesn't want his wife saying, "Don't worry, darling, it doesn't matter."

- *Don't blame yourself.* And don't let him blame you. Even if his ED is rooted in relationship conflict, you are not the cause of the problem. Sex is a cooperative effort. So is relating. After an erectile failure, however, is not the right time to analyze your relationship.

A man and his partner can probably alleviate or prevent many garden-variety erection problems by following the advice given here. What if the problems are caused by deeper or physiological issues?

The Causes of Erectile Dysfunction

"I was terrified at the thought of having a penile implant," says Brian, 52, "but I'd been suffering bouts of ED for almost a year. I thought it was probably time to do something about it, even if that turned out to be surgery."

Brian and his longtime partner, Maggie, 50, were very discouraged about his erection problems by the time he sought help from his doctor. Though he sometimes had morning erections and sometimes was able to get an erection for masturbation, he was increasingly unable to become erect during lovemaking. When he did get an erection, he would quickly lose it. Both Brian and Maggie became, in her words, "obsessed with the state of his penis." They spent so much time watching his penis when they attempted to make love that they'd turned sex into a spectator sport.

"We were both suffering from performance anxiety," Maggie says. "I was convinced I could make him get and keep a good erection if only

I could get it right when we made love. We both felt like we'd been tested and found wanting every time we tried to have sex."

"I felt doubly bad because I left her hanging so much of the time," Brian says. "I would offer to bring her to orgasm but she would often be too upset for that."

His doctor told him that the morning erections he sometimes experienced and his ability to get an erection sometimes during masturbation indicated that his problem might not be entirely physical or, if it was largely physical, his condition probably wasn't as far advanced as he feared. Routine medical tests showed that Brian had very high cholesterol levels, no surprise given his diet rich in saturated fats and dairy cholesterol. The same substances that clog the arteries of a man's heart, his doctor explained, also clog the arteries of his penis.

The damage done by a poor diet and high cholesterol levels had caused some problems with ED for Brian. His response, and Maggie's, had exacerbated the condition. His doctor prescribed a low-fat diet and medication to bring down the cholesterol; he also recommended several sex-therapy sessions both alone and with Maggie.

Brian says, "We've learned how to make love without so much emphasis on an erection and intercourse. It's really a better, more sophisticated way of making love. We both feel closer to each other now than we did."

Maggie adds, "We shouldn't have waited so long to get help. We were both positive he would need a surgical implant or some dramatic cure. He could have been on medication a year ago, and we could have saved ourselves that ride on an emotional roller coaster."

As Brian's case illustrates, ED has a psychological component even when the root cause is physical. Repeated erectile failures put stress on a man and his partner. The cycle of failure, performance anxiety, guilt, and blame is hard on any relationship. Some common physical causes of ED are the following:

- *Diabetes.* A major physical cause of ED, diabetes can also accelerate other causes. For example, penile artery damage from cholesterol may become significant in a shorter period of time than it would if not complicated by diabetes.

- *High cholesterol.* Recent erectile dysfunction research has led authorities, such as Irwin Goldstein, co-director of the New England Male Reproductive Center at Boston University Medical Center, to conclude that high cholesterol is "probably one of the leading causes of impotence in this country." The penis is a vascular organ, made up of layers of venous tissue and blood vessels. High cholesterol adversely affects erectile tissues.

- *Medications.* This is another major cause of ED. A study reported in the *Journal of the American Medical Association* showed that 25 percent of all sex problems in men were caused or complicated by medications and other drugs. Tranquilizers, antidepressants, some high blood pressure drugs, corticosteroids (taken for arthritis), analgesics (for pain), alcohol, tobacco, and recreational drugs (cocaine and marijuana) affect libido and performance in men.

- *Prostate problems.* Chronic pain and swelling in the prostate area can affect sexual functioning in an indirect manner if a man finds erection or ejaculation painful or uncomfortable. Though studies show 80 percent of men can return to sexual functioning after prostate surgery, many don't, indicating a possible psychological barrier.

- *Major illnesses.* Heart disease, cancer, neurological and other diseases that don't directly affect the genitals can still cause temporary ED as a result of medication side effects or depression. And heart disease generally indicates damaged blood vessels, which affects the blood flow to the penis.

- *Chronic alcoholism.* Shakespeare noted in *Macbeth* that alcohol provokes desire but takes away performance. In the later stages of alcoholism, desire ebbs, too. Testosterone production is impaired and penile blood vessels show considerable damage. Liver damage may lead to an increase of estrogen in a man's body. ED is almost inevitably a consequence of long-term alcoholism.

Some common psychological causes of ED are the following:

- *Anger.* Unacknowledged and unexpressed anger can sit on the end of a penis and hold it down. As noted in previous chapters, repressed anger, whether at the partner or not, has a devastating effect on sexuality.

- *Intimacy conflicts.* Maybe your penis is trying to tell you something about your relationship. Conflicts that have been ignored or papered over for years can eventually cause sexual functioning problems.

- *Depression.* Libido is often a casualty of depression, even low-level depression, especially if prolonged. A bout of ED can increase a man's feelings of discouragement. Although antidepressants such as Prozac may lift the depression, the drugs may fail to lift the penis.

- *Stress.* At midlife, a man has to learn stress management or face increasing bouts of ED. When he was young, he could get and maintain an erection in spite of stress. That's less likely now.

- *Worry.* Concerns about job security, personal finances, and family issues such as problems with teenage children and aging parents can also create a psychological climate for ED. If a man is feeling powerless in the world, he may convey that message to his penis. Generally, worry and stress are short-term situations. They may result in brief periods of ED that can be overcome in a good relationship.

- *Performance anxiety.* As mentioned earlier, one occurrence of ED can set up a cycle of failure, anxiety, and more failure. In fact, performance anxiety is probably the most common contributing or secondary psychological cause of ED.

In addition, negative attitudes about aging—both the man's and his partner's—can lead to ED. If a couple has surrendered to the belief that they are old and no longer sexually attractive and desirable, they aren't likely to have good sex. Desire begins in the brain, and so does performance. Especially in the middle and later years, the ability to function sexually depends on the belief that one can and will.

Erectile Dysfunction Remedies

"Alice and I stopped having sex five years ago," says Jeff, 52. "I had a few episodes of ED, once unable to get an erection, once losing it as soon as I got it. She assured me it didn't matter, and, since our sex life had been going downhill for years, I believed her. I thought it didn't matter that much to me either. We kept to our separate sides of the bed. Without telling her, I masturbated once or twice a week.

"Then I had a little fling with a woman I met on a business trip. Nothing emotional, it was just a purely sexual affair. No problems with erections. I went home to Alice in an erotic frame of mind. We made love for the first time in six months. It wasn't great, but it was better than it had been in a while. I was pretty sure she had an orgasm, not faked one, but I had never been completely sure about Alice's orgasms.

"To my surprise, she cried afterward. She told me she'd missed making love to me. I was shocked. We began treating each other with a little more tenderness after that night. I had another erection problem, and we decided to see a therapist together. Therapy was good for us. We forged a closer, more intimate connection to each other than we'd had since the early days when we were struggling and the kids were babies. Once we got closer, the ED thing didn't happen again.

"My erections are pretty good, partly because we've opened up our lovemaking style. I've never told her about the fling; I don't think it would serve any purpose to tell her. But other than that, I'm not keeping secrets from her."

For Jeff, therapy was the ED remedy. Depending on the cause of ED, there are several ways of treating it. The most popular are the erection enhancement drugs (Viagra, Levitra, and Cialis), but other remedies are available as well. Before you take any erection enhancement drugs, you should check in with your doctor, especially if you have a cardiac condition that may prohibit you from taking them.

Erection Enhancement Drugs

VIAGRA: Viagra was the first erection enhancement pill. Before Viagra, approximately 0.5 million men a year sought treatment for ED, either from medical doctors or therapists or through treatment that combines the two disciplines. Informed estimates put the number of men suffering from ED at much higher levels, perhaps as high as 30 million. Viagra has lured these guys out of the ED closet. Men who didn't want to talk about the problem with a therapist or submit to implants, injections, or other treatments have been lured by the promise of an instant cure. Open mouth. Insert pill. Wash down with water. Become Man of Steel.

Dubbed by author Erica Jong as "the perfect American medication" because "it raises the Dow Jones and the penis, too," the ED pill of the 1990s has supplanted the birth control pill of the 1960s in the breadth and depth of media coverage generated. When Viagra was first launched, pharmacies were actually broken into by overeager men, and the media had a field day. Questions never raised in public before became the talk of the town. Would aging men leave their wives for younger women now that they had newfound potency? Would women who were secretly pleased that their husbands were no longer sexual revolt? And would this little blue pill begin a new sexual revolution? Well, the revolution didn't occur, and relationships didn't tumble any more than they had in the past. What did occur is that the success of Viagra created competition among pharmaceutical companies and now men have a choice of drugs.

Viagra, like the other vasodilator drugs discussed below, does not work instantly. Combined with arousal (a desire to be sexual) and physical stimulation, Viagra works in about 30 to 60 minutes and is active for about 4 hours. Viagra works faster when taken on an empty stomach or after a light, low-fat meal. After sex, a man's erection will typically dissipate.

Viagra comes in three doses, 25 mg, 50 mg, and 100 mg. Men are usually started on 50 mg, but many men move up to the 100 mg dose. The medication is considered safe for men with a host of health problems, like diabetes and high blood pressure, for example. However, men who are taking medications that have nitrates in them should not take Viagra.

LEVITRA: Chemically similar to Viagra, Levitra is marketed as more powerful, and research supports that its effect is felt within 15 to 45 minutes and lasts 24 hours. That doesn't mean that a man can perform for 24 hours, but that the drug will support an enhanced ability to get erections for 24 hours after having taken the pill. Levitra can be taken with or without food, so it can be taken during a romantic dinner or whenever the man senses the time is right. More than three-quarters of men (and their partners) find Levitra to be effective in treating ED.

The side effects are headache, flushing, upset stomach, and nasal congestion. An advantage of Levitra is that it does not seem to be associated with blurry vision and the other sight issues that have occurred in a small number of Viagra users.

CIALIS: According to a recent report, more than half of men who took Cialis were able to have an erection as much as 36 hours later. Because of this, Cialis advertisements stress sexual spontaneity. Like Levitra, it can be taken with or without food, which adds to its convenience. The drug takes effect in 15 to 45 minutes, like the other ED pills. The success rate of Cialis is similar to the other ED drugs; more than three-quarters of men who take it are able to maintain an erection.

As with the other ED pills, some men who take Cialis have reported side effects. Known negative effects are flushing, headache, stomachache muscle pain, and nasal congestion, which are common to all these drugs, plus limb pain and back pain.

Approximately 20 percent of men do not respond well to any of the ED drugs. Typically, these are men who have or have had one or more of the following: poorly controlled diabetes, non-nerve-sparing prostate surgery, severe psychological issues, and/or other serious illnesses or impairments. If you do not have a cardiac condition that prohibits the use of an ED pill, there's no harm in trying one of the drugs just to see if it might work. If your ED is physically based, and the ED drugs are not appropriate because of a heart condition requiring nitrates, it makes sense to attempt the low-risk alternative interventions mentioned later in this chapter.

If one of the ED pills is being considered, it is important to discuss the risks, benefits, and likely success of this intervention with your doctor and pharmacist. The popular media have both praised these drugs and warned consumers away from them, making it difficult to accurately assess what you read in the popular press.

ED PILLS—QUESTIONS AND ANSWERS: The following are the most often asked questions about erection enhancement pills:

- *How do the erection enhancement pills work?* Here's a simplified physiological explanation of erection: When a man becomes sexually aroused, his brain signals the nerve cells surrounding his penis. These cells release nitric oxide, which causes the penis to make a chemical called cyclic guanosine monophosphate (cGMP). cGMP increases the size of the blood vessels in the penis; these vessels fill with blood, causing an erection. The body also produces phosphodiesterase 5 (PDE5), which is an enzyme that breaks down cGMP and thus prevents the penis from filling with blood. Impotent men often have increased levels of PDE5. The primary ingredient of ED pills enhances the action of cGMP and simultaneously inhibits the effect of PDE5. Thus the ultimate effect of the ED drugs is to significantly increase blood flow to the penis, which leads to an erection. The drugs boost the natural process through which the arteries of the penis dilate and block the body's chemical (PDE5) that prevents this from happening.

- *Should I buy ED pills over the Internet?* No. Make it personal and discuss your situation with your physician. Everyone has a unique medical history, and the specific drug and dosage that are right for you can be determined only after your doctor has conducted a comprehensive physical examination, taken blood tests, and delved into any relationship issues. Never take medication prescribed for someone else, and be aware that taking more than the recommended dosage may be harmful.

- *Can these pills alone produce an erection?* No. The pills can restore erection capacity but have no effect on libido. A man who can get aroused but who cannot get or sustain an erection may be helped by an ED pill, but a man who has lost his desire for sex will not be affected. You can't take a pill, sit back and watch television, and wait for the magic to happen.

• *Will ED pills give a man who does not have an erection problem a better erection?* No. Many older men lament the quality of their erections. They complain about not being as hard as they were in their youth. True, most men have more rigid erections at 19 than they will have at 59. These pills can't change that. The erectile tissue in the penis has a finite number of receptors for cGMP. If you have normal erections, a pill won't make them extra-normal by creating more or bigger receptors.

• *Will these pills help a man last longer before ejaculation?* No. None of these pills is supposed to create a prolonged erection. These pills, like most medications, have a very specific purpose: They increase blood flow to the penis in men whose bodies no longer do this on their own. In fact, if you experience a prolonged erection, you should seek immediate medical attention because this indicates an adverse reaction to the drug.

• *Can these pills help a man become erect again after orgasm?* With or without a pill, men need a refractory (recovery) period between erections. Levitra and Cialis have relatively longer effective times than does Viagra, and so there is at least the possibility of a second erection. On the other hand, orgasm signals the body to stop producing cGMP, which allows PDE5 to gain control and shut the erotic system down. In young men, the refractory period can be brief, but in older men it can last hours or even days. With the aid of an ED pill, some men may be able to have a second erection with a second orgasm, but none of these pills makes a man a sex machine.

• *Are some men immune to the effects of these pills?* As noted earlier in this chapter, men who have poorly managed diabetes, severely blocked arteries, longstanding high blood pressure, and nerve damage from injury or surgery may not respond to an ED pill. Also men whose erectile problems are caused by severe and chronic psychological issues may be unaffected by the pills. The good news is that other treatments are available (discussed later in this chapter).

- *Can women take ED pills?* When women are aroused, they also have blood flow to the genitals, a condition called *vasocongestion.* Because blood flow is a factor in female sexuality, it is no surprise that the oral ED medications have been considered for women. In fact, studies show that some women report a greater feeling of satisfaction after taking an ED pill. So, why aren't these drugs big sellers for women? The answer is that women's sexuality is not as simple as that of men, and blood flow is not the main problem for women. The biggest issue women struggle with is libido (the desire to have sex), and the ED pills do not directly target that issue. For women, libido has many emotional and relationship factors and is also controlled by a number of hormone factors that are not yet fully understood.

ED PILLS AND YOUR PARTNER: You might think that ED medications have been universally considered a godsend for all couples who use them. Although the drugs may solve erectile problems for men, they do not offer a solution for deeper relationship issues.

For couples whose main problem has been unsatisfactory sex owing to the man's diminished erection capacity, ED drugs can be a blessing. John and Delores, married for more than 20 years, were struggling with his ED for several years. His physical problem had devastating psychological consequences for both of them. "I blamed myself for not being able to excite him anymore," Delores says. "I thought I was doing something wrong in bed. And I tried everything, from new sex techniques to sexy lingerie, candles, and flower petals on the bed. I tormented myself about my shortcomings. Deep down I suspected he was having an affair."

John adds: "I tried to reassure Dolores, but I wasn't very good at it. How can you convince a woman of her desirability when you don't seem to desire her? I knew it was my problem, but I wasn't able to talk to her about it. I thought if I laid it on the line to her, she might want to leave me or at least have an affair."

Finally, John's urologist insisted he get some help in talking to Dolores. John had been diagnosed with vascular blockage in the blood vessels supplying the penis when they came to see me. Shortly after that, they tried penile injection therapy. "I couldn't get used to sticking a needle in my penis," John says. "Dolores found it hard to handle, too."

When Viagra pills became available through prescription, John practically stood on line to be one of the first to try it. The drug worked well for him and Dolores says they have been enjoying a second honeymoon. John notes, "Viagra gave me back my potency, something I thought I'd lost."

For some couples, the erection enhancement drugs have proved to be a mixed blessing. Some couples in long-term relationships have accommodated to being nonsexual. The woman may be secretly relieved that her husband is impotent because she lost interest in sex years ago. Avoiding sex may help both of them avoid intimacy. They may have serious relationship issues that they've chosen to sweep under the rug. Then, along comes a small pill. "The possibility of having sex again is unsettling," a female patient admitted, after her husband, who had been diagnosed with blocked arteries, decided to try an ED drug. She had handled his ED with grace but was not sure how was she going to handle his renewed potency. They were an affectionate couple, even without the sex, and she was happy with the status quo. For men whose partners are like this woman, be patient. If you spend some time courting her and seducing her, she's bound to happily come around.

For other women, resuming sex with their partner is eagerly anticipated, but some may find their bodies less accommodating. Depending on a woman's age and physical condition, it might not be that easy to jump back into bed. Postmenopausal women who have been sexually inactive may be surprised to find thinning vaginal walls and lack of lubrication make intercourse painful. For these couples, it is important to ease back into a sex life at a slow pace. Just because the man takes a pill and gets an erection doesn't mean the woman is automatically able to enjoy sex. These men need to be patient and work with their partners as they both return to their sexual selves.

A man's sudden ability to get an erection again can also create a crisis for him. "I don't have an excuse anymore," a male patient told me. "My wife expects me to be able to make love now that I have the pill."

Remember, the ED pills restore erection capacity, not libido. A man who is depressed, stressed, hurt, or angry won't resolve those problems by taking one of these pills. Some men have developed psychological problems as a result of their erection difficulties. They may be too concerned about adequacy, aging, and overall success issues to feel desire. For men in any of these situations, the ED pills may present a new set of problems rather than help solve the existing ones.

For some couples, the ED pills have been dubbed *chemical home wreckers*. Once their erection capacity is restored, some men are tempted to wander. Some men still fear sexual failure and do not want to take the risk with their partners. For a man such as this, another woman is a safe testing ground. If the pill doesn't live up to his expectations, he can tell his extramarital partner that guilt prevented him from acting on his desire as he hurries out of the room. With his wife, however, he would have to acknowledge the failure, and she might expect him to deal with the root causes of his ED.

Other men may realize their marriages were based on accommodation, complacency, or the meshing of neuroses. Such a man may come to the conclusion he'd stayed married only because his ED hadn't left him with many other options. How many unhappy marriages are held together by a woman's loss of interest in sex and a man's lack of ability to perform? With advent of ED pills, these men have, or perceive they have, choices.

Will we see a flurry of divorces that can be blamed on Viagra? There is some basis to this concern, but it is not nearly what was feared when the pill first came on the market. A minority of men who once felt too inadequate to leave may now do what they've long wanted to do. For some couples, the ED pill, although not the cause of their relationship problems, may force them to examine issues they've been ignoring. Inevitably, some couples will decide they don't want to be together anymore, and the ED pills may be a convenient peg on which to hang their divorce.

In other situations, ED drugs may help strengthen a marriage by forcing the spouses to face their relationship issues. "I was disappointed," a male patient confided, "and so was my wife when Cialis didn't change our lives." He and his wife expected a regained erection capacity to solve their emotional problems. Instead, it destabilized their relationship. They were overwhelmed by the possibility of regular erections. This couple, however, stayed together because they took the opportunity to go into therapy and were able to resolve their issues.

For some couples, ED drugs can open the door to the room where they have stored all of their relationship problems. However, it is possible for the partners to work together to clean out that room, making their relationship better and stronger. Jeff and Sally are one of those couples. They were in therapy before he began taking an ED pill. Jeff's restored erection capacity threw the couple off balance. "His expectations are unrealistic," Sally groused. "He thinks we're going to have sex every day or at least five times a week. I don't want to go back to the way it was, him chasing, me giving in and not being satisfied."

In addition to working on issues of buried anger and resentment on both parts, Jeff and Sally had to learn how to become better lovers. Erections don't guarantee sexual satisfaction, particularly for women. "I feel rejected by her," he complained.

Years of ED had left Jeff with a fragile ego. He needed to be wanted and appreciated. When he came to the conclusion that Sally preferred him impotent, he was devastated. Their story has a happy ending because they were able to work through their anger and resolve the differences that kept them on opposite sides of the bed—even after Jeff added the magic pill to the medicine cabinet.

Other Therapies

Men who cannot or do not want to take an ED drug have several options for treating their ED. Testosterone supplementation is one such treatment and is discussed in Chapter 11.

INTRACAVERNOUS INJECTION THERAPY: Before the ED oral medications were developed, well over 1 million men could hear the words *sharp object* and *penis* in the same sentence and not flinch. Well, maybe they flinched, but they gutted it out because of the promise of being able to resume their sexual life. And, in fact, the promise delivered. Intracavernous injection therapy (IIT) involves injecting a mixture of drugs directly into the shaft of the penis. The drugs work to enlarge the blood vessels, increasing blood flow and causing an erection.

A very fine gauge needle is used, and men administer the injection to themselves. Because the medicine goes directly into the penis, rather than being delivered throughout the body, the side effects are minimal. In fact, the biggest concern is scarring due to poor injection technique. Consequently, it is suggested that men limit themselves to a maximum of 12 injections a month. Of course, injection therapy is not spontaneous, nor is it as easily portable as a pill: IIT involves an injection kit and a medicine that is best kept refrigerated.

The upside of injection therapy is that it is very effective. Studies have demonstrated a near 90 percent success rate. Note that, as with the oral medicines, penile stimulation is needed to achieve an erection.

VACUUM PUMPS: When the romance and drama are put aside, an erection is actually a cardiovascular event. Not very sexy, but that's what's involved on the physiological level. It simply involves blood flow into the internal caverns of the penile shaft. Vasodilating medicines are one way to bring blood to the penis. Another way of getting blood into the area is to pump it in through a low-tech gadget called a vacuum pump. Vacuum pumps have been around a long time, predating both IIT and the ED pills.

A vacuum pump is a hollow tube with pump action that is placed over the penis. To use the device, the man slips the tube over the penis until it is flush against the pubic bone, creating an airtight seal. He then uses the pumping action to pull blood into the penis. Once the penis is erect, a thick rubber band is slipped off the tube onto the base of the penis; this keeps the blood in the penis, maintaining the erection. Men are advised to shave their pubic hair so that it is not pulled when the rubber band is removed.

The pump provides an erection strong enough for intercourse in about 75 percent of men. An erection achieved through a vacuum pump is not generally fully hard but is firm enough for penetration. Note that the man should not keep the erection for more than 30 minutes; longer restriction of blood flow could result in nerve damage.

SURGICAL IMPLANTS: A last resort for many men is an irreversible surgical procedure. Some men opt for a penile implant, which cannot be removed without significant damage to the penile tissue. The surgery involves implanting two silicon chambers into the penis, a saline reservoir into the abdomen, and two small bulbs into the scrotum. One bulb is pressed and saline solution is released into the chambers to create an erection, the other bulb opens the chambers so that the saline solution can flow back into the reservoir.

The procedure is expensive but may be covered by insurance when it is used to correct an organic condition, which is really the only justifiable basis for its use. This is clearly one of the most invasive forms of treatment and recovery requires a few days of hospitalization. Implant surgery is used as a last resort treatment for a motivated man who has not succeeded with other available solutions to ED. On the other hand, most men who have undergone the surgery report satisfaction.

Counseling

Whatever the cause of ED, therapy is a wise consideration because the issue is typically emotionally loaded. Successful therapy might involve focusing on the following goals: improving or resolving personal conflicts and issues, improving or resolving relationship issues, and strengthening the relationship by building and deepening intimacy.

Because ED has such confusing and painful psychological implications for a man and his partner, each partner can almost always benefit from talking about his or her feelings and fears with a counselor. A satisfying sexual relationship isn't likely to thrive when a couple is acting out significant conflicts in the bedroom.

The best results are likely to be had with a counselor who specializes in sexuality and relationship issues, and whose experience and credentials are consistent with that specialization. In other words, a counselor who has had advanced training and has specialized in those areas for a number of years is preferable. Therapy duration is likely to last several months on a weekly basis when there are both sexual and relationship issues, but may last only a few weeks when the sexual issues are not complicated by significant intrapersonal or interpersonal issues. In all cases, complying with the counselor's suggestions and the "homework assignments" will likely lead to a resolution more quickly.

SOME GUIDELINES FOR A RETURN TO INTIMACY

- *Express a desire for intimacy, the kind of intimacy that is fully clothed.* Some couples who have experienced a long nonsexual interlude have also lost touch emotionally. An awkward distance exists between them, but they can diminish that space by beginning to tell each other how they feel. A man who has experienced erection problems for a long time may have stopped being affectionate. Touching, kissing, holding, and stroking reminded him of his erection issues, and he might have also feared arousing his wife or giving her false hope. He needs to tell his partner why he withdrew affection. She has probably been hurt more by his lack of affection than by his inability to achieve an erection. Feeling hurt, angry, confused, and rejected, she has withdrawn, too. She needs to tell him how she feels and listen to him talk about his feelings. A sensitive talk will help span the distance between them.

- *Men (and women) should get a medical evaluation after a long period of not having sexual relations.* A man should never start taking an erection enhancement drug, or any prescription drug, without a medical evaluation. An erection problem can signal an underlying medical condition, such as diabetes, high blood pressure, or cardiovascular problems. Even if he knows he has medical problems and is being treated for them, a man should still see a doctor if he hasn't had a physical examination in the last 6 to 12 months. A woman may suffer from vaginal thinning, lack of lubrication, or other problems she hasn't recognized because she hasn't been having sex. She should let her doctor know that her husband is planning to take an ED drug and ask if there are any steps she should take to make sex more comfortable for her.

- *Take it slowly.* Men should not be too anxious to use their new erection. It will still be there in a few minutes, and you can get another one tomorrow. Be loving with your partner. Do a lot of touching, caressing, and cuddling. Don't forget that she's had a long period of absence and cannot turn on instantly. Women need to take responsibility for their own arousal. If your partner hasn't made love to you in a while, he'll need your help in guiding his hands and mouth where you want them to be. Don't be embarrassed to touch yourself.

- *Pay attention to the problems underlying erection disorders.* Younger men often get into trouble by listening to their penis when they should be listening to their brain. The young penis is eager and headstrong. It can lead a man into trouble. Mature men don't listen to their penis as often as they should. In older men, an erection problem can signal an underlying intimacy or emotional issue. Many men have erectile problems because they are under stress, are depressed, or harbor feelings of anger or hurt in their relationships. Taking a pill may or may not produce an erection. If it works, the man may be able to take a pill and bypass the real problem. But that will often prove to be a costly relationship mistake.

What does the tremendous interest in erection enhancement drugs tell us about ourselves? A lot of men, and perhaps their partners, too, are really unhappy with their sexual performance and perhaps with the state of their relationships. Perhaps the advent of ED pills is a call to action on many sexual and relationship fronts—for women as well as for men.

SIZZLER #12

Beyond Intercourse

Robert was fired for the first time in his life at the age of 52. He hadn't seen it coming. Though his wife, Donna, was working, early retirement for either of them wasn't in their financial plan. For several weeks, he was in denial. Telling everyone that "this is the best thing that ever happened to me," he threw himself into job searching with gusto, and he made love in the same way. Donna, who had been prepared for a job loss—ED link, was pleasantly surprised. Then about 2 months into involuntary unemployment, Robert failed to get a job he'd thought he'd clinched in the interview; the predictable finally happened. No matter how hard he tried, he couldn't get an erection.

Donna was reassuring, supportive, and sanguine. She could live without sex until Robert found a job, she reasoned. Eventually, he did find another job, but it was a lower position than he'd once held. Unfortunately, his potency did not return. After a few failures, he avoided all sexual activity.

"I want you to satisfy me," she finally told him in exasperation. "I don't care if you don't have an erection. I still want sex."

"I can't satisfy you if I can't get an erection," he countered, his face red, expressing both his shame and his anger.

"Oh, yes, you can. You have no idea how many times I've faked an intercourse orgasm. Ninety percent of my orgasms have occurred during oral sex or when you were masturbating me before or after intercourse. I usually fake another one to make you feel good."

He felt, he said, like a character in an episode of Seinfeld. She'd taken something away from him, and he had to be alone for a while. He picked up the car keys and headed for the door.

"I'm going to masturbate while you're gone!" she shouted after him, overcome with embarrassment as soon as she'd said it.

She poured herself a large glass of wine. Sipping it, she tried to conjure erotic images but succeeded only in remembering the look on Robert's face when she told him the truth about her sexual responses. She paced the floor. Feeling alternately guilty and sad, then angry and resentful, Donna finally acknowledged that she was too wound up to do anything but seek release in a purely physical sensation, such as an orgasm.

Shedding her clothes, she stepped into the big marble shower for two, which had been a realization of their erotic desire when they remodeled the house. Sighing, she remembered the wonderful lovemaking they'd shared under the twin sprays of water. She closed her eyes and willed herself to imagine his mouth in place of her hand on her vulva.

"Pretend you're standing under a waterfall in Bali with Robert on his knees in front of you," she whispered to herself.

Slowly the fantasy began to take on life. She could almost smell the fragrance of exotic flowers in the steamy air. Her fingers raced in circles around her clitoris, the water cascading between them, increasing her arousal.

"Donna," Robert said. But of course, she was imagining his voice, wasn't she? "Donna," he repeated.

She opened her eyes and saw Robert standing in the bathroom, watching her, his eyes glazed over with longing. Reluctantly, she pulled her hand from her body and beckoned to him with it.

"Satisfy me," she begged in a husky voice.

He kicked off his shoes and came into the shower, fully dressed, moving like a man in a hurry to rescue a woman from drowning. His fingers caressed her vulva as his mouth hungrily sought hers. Her mouth sobbed into his. He stroked her to orgasm, then pulled her body tight against his. Through his wet clothing, she felt his erection.

She helped him shed his pants, sodden with water, and she sank down to her knees. Eagerly she took his stiff penis into her mouth as he raised his arms to grasp the showerhead. She stroked herself while she fellated him and had another orgasm in time to his own.

CHAPTER THIRTEEN

Sex and Health

"What has grilled trout and steamed broccoli got to do with sex?" James asked his wife when she told them they were going on a diet and beginning an exercise program to improve their sex life.

Grilled trout, steamed broccoli, and other healthful foods don't have an aphrodisiac effect. They don't influence potency or strengthen and don't provide multiple orgasms. Yet the older you are, the more your sex life depends on maintaining good overall health habits, including diet and exercise. Studies of middle-aged and older adults repeatedly show that those in good health have more active sex lives than those who aren't. And many of the health problems suffered by people as they age are brought on by or made worse by bad health habits. Earlier in the book I pointed out the connection between smoking, heavy drinking, and the consumption of a fatty diet and the loss of desire and sexual performance problems. If you can stay healthy, you greatly improve your odds of staying sexy.

There are several components of a healthful lifestyle. Each has an effect on sexual desire and performance.

The Sex Diet

"The wrong foods can put a crimp in your sex life," says David, 49. "I would not have believed this was true until my doctor put me on a diet to lose fifteen pounds and cut back my cholesterol levels. I eliminated a lot of fat from my diet, cut my consumption of red meat and dairy products, added more fruits, vegetables, grains, and fish. That's it. I made no other life changes. I already had a reasonable exercise routine. With the dietary changes, I lost the weight and—here was the surprise—my sex life improved a great deal.

"I lost that sluggish feeling that had been dragging me down for several years. My erections were firmer and more frequent. I had more interest in sex. My wife was so delighted with the change in me, she went on the diet, too."

At midlife, what you eat does have an effect on how often and how well you make love. Dietary changes can raise libido in both men and women, improve male erections, and possibly influence the quality of orgasms. (If you have greater desire for sex and a stronger erection, you'll likely experience the orgasm more intensely.) No one food or group of foods has special erotic powers. But one food group can have a detrimental effect on sex: fats. A diet high in saturated fats has both short-term and long-term sexual consequences.

In the short term, both men and women who consume too many fats suffer from feelings of sluggishness and low energy that may decrease their libidos. They are probably overweight, another factor that can pull down the libido. Because they don't look and feel their best, they may not think of themselves as sexy and desirable to their partners. The couple on the couch passing the potato chip bowl back and forth as they watch television are probably not thinking about sex.

In the long term, a diet rich in fats raises cholesterol levels, which can lead to erectile dysfunction (ED) in men. It can have a similar, though less obvious, effect in women. When the arteries in the pelvic area narrow from the accumulated plaque of cholesterol deposits, blood doesn't flow into the area the way it once did. Arousal feels more diffuse, less intense. Finally, high cholesterol levels lead to heart problems in both men and women.

Here are some important diet tips for a great sex life:

- *Cut saturated fats.* Start basing some meals around grains, legumes, vegetables, and fruits. But don't cut out all fats, some are essential and are healthful additions to the diet. Foods such as salmon and sardines contain omega-three fatty acids, a good dietary fat.

- *Get advice from a nutritionist or an internist.* Ask a health-care provider how many calories you should consume daily. Take into consideration your activity level and any medical issues.

- *Do some background reading on vitamin supplements.* Scientific opinion is divided on the value of specific supplements and on the amount of each that should be consumed. A multivitamin containing antioxidants and minerals is probably a good addition to the average person's health program.

- *Drink alcohol in moderation.* A glass of wine with dinner may have health benefits, but an excessive amount of alcohol inhibits desire and limits performance.

How Exercise Influences Sexuality

"Regular exercise can improve your love life, especially if you work out together," says Terry. "My husband and I joined a gym together last year. We decided we weren't getting enough exercise after we spent a weekend hiking with friends. They're a few years older than we are, and they were walking circles around us.

"After a few months at the gym, we began looking and feeling better. We were more attractive to each other, and we had more energy. Naturally, we started having more sex. Energy feeds energy. Exercise was the jolt our sex life needed. One of the myths about aging is that your body has to get soft and shapeless. That only happens because people don't use their bodies, not because they age."

The physical and psychological benefits of regular exercise have been well documented. Even the most inactive person knows that it promotes cardiovascular conditioning, lowers blood pressure, helps keep weight under control, and tones the body. Recent studies have shown that regular exercise also enhances sexuality. In one study of couples who exercised regularly, every age group from the 20s through the 60s reported more sexual activity than was average for their contemporaries. In another study, couples in their 60s who exercised regularly reported having more sex than the average reported by couples in their 40s who did not exercise. A large study of the effects of exercise on sexuality found that 97 percent of the men and women in their 40s were sexually active and 92 percent of those in their 60s were. All of the men and women in both age groups in this large study who were sexually active were exercisers. Is that incentive enough to get off the couch? If not, how about the following facts?

- People who work out have better body images and a greater sense of well-being, factors linked to increased sexual activity.

- Those who exercise have improved cardiovascular health, which probably aids erections because it helps keep critical blood vessels unblocked. The vessels leading to the penis need to be unrestricted for a man to maintain a firm erection for a reasonable length of time.

- Exercisers reach orgasm more easily and more often than people who don't exercise regularly, according to research by the Center for Marital and Sexual Studies in Long Beach, California.

- Active women have good circulation, which creates increased blood flow and allows the genitals to engorge fully during arousal.

The Health Benefits of Sex

"The mind and body are powerfully connected," says Kate, 49, a medical writer. "And there is a growing body of evidence indicating that our brains respond to sexual pleasure in the body by influencing resistance to and recovery from disease. When my sister had surgery for breast cancer last year, I gave her articles on the link between orgasm and recovery. She was embarrassed to have her baby sister advising masturbating to orgasm as a form of physical therapy. But the research convinced her. I honestly believe that everyone can influence his or her health, including the outcome of illness and surgery, by encouraging sexual pleasure, if not in a relationship, then through masturbation."

A study published in the *British Medical Journal* concluded that men between the ages of 45 and 59 who have regular sex were generally healthier than were men who don't. Other studies have shown a correlation between the frequency of orgasms in women and good health. In the past decade, a surprising amount of research has shown how important sexual pleasure is to health, including the following:

- Improved appearance of the skin from the increased blood flow that accompanies arousal and orgasm

- Diminishment of some of the genital signs of aging, including vaginal dryness and atrophy in women and poor erections in men

- Strengthening of the immune system

- Relief of mild pain, such as headache or backache, through the release of endorphins in the brain

- Release of physical and mental tension and stress

- Elevation of mood

- Mild cardiovascular benefits

- Lasting psychological benefits

It may be obvious to most people that sex releases tension and elevates mood. But how does it strengthen the immune system? The state of euphoria felt after orgasm is brought on by the release of endorphins, which leads to increased levels of T cells, white blood cells that are responsible for immunity and help resist cancer. The profound sense of relaxation that people experience after good sex is a welcome antidote to stress. And unrelieved stress takes a toll on the immune system, making us more susceptible to colds, infections, and other illnesses. Positive moods foster resistance and recovery, whereas negative moods, such as depression, anger, and fear of pleasure contribute to health problems. After sex, the muscles relax, tension ebbs from the body, and a general sense of well-being contributes to continued good health.

People who have satisfying sex lives are more likely to have good relationships, too. Good sex increases self-esteem and reduces anxiety. Couples have fewer arguments and feel more closely connected to each other. Some studies have shown that couples who report sharing satisfying sex lives have fewer problems communicating their needs and desires. A couple who is happy together in bed is likely to be happy together in life.

The Sexual Effects of Illness and Disability

As we age, many of us who would like to be sexually active are thwarted by chronic illness, disability, and/or medications. Some conditions affect sexuality in indirect ways. When a person feels sick or is in pain, he or she is not usually interested in making love. The following sections discuss common medical problems and their effect on sexuality.

Diabetes

Diabetes has the greatest direct effect on sexuality of all the diseases that commonly have a midlife onset. Diabetic men have a far greater chance of becoming impotent than other men, and in fact ED can be the first sign of disease. In women, diabetes can cause vaginal dryness, loss of sensation in the genitals, and make achieving orgasm more difficult. It can also lead to increased risk of succumbing to yeast and urinary tract infections, which preclude sex until cured.

Patients can manage their diabetes by rigorously following the medical and dietary regimes prescribed for them. If they do, they are able to mitigate the sexual effects of the disease. Nearly half of all diabetic men suffer ED for psychological reasons. For some men, the erectile problems they experienced early in their illness—before undergoing treatment—may have left them feeling anxious, inadequate, and fearful of more failures.

Women who keep their diabetes well under control minimize any sexual effects of the disease. At menopause, these women are particularly good candidates for estrogen-replacement therapy because diabetes often leads to lower estrogen levels and intensifies the negative effect of hormone loss. Make sure your doctor monitors your estrogen levels carefully at the onset of menopause.

HOW TO HANDLE: A sex therapist can help you get over the psychological effects of ED. According to one study, more than 75 percent of diabetic men with ED were able to overcome their problems through counseling. Several of the available ED treatments (discussed in Chapter 12) have proven successful in diabetic men. If you are a man, talk to your doctor about all your options. Women with diabetes should become familiar with all the indicators of low estrogen and do everything they can to boost their hormone levels.

Comments: A 59-year-old man with diabetes says, "I was having erection problems for almost a year following the onset of diabetes. It wasn't necessary to suffer that long. I was backward about bringing up the subject of sexual functioning with my doctor. Finally, in exasperation, my wife did. Because it had been so long, I had to use injections to get an erection for several weeks. Meanwhile my wife and I began seeing a therapist. After a few months of therapy, I was able to have an erection without the injection. I've been fine for the past two years. To remain sexually active at this age with diabetes requires two things: Following the diet-and-exercise routine and taking medication as prescribed and making love often without putting undue stress on erections and intercourse. If you don't force the erection, it will come."

Stroke

A mild stroke may have little or no effect on sexual functioning. More severe strokes obviously affect sexuality because they impair a person's ability to move freely. Even memory loss can affect sexual functioning if the patient has forgotten some aspects of lovemaking. But the mental interest in sex and the drive remain.

HOW TO HANDLE: After a mild stroke, a man or woman may need more patience and tenderness from a lover. Initial lovemaking sessions may be tentative, even awkward; but that stage will pass quickly. When a stroke has resulted in some degree of paralysis, sex, rather than being a part of the past, may assume greater importance to the patient. With medical guidance and consultation with a sex therapist, many couples are about to find ways of making love that bring pleasure to both partners. The stroke victim may have heightened sensitivity and perceptions in the areas undamaged by the stroke. Erotic massage to the unaffected body areas may be very arousing.

Comments: A 48-year-old woman says, "After my husband's stroke, he had mild temporary paralysis and some forgetfulness for about six months. The doctor told us it would be good for both of us to resume our sex life, but he said we should put aside our performance standards for a while. When we made love, our familiar routines didn't exactly work. It was like dancing with someone who had forgotten the steps. But on the plus side, we developed some exciting new steps because we were in a sense new to each other."

Heart Attack
Many people mistakenly believe that a heart attack signals the end of one's sex life. Most heart attack patients are encouraged to resume sexual activity at the same time they begin other physical activities. Making love typically is no more strenuous than climbing a flight of stairs. Less than 1 percent of heart-attack fatalities occur during sex—and the majority of those people are in bed with an extramarital lover, not with their spouse.

HOW TO HANDLE: The major effect of a heart attack on sexuality is psychological. People fear another attack, and they need reassurance. Regular pleasurable sexual activity may actually reduce the risk of further problems, particularly when combined with exercise and dietary and other lifestyle changes. With the doctor's approval, people who suffer shortness of breath from climbing stairs can take a dose of nitroglycerin shortly before engaging in lovemaking.

Comments: A 55-year-old man says, "My heart attack five years ago actually gave me a new lease on life. It scared me into better health habits and made me appreciate sex more than I had in years. Initially, I was a little fearful, but I soon got over that. Sex is better now than it ever was. When you have a brush with your own mortality, it heightens your senses and intensifies your appreciation of life."

Coronary Artery Disease

The majority of people who suffer from coronary artery disease (CAD) are able to lead satisfying sex lives. Unless angina pains are severe, unpredictable, and accompanied by shortness of breath, your doctor will probably encourage sexual activity. The emotional benefits of lovemaking are important.

HOW TO HANDLE: With your doctor's approval, you may want to put a nitroglycerin tablet under your tongue before beginning lovemaking. Until your condition stabilizes, make love in the most familiar and comfortable patterns. Unless you have been given medical orders to abstain, abstinence is rarely part of the long-term healing process.

Comments: A 57-year-old man says, "My wife was the one who feared making love after I was diagnosed with coronary artery disease. I accepted my doctor's advice on the subject, but she was very protective of me. She had to see a counselor to get over her fear of losing me. In our first few lovemaking sessions, I pleasured her, giving her orgasms via oral sex."

Cancer

Both the psychological effect of a cancer diagnosis and the pain accompanying treatment can be sexually debilitating. Add to that the devastating physical effects of chemotherapy. Many people lose weight and lose their hair. It's not unusual for a cancer patient enduring radical treatment to suffer periods of body loathing. For men and women suffering gynecological cancer, the sexual issues are magnified. While the disease itself may not render the patient incapable of having sex, it wreaks havoc with desire and feelings of desirability—primary sexual motivators.

HOW TO HANDLE: Most cancer patients and their spouses will benefit from sex therapy. They may need to learn alternative ways of lovemaking, and they almost certainly need some help with the psychosexual ramifications of cancer treatment. In the early stages, survival, not sex, may be the primary concern. As recovery progresses, sexual healing needs to take place, too.

Comments: A 49-year-old breast cancer survivor says, "I withdrew sexually following my cancer diagnosis. I didn't even want to be touched by my husband. He persisted in being affectionate until I responded to that. I had a partial mastectomy and reconstructive surgery so the recovery was long. And I will never look exactly the way I did. I didn't want to make love for weeks after the doctor said I could because I hated my body. My husband bought me twelve beautiful silk camisoles, very expensive ones with lace. I wore them to make love. The camisoles carried me over the worst days. Gradually I have gained enough body acceptance to let my husband see and touch my breasts during sex."

Arthritis
In a severe form, arthritis can be crippling. Even in its mildest forms, the disease can leave a sufferer with stiff joints, making some sexual positions uncomfortable. Some men and women experience cramping and slight disfigurement in their hands, which makes them reluctant to use manual stimulation fully during lovemaking.

HOW TO HANDLE: Before sexual activity, take the anti-inflammatory agents recommended by your doctor. Ask your doctor about using herbal remedies to ease pain, such as yucca, ginger, or Boswellin. Taking a hot bath or using a heating pad before sex may also help. You and your partner can share the bath as foreplay! If some intercourse positions are uncomfortable, experiment with others or adapt the favorites with the use of pillows and other supports.

Comments: A 50-year-old woman says, "When I developed arthritis in my hands last year, I felt old. Every time I looked at my hands with their swollen joints, I felt like an asexual old broad. Just when my husband needed more manual stimulation of his penis, I wanted to hide my hands so he wouldn't notice them. We had always made love with the lights on, and we started turning them off. Now we light candles."

Surgery
Sexual relations after major surgery will almost certainly be curtailed for some period of time. Depending on the type of surgery and the recov-

ery process, abstinence may extend for weeks, even months. In addition, postoperative depression, a common condition, can dampen libido. At midlife, regaining sexuality may be a little more difficult than it would be for a younger patient.

HOW TO HANDLE: It's important for the patient to seek and the partner to give physical affection during the recovery process. Touch has been shown to have therapeutic value, and it will make it easier to restart your sex life when the patient is ready. The partner of a surgical patient needs to remain sexually active through fantasy and masturbation; this is beneficial for the individual and for the relationship. The healthier person will probably have to take the sexual initiative. Talk to a doctor and/or therapist about how and when to resume sexual activity.

Comments: A 51-year-old man says, "After a car accident, my wife needed three major surgeries, on her back and both legs. She is an enormously vital, alive, and sexual woman. When we couldn't have intercourse, we masturbated each other or I performed oral sex on her. We even played with each other when she was in the hospital. We probably made love more during the six months she was laid up than we had the prior six months because we needed each other so much more then. When we were able to have intercourse again, we used the 'love stool,' which was a gift from our best friends. It's a padded and adjustable device that straddles the recumbent person's lower abdomen. We used it to support my weight in the missionary position, because flat on her back was the most comfortable sex position for her but she couldn't stand any of my weight on her."

Chronic Back Pain

Back pain is a common complaint among midlife Americans, partly because they don't get enough exercise. Weak stomach muscles contribute to the possibility of back injury and make lifting heavy objects a particular risk to the back. Pain can limit one's sexual options by making it difficult to find a pleasurable position for intercourse. It can short-circuit the libido or create enough distraction during lovemaking to quell or dull sexual responses.

HOW TO HANDLE: Stretch and take a hot bath before lovemaking. It also may help to do some muscle-stretching exercises. (Check with your doctor, of course, before doing any exercise.) Work with your partner to adapt positions to meet your physical limitations because the standard missionary position may be the least comfortable one. Chapter 5 describes several positions; the scissors position may now be the most comfortable one for you.

Comments: A 56-year-old woman says, "After my husband first hurt his back helping our son move a sofa, we thought our sex life was over. Every time we tried to have intercourse, he would yelp in pain, lose his erection, and that would be that. We agreed not to try intercourse for a while, but to have oral and manual sex. Then we realized we could make love in a big chair, with me on his lap, my weight supported by my folded legs on either side of him. His back has improved through regular physical therapy sessions, and we have gradually added some more intercourse positions. Losing his gut has helped him a lot, both with the back and intercourse."

Sexuality After Illness
The following suggestions will help you and your partner restore your sexual relationship as soon as possible after one of you has recovered from a major illness or surgery.

- *Share the crisis.* It's easy to let illness divide you into the roles of patient and provider. Think of your partner's illness as yours, too. If you are the one with the illness, empathize with your partner's fears and concerns.

- *Research the problem.* It helps to learn everything you can about the disease, its immediate psychological and sexual effect, courses of treatment, and side effects. Be frank about sexual concerns in talking with your doctors. Consider a consultation with a sex therapist, too. Most physicians have not been trained in sexuality. When you know what to expect, you can plan coping strategies.

- *Expect a full range of emotions.* Anger, sadness, fear, and other strong feelings accompany major illnesses or surgery—for both partners.

- *Don't plan on being the sole full-time caregiver.* If you are the healthy partner, remember that you need time for yourself; if you are the recovering partner, remember that more than one person cares about you and can help.

- *Be affectionate with each other.* Even if you don't feel like being sexual, don't withdraw from physical affection. Both partners need closeness and physical contact through holding hands, hugging, kissing, and cuddling.

- *Don't stop thinking about sex.* If your partner is too ill to make love, don't stifle your sexual thoughts and fantasies out of guilt. It's okay to have these thoughts. They keep the fire burning.

- *Masturbate.* Explore your own sexual feelings while you are waiting for your lover's recovery.

- *Remember that sex is more than intercourse.* Making love does not require an erection, an orgasm, intercourse, or ejaculation.

- *Have a positive attitude when you can have sex again.* Don't worry about functioning. The attitude you take about your sexuality is far more important than any physical limitations you may have.

- *Do your homework.* Look for books and articles about the lingering or ongoing physical, psychological, and sexual effects of your particular illness or disability. In some cases, there are support groups for patients and their partners. And some associations may have helpful information, including where to find specialty products, such as the love stool, that facilitate sexual expression for the ill and disabled.

Why a Hysterectomy Doesn't End
Your Sex Life

"Having a hysterectomy is a psychologically traumatic event for a woman because you are losing the part most closely identified with womanhood," says Donna, 49. "I had one two years ago. I believe it was necessary, and I felt better physically afterward. But I had lingering depression and no interest in sex for several months. My husband's tenderness really got me through the rough period. He was very romantic, as though we were newly involved with each other. Bringing flowers, making dates, writing me love notes in shaving foam on the bathroom mirror, remembering all the little things I like when he did the food shopping are just a few of the ways he courted me. I felt womanly again, and the sex followed naturally."

Though the numbers have gone down dramatically in the past decade, hysterectomy is still the most commonly performed surgery on women. A hysterectomy involves removing a woman's uterus and sometimes her ovaries and fallopian tubes as well. Prevailing medical thought now is that the operation has been unnecessarily performed on many women, particularly for the treatment of fibroid tumors, which often either do no harm, respond to other forms of treatment, or shrink or disappear after menopause.

For many women, plagued by pain or discomfort and heavy bleeding or other problems, hysterectomy is a relief. They find that sex after surgery is better than it was before. Other women report a loss of sex drive. Some question whether their surgeries were necessary and feel angry or betrayed by their doctors, especially if they have lost interest in sex. Many of the concerns women have about hysterectomy are yet unproven. At present, there is no evidence that the surgery has any of the following effects:

- Causes weight gain

- Prohibits sexual functioning, including intercourse

- Accelerates the aging process

We still do not know, however, all there is to know about the effect of hysterectomy on a woman's sexuality. Some researchers believe the uterus, which continues to produce hormones (including testosterone) in small amounts after menopause, plays an unrecognized role in sexual functioning. We do know that the removal of the ovaries and the loss of estrogen they produce leads to menopause and the attendant symptoms such as thinning of the vaginal walls and a decrease in lubrication.

If you have experienced a loss of sexual desire after undergoing a hysterectomy, consider these tips:

- Think about short-term hormone-replacement therapy (HRT) or bioidentical hormone treatment. HRT may be of particular concern if your ovaries have been removed.

- Add alternative estrogen sources, such as soy-based products, to your diet.

- Exercise regularly and improve your diet.

- Try testosterone supplementation, at least temporarily.

- Be honest with your partner about your feelings and ask for his support.

- Consult a therapist.

If your partner has undergone a hysterectomy, you can support her by trying these ideas:

- Learn as much as you can about the sexual side effects of having a hysterectomy and about HRT.

- Accept her feelings and do not try to make her see how irrational they are.

- Be supportive and understanding; do not pressure her for sex. Let *her* set the pace.

- Make her feel desirable by your compliments and gestures.

- Behave in a romantic way.

- See a therapist with her if she asks.

Overcoming the Sexual Side Effects of Medications

Often it's the medication, not the illness or injury, that precipitates a sexual problem. Prescription medications are one of the most common factors affecting erectile capacity. With more than 95 million Americans taking prescription medications, drugs eventually touch all our lives. At midlife, many people are taking drugs to lower blood pressure, regulate heart conditions, alleviate depression, control ulcers, and treat minor conditions (infections, aches, pain, colds, and allergies). A middle-aged man whose erection ability is already affected by age may lose that ability altogether when blood pressure medication is added to the equation. A middle-aged woman with some body-image and other aging issues may lose her fragile libido altogether when she starts taking medication for depression.

A prescription can push a person over the sexual edge. And more than 200 of the commonly prescribed drugs can, according to the manufacturers' own literature, influence sexual performance or enjoyment. The antihypertensives, the medicines used to control high blood pressure, have the highest incidence of interfering with erections and ejaculations, and the antidepressants have the highest incidence of inhibiting desire. Doctors rarely mention sexual side effects when prescribing drugs, and patients who don't read the fine print in the accompanying product literature often fail to connect the sex problem with the medication.

The main potential sexual side effects include the following:

- Decreased libido

- Increased vaginal dryness

- Problems getting or maintaining an erection

- Loss of sensation in the genitals

- Difficulty with ejaculation in men and with orgasm in women

Sometimes it's difficult to determine if a sexual problem is directly related to a medication. A depressed person, for example, may lose interest in sex because of the depression and/or because of the prescribed drug. If you can trace the beginning of the problem to the start of medication, you have good reason to suspect the drug. What can you do if prescription medication is interfering with sexual desire and functioning?

- Talk to your doctor first. *Don't take yourself off any medication.* Ask for alternative drugs that may not have the same side effects. If there are none, would a change in dosage help?

- If you haven't done this before, fill your doctor in on your sexual history. Be honest about the rest of your medical situation, including whether or not you smoke, how much you drink, and what over-the-counter medications you use. All this information helps a physician evaluate the contribution of prescription medication to a sex problem.

- Make the positive lifestyle changes that might enable you to reduce your dosage or go off medication altogether. Stop smoking. Reduce alcohol consumption. Take some of the fat out of your diet, and start a regular exercise program.

- Have sex frequently. The more you make love, the more you will want to make love. Abstinence at midlife is not conducive to sexual functioning later on.

- With your doctor's knowledge and input, explore alternative and holistic remedies. You will need to do a lot of research in this area. Look for fact-based books and articles that back their claims with research rather than anecdotal accounts. Remember that anyone can post anything on the Internet: Valid research papers reprinted from reliable sources coexist with pure drivel.

Rejuvenating the Mind–Body Connection

You've read about the effects of hidden anger and resentment, depression, fear, anxiety, and other psychological factors on sexuality. How does an intense dislike of your aging body affect your sex life? For many people, the answer is badly.

"It's hard to make love on the same day I've looked at myself in a mirror," a 53-year-old woman said ruefully. "My friends have either had or are considering having their first face-lifts. My husband doesn't even want to hear about it. He thinks the whole idea is ridiculous. 'I love your wrinkles,' he says. Maybe he does, but I don't. My wrinkles are taking my libido down with them."

Whether it makes sense to the people who love them or not, some women—and some men, too—stop feeling sexy when their mirror image tells them they are looking old. They will endure the pain or discomfort of face-lifts; liposuction; tucks to the breasts, abdomen, and butt; hair transplants and the cost and agony of whatever treatment promises to restore a measure of youthful sex appeal. The link between a younger-looking image and feeling desirable is a strong one in Western culture.

"Healthy and fit isn't quite good enough," a female patient in her 50s told me. "I need to look younger and *sexier*, too."

For many people, the suggestions given in Chapter 1 will help them gain acceptance of their bodies as they are now and will help them feel more sexually desirable. For some others, nothing short of surgical intervention will jump-start their libido. As baby boomers age, the number of people submitting to plastic surgery and other forms of invasive self-improvement will continue to increase. And so will the number of products designed to hide your expanding waistline and balding head. After age 50, we may all be a little vulnerable to the sales pitch when the promise is a more youthful appearance and a reinvigorated sex life.

What can you do if *your partner* is determined to have a face-lift or other surgical procedure?

- Make sure your partner has researched the surgery, the doctor, and the hospital or outpatient facility thoroughly. Help him or her evaluate the risks and make a reasoned choice. Many people decide to have cosmetic surgery because their friends are doing it. We each bring our own set of risk factors to any medical situation.

- Walk the narrow line between being supportive and appearing to welcome the prospect with too much enthusiasm. He or she should feel free to cancel the procedure—up to the last minute. Most of us would find it hard to change our minds about surgery if we believed our partners were anxiously awaiting the new, improved us.

- Express the sentiment that you love your partner the way he or she is now and that you will still love him or her after surgery. Let your partner know that the decision is not yours to make.

- Be loving and affectionate before surgery and during recovery.

If *you* are the one determined to have a face-lift or other surgical procedure, here are a few suggestions:

- Research the procedure, the doctor, and the hospital or outpatient facility thoroughly. Don't choose a doctor based on personal references alone. You should ask to see before and after photos of other patients. Also ask about the complication rates. How many patients have infections, scarring, or other unsatisfactory results?

- Set realistic expectations. You will not look 21 again. Traffic won't stop when you cross the street. You won't be a 20-year-younger version of yourself. Ask your doctor what it is reasonable to expect. Most people look a little younger and more rested and relaxed after a face-lift. They don't look like Demi Moore or Tom Cruise.

- If you are suffering from loss of libido or some other sex problem, surgery probably won't solve it. Work on increasing desire and improving sexual functioning, as discussed throughout this book. Talk to your doctor and consider other treatment before submitting to the knife.

- If you have reached a carefully evaluated decision, don't let anyone make you feel guilty about it. There's nothing wrong with wanting to looking your best. Enjoy.

- After surgery, find ways of feeling good about yourself that aren't appearance based. Eventually, your skin will sag again.

"I didn't want to appear vain," a patient said about his hair implants, "but I hated my bald head. I looked in the mirror and saw my father. Now that I have a modest crop of hair, I see a virile guy, still young at fifty-five."

Vanity implies an excess of pride or self-importance, but most people who undergo surgery and other procedures aren't excessively proud. They're worried that the way they look inhibits their partner's desire for them.

"I can't believe the difference a mini face-lift and some minor tucks have made in my sex life," says Deborah, a very attractive woman in her early 50s. "My husband will deny it to his dying day but he wasn't as interested in me sexually before the surgeries as he is after. I don't blame him. I didn't turn myself on either.

"Now when he looks at me, he sees a woman who is more like the one he fell in love with. I feel exhilarated, sexually charged. We are feeding off each other again. It's wonderful. Would I have another tuck in five, ten years? Maybe. Probably. Why not?"

Regaining Desire Lost to Illness, Disability, or Physical Signs of Aging

As couples age, they are more likely to be confronted with illness, injury, or disability—conditions that may have important consequences for their sex lives. Also, they are more likely than previous generations to want to overcome issues surrounding the physical signs of aging. Men and women over 50 today don't accept the same limitations their parents and grandparents did. They expect to look and feel younger. Inevitably, their expectations will clash with the reality shown in their mirrors.

Some couples will stop making love in response to these situations. By regaining their passion for each other, their enthusiasm for life and love-making, and their erotic creativity, nearly every couple can surmount the medical obstacles to good sex. Here's how:

- *Don't pull away from each other.* Now is when the need for touch, affection, and pleasure is greatest. Illness can cause the sufferer to withdraw into the self. Resist the temptation to do that. Reach out to your partner. If you are the healthy one, don't take your partner's withdrawal as personal rejection. It isn't. Reach out and coax your lover back to you.

- *Be supportive.* Review the sections on sex and illness and disability earlier in this chapter. The same advice can help men and women who are avoiding sex because they hate the way they look. Don't belittle a partner's dissatisfaction with an aging body. A preoccu-pation with sags and bags may not seem as significant as a heart attack, but it can be sexually debilitating, too.

- *Do what you can to look better and to help your partner look better.* Studies have shown a direct correlation between the time required for a woman to resume sexual activity after a mastectomy and the effort she puts into improving her appearance. Wigs, pros-theses, and special clothing are necessities, not luxuries, for the recovering breast-cancer patient. Whether you're getting over an ill-ness or making the mental adjustment to the physical signs of aging, do everything you can to look better today. A couple in their 50s who were despondent about their son turning 30 reignited their sex life by getting his and her makeovers. "It was expensive," he says, "but a lot cheaper than divorce."

- *Give yourself and your partner a sensual treat every day.* Take time to smell the flowers. Savor the texture of different foods in your mouth. Wrap yourself in a cashmere throw.

Here's a final consideration: Go ahead and investigate the available antiaging products, but don't allow yourself to be taken in by outrageous claims. The marketplace is flooded with antiaging remedies from expensive face creams that promise to eliminate fine lines to over-the-counter hormones such as melatonin, dehydroepiandrosterone (DHEA), and pregnenolone that claim to be life extenders. Manufacturers prey on the hopes and fears of an aging population, and much of the hype has no substance. Nonetheless, there are some worthwhile new products that may help you cheat time, at least by minutes, if not years.

The face care products featuring alpha- and beta-hydroxy, for example, are more effective than any previous beauty aids at diminishing the appearance of fine lines and age spots. Read the labels and, as always, do your research. New products are being developed all the time; and although some may be very effective, others might be a waste of money.

When it comes to over-the-counter hormones and similar products, be sure to do your homework. Be skeptical when reading product literature, and talk to your doctor before taking any of these drugs; they may not be right for your unique needs and some may affect the efficacy of prescription medicines. Antiaging medicine is, for the most part, an idea whose time is not quite here.

Makeover Sex

While Jim's wife, Katie, was dying of cancer, he hardly even saw himself when he looked in the mirror to shave or comb what was left of his hair. For 2 years after her death, he did not look at another woman. Then one bright autumn day as he was having a solitary lunch at a sidewalk cafe, he noticed another lone diner, a woman who must have been in her late 40s or early 50s. Even in repose she looked vibrant, lively. He wondered what it would be like to make love to her.

Later at home he looked, really looked, at himself in the full-length mirror on the inside of his bedroom door. Standing sideways, he studied his profile. Potbelly. Slight double chin. Head-on, he couldn't escape the bags around his eyes. The shiny pate and the fringe of graying hair surrounding it didn't bother him as much as those sagging eyes. He looked as if he would never smile again, and he was smiling when he drew that conclusion.

Jim embarked on a diet-and-exercise program. The potbelly shrank. He could discern muscles developing again beneath the fat. But those eyes. He thought of the woman he'd seen at the restaurant. She wasn't much younger than he was, probably 5, maybe 10 years. Would a woman like that even consider a man like him? Probably not, he concluded, because of those damn saggy, baggy eyes.

He told his friends, grown son, and colleagues that he was having his eyes fixed because the drooping flesh was narrowing his field of vision. They believed him or pretended they did. The surgery was easier than he thought it would be. After a few uncomfortable days, he healed quickly, and he was rewarded for his mild suffering with a new look. The excess flesh on his eyelids and beneath the eyes was gone. When he smiled now, he reminded himself of the actor Ed Harris. He was handsome again.

Jim went back to the cafe where he'd seen the woman who had turned his erotic pilot light back on. It was winter, and the outdoor tables were in storage. He sat inside at a table for one, close to a roaring fire. She wasn't there. He made a habit of dining there two or three times a week, but he didn't see her.

Just as he was about to write off romantic fantasy, a woman asked in a soft, hesitant voice, "Do you mind if I share your table? There's not another one free."

His heart leaped. He looked up into the lovely green eyes of a woman who wasn't his fantasy, but he didn't care. Confident of his clear gaze not obscured by folds of flesh, he held her eyes for several heartbeats. He certainly didn't care that she wasn't his mystery woman. Standing, he pulled out a chair for her.

"Please," he said. "I often come here and dine alone, wishing someone would join me."

"Oh, you're being kind," she said, laughing, as she took the chair he offered.

They sat together at the little table and talked through lunch, dessert, wine, and finally a selection of appetizers. He suggested a movie, followed by dinner at another restaurant. And she eagerly agreed. On that first long date, they learned a lot about each other's marital histories and tastes in food, movies, and books. A widow, she had lost her husband to cancer, too.

At the end of the evening, Jim escorted her back to her apartment. At her door, he took her in his arms and kissed her, gently at first, then with growing passion. He knew they would become lovers, not tonight, but soon. When he held her in his arms, he pressed against her, just enough to let her feel the promise that he felt growing inside.

Two weeks later, Jim made dinner for her at his place. He had set the stage for seduction, and she didn't disappoint him. She came with a tote bag in place of her classic handbag. He saw something silky peeking from the top.

After a leisurely meal, he began making love to her on the sofa in front of the fireplace. The lovemaking lasted a long time. It fulfilled the fantasies he'd begun to nurture since the day he'd noticed the woman alone at the sidewalk cafe. The man he'd seen in his mirror that night was gone. An old man, a sad man, he had disappeared into the glass. In his place was Jim, mature, sophisticated, a lover extraordinaire.

The woman in his arms returned his kisses, touches, embraces. Her heart beat loudly in his ears when he lowered his face between her breasts. They were vital, alive, and together—and he was going to bring her joy.

CHAPTER FOURTEEN

Making the Dating Scene

Betty, 54, has been widowed for 4 years, although she still wears her wedding ring. She lives in the same apartment as when she was married, and has kept most of her husband's possessions. Although she is not proud of it, she makes it known that she is a widow to distinguish herself from the divorcées.

Betty does not find it easy to talk to new people. Several of the men she has dated—at the persistent urging of her family—issue a similar report: "Her eyes look through you rather than at you. Not only is the person who lives behind those eyes inaccessible, she doesn't even *try* to relate. You get the impression she is waiting for you to prove something, or trying to spot a flaw, or sizing you up and finding you wanting."

Undoubtedly, there are a number of widows and widowers who, after a period of mourning, are able to court a new intimacy. Unfortunately, Betty is not among them; she is having a very difficult time facing life.

In midlife we approach dating with two minds. Meeting someone new is exciting, but along with the excitement may be low-grade terror. What to wear? What to say? Where to go? Do I have sex or not? If you're like Betty, you feel loyal to a partner who has died and believe that becoming close to another will be an act of betrayal. If you are divorced, you may still be dealing with a complex and confusing interplay of emotions, such as anger, guilt, sadness, fear, relief, and excitement. Whatever your situation, all those feelings are compounded when it's not just any first date but perhaps your first date in decades.

New Beginnings

The end of a relationship in midlife need not be the signal that life has come to a halt and is never to be resumed. Many people have succeeded in the face of widowhood or broken relationships, despite the initial feeling that rebuilding one's life is a hopeless task.

The process of recovery, however, is not likely to proceed without setbacks. Some days will pass easily, and it will feel good to be alive; these may be followed by days filled with monumental distress. Some problems, the pragmatics of a new living arrangement, for example, may be resolved smoothly; others, such as developing a new social network, may not be solved for months. If you've been coupled for a number of years, you may lose some of your couple friends or feel as if you no longer fit in. Remember that some emotional issues may take quite a bit of time to resolve, such as strong feelings toward your former partner, feelings of injustice, fear of making it alone, and guilt about new involvements.

Whether a relationship dissolves through a breakup or death, one lesson of midlife daters stands out clearly: Moving immediately into a new committed relationship is often a mistake. Most people need to go through a difficult emotional struggle and healing period before they can once again love judiciously and fully. Emotional wounds close slowly.

On the other hand, it is important to seek support and help from friends and family. Nonromantic relationships are key to a successful reconstruction process. If you would like to seek new friendships, get involved in activities that are meaningful to you: Volunteer at a school, hospital, or library; campaign for your favorite political candidate; take a class at your local college, art institute, or dance studio; join a gym; or become involved in the Chamber of Commerce or your church or synagogue. These are healthy and positive ways to fill your time, learn new skills, and meet people who share your interests.

Don't forget to take a look at your general attitude toward life and your own self. As discussed throughout this book, once we pass age 50, it can be difficult for some of us to maintain a positive self-image. Remember that any potential partner who is around your own age is struggling with the same issues. Learn to accept yourself—blemishes and all—and limit your negative internal conversations. When you have a confident and upbeat attitude about yourself, others will, too.

Getting Out There

When you're ready to consider opening a new chapter in your life—meeting a new companion, perhaps a lifelong partner—you have but one choice, and it doesn't involve sitting on the couch. To begin writing that new chapter you need to get out there and reconnect with old friends, meet new people, and go on dates. Many midlife singles realistically expect that the initial dating experience may be awkward.

Dave, 53, married Jan when they were in their early 20s. After their divorce, Dave thought back to his first date, which took place when he was a junior in high school; he remembers being paralyzed by self-consciousness. "That was exactly how I felt on my first date after Jan and I split," he said. "I went home that evening and called an old friend who had divorced a few years back and is now living with someone. 'Mark,' I said, 'I can't do this. No way! I'm going to die alone!'"

His friend laughed and told Dave that, although his experience wasn't quite that dire, dating was not easy. He urged Dave to stay with it and gave him some good advice: "Begin with mini-dates, a drink after work, lunch, or simply be out front and suggest an initial meeting that is brief."

Some midlife singles are like Dave and dread returning to the dating scene, but others find the experience uplifting, especially if their old relationship was not ideal. Kimberly, 56, who had been married for 30 years, was more positive: "Meeting new people was a very potent antidote to the indoctrination imposed on me by my husband—'You are a cold, aloof, unlikable person.' I didn't really feel that way about myself, but I wondered at times, 'Could he be right?' If he was, I have changed dramatically or my coldness was in reaction to him because this has not been my experience with other men. I feel comfortable and natural offering myself without guile to many of my dates. I am pleased to find how communicative and outgoing I can be. Many of the men I have seen are easy to talk to, we discuss each other's feelings, neutral topics now and again, common interests, and the like. There is an easy flow that has developed after a few dating experiences. I have discovered latent social skills and personal charm I didn't appreciate because it was so at odds with the feedback I received from my husband. Rather than a reminder of a tragedy—my torn marriage—dating has been a renewal for me."

The dating experiences of Dave and Kimberly illustrate the extremes you might encounter when you start dating again. Most midlifers will have experiences that fall between these polar ends. Dating will bring ups and some downs, but most of the newly single adapt quite well. After going out a few times, they come to terms with their new life. Lynn, 51 and newly single after 18 years of marriage, says: "After five or six dates there was a gradual settling down. Meeting a new person became less frightening when it occurred to me that people are fundamentally the same. While I was worried about being judged, I hadn't considered that the other person was probably worrying that I was judging him. When I stopped preoccupying myself with my own uneasiness and instead put my date at ease, my discomfort disappeared. You might say I got over myself! From there on, it became much more fun. I was no longer tongue-tied. I am amazed at how personal and intimate conversation can become in almost no time at all."

Going Online—Or Not

The 21st century presents a whole new world to the midlife dater. For many in the over-50 crowd, the hard-wired telephone was the most high-tech option available last time they set up a date. Today, the newly single is wondering not only about where and how to meet but also about the pros and cons of using the Internet. And for some older daters, the whole idea of online dating can seem intimidating. If you haven't yet thought about going online, take a look at these advantages of using an Internet dating service:

- *Wider range of choices.* Online dating services have thousands, sometimes millions, of members; you'd have to do an incredible amount of socializing to meet as many people as you can by joining an online dating service. The greater the number of members, the more likely you'll find someone who will accept you just as you are.

- *More likely to find singles.* In practically any forum for meeting people—bars, clubs, and the like—you'll find individuals in committed relationships who are looking for casual sex. Although married people may list themselves with a dating site, the great majority of members are single and looking for a partner. What's more, several sites conduct a basic screening to confirm that their subscribers are single, although people can slip through the cracks.

- *More preference centered.* Many newly single midlife daters are very selective, looking for a particular person with specific interests and with values that are consistent with their own. Dating sites can help people find others with similar core beliefs, religions, ethnicities, and cultures. Some sites are geared specifically to baby boomers and members of "generation Jones," those born at the tail end of the baby boom.

- *More affordable.* In a single evening, you may buy a couple of drinks, something to eat, and perhaps tickets to a movie or other event—do the math...dating is expensive! And, if the date turns out not to be a potential partner, you may feel that you've made a poor investment. Online dating typically involves a getting to know you process before the pair commits to an expensive offline date. The couple talks via email and the telephone before even a mini-date (a brief date) is scheduled. Furthermore, the monthly cost of most online dating services is cheaper than a traditional dinner and a movie.

- *More convenient.* Lots of people, especially women, don't feel comfortable going alone to bars, clubs, and singles hangouts. And even if that is not an issue, most newly single baby boomers have little free time after taking care of their careers, children, parents, and other responsibilities. Online dating begins at home and is time-efficient; no need to get back into your car or to worry about what to wear. You can date while doing your laundry or helping your teenagers with their homework.

- *Better background information.* With traditional dating, potential partners barely know each other before they've committed to an entire evening together. You make or accept a date because you like the other one's looks or because your friend set you up. More often than not, in the middle of the first date you discover something you really don't like about him or her. Online dating doesn't guarantee a wonderful first face-to-face date, but it does offer you more chances and more time to get to know the other person *before* you agree to meet.

- *More opportunity for risk-free flirtation.* In the bar scene, flirting can lead to trouble, especially when fueled by alcohol. Just ask the guy who thought he was keeping it friendly only to get slapped or the woman who was followed out of a bar by a guy who began with charming banter but then crossed the line. Flirting can be fun when it works; it can be scary or humiliating when it doesn't. Online dating services allow you to try out flirting. If it is reciprocated, great; if not, no big deal.

- *Safer.* Online correspondence may not be guaranteed safe, but no one's going to slip something into your drink, follow you home, or take advantage of the fact that you've had too much to drink. If you use a dating service that is security conscious, the person has been screened and has submitted a profile. You have also had ample opportunity to check out the person by email and telephone before you get together. If you sense that you're not compatible or if you're spooked, you don't have to meet at all.

- *Better social opportunities.* Several of the more popular Internet dating sites put together social events for members only. Thus you have an opportunity to meet some of the singles whose profiles you've already screened and to mingle with others who have likely had at least some preliminary screening. Because you have already interacted with at least some of the others at the gathering, you won't feel as if you were meeting total strangers.

• *More disclosure.* Online dating is like a plane flight during which you feel free to reveal things to your seat mate because you won't likely see him or her again and you have anonymity. Getting to know someone through email gives you a pleasing sense of freedom; if the other person responds negatively to something you've disclosed, then you simply stop writing to him or her. If you get a positive or sympathetic response, then you have found a potential partner!

Other Dating Options

Although online dating is loaded with advantages, other more traditional options have value and should not be forgotten.

Setups

Many boomers have a rich social network, and although they may lose some friends when their status changes, especially if through divorce, others will remain loyal. When you're ready to venture out, it is often a good idea to tell your friends that you're now ready to date. After all, your friends have a sense of who you are and may act as unofficial matchmakers. Sure, some of your dates will turn out to be mismatches, but others may be right on target.

Margaret, 52, attests to the bright side of setups: "I have a best friend, Dawn, who has known me since high school. She's the confidant I leaned on all through Mike's losing fight with colon cancer. About a year after Mike's death we were having coffee and Dawn mentioned Christian, a friend of her husband's. She said that he was divorced almost three years and had great character, a lively sense of humor, and was looking. 'He'd be perfect,' she said. At first, I was resistant, but feeling close to Dawn, and trusting her judgment, I conceded. It was a great decision; Christian and I are still together!"

Of course, most of us have heard the horror stories as well—the matches made in hell—the deeply religious woman matched with a dogmatic atheist, the 6-foot-tall woman matched with a man barely 5 feet, and the ultra-liberal matched with an anti-everything conservative.

However, don't risk losing an opportunity; if you're not sure, you can always try a mini-date.

Singles Events and Activities

Most communities have events for singles—tennis, bowling, hikes, book clubs, dancing nights, cycling clubs, church- or synagogue-sponsored socials, gym and athletic club events, and weekend getaways. Frequently, local newspapers have listings of social events of a general nature and of those specifically geared to singles. For women, who often feel they out-number men at many events, the unfavorable male-female ratio is often softened by choosing athletic activities and other events that tend to draw more men.

Jen, 58, has been single for 2 years: "Unlike my single friends who have become discouraged because all the good men are either taken or gay, I am persistent and resilient. I joined a gym, got in great condition, and then started frequenting athletic gatherings to meet men. Sure enough, the ratio was more favorable, still lopsided, but better. The upside is that I am enjoying being in shape, my doctor is happier with my numbers—I even asked him if he had single friends, but he didn't—and I am going out on more dates. I still haven't met my Mr. Right, but I have increased my chances."

Professional Matchmaker

A minority of boomers have taken the express highway to finding a mate: They've paid for the services of a professional matchmaker. The screening process is usually extremely extensive; the prospective enrollee may feel as if he or she were applying for a high-level FBI job. On the other hand, knowing that their matches will also have undergone as extensive an investigation can be comforting. Before hiring a matchmaker, be sure to check out his or her success in creating compatible matches; you might want to ask about the number of clients he or she has and the number of available singles there are to choose from. The primary disadvantage is the high fee, which can reach $20,000 or more.

Frank, single for 5 years, took the professional matchmaking plunge just as he turned 60: "I had been dating for five years and I just got to thinking, how much time do I have left? It occurred to me that, at my age, time is more important than money. If a professional can match me with a lifelong companion, someone I can live out my life joyously with, it will be worth every penny. And that's what happened! It was expensive, the intake took several appointments, but I hit the jackpot on the third date. That was four years ago and we're still together having a ball, traveling, enjoying similar interests and talking endlessly, sometimes well into the night. My dream of meeting a soul mate has been realized, and I couldn't be happier."

Speed Dating

If you can jump into conversation quickly and don't mind a dizzying pace, speed dating might be for you. Speed dating involves a form of musical chairs played with 10 to 15 unattached couples. An equal number of men and women gather at a restaurant, bar, or club and enjoy a brief, casual social time before each man (or woman) sits at his own table. Then each woman sits across from a man and engages in conversation. Every 3 to 8 minutes, depending on the setup, the men shift tables and meet another woman. At the end of the event, the participants tell the director which, if any, of the prospects they'd like to meet. If two people both choose each other, the director shares their contact information; the choice must be mutual before the director will release any personal data.

For some people, speed dating is a nightmare because the pressure of having to make an instant impression is too much. However, others find it to be an efficient way to conduct a number of screenings in a short period of time.

Paul, turning 50, loved it: "This was great for me. Hey, I'm hyper, love the challenge of pressure and have plenty to say—and I can say it fast. I go to an average of one speed dating event a month, and I find that it really saves me time and money. I meet at least 15 women at each event. For me there's nothing like meeting someone in person. And, yes, I am pleased that I don't have to buy dinner for women I have little or no interest in."

Ten Great Conversation Starters

Paul's experience aside, for most boomers, first-time meetings can be tense, regardless of how the meeting was arranged. Even after emails, phone exchanges, and perhaps a mini-date, the first full face-to-face date can be anxiety producing. What if there's a lull in the conversation or you find yourself at a loss for words? The best counter to first-date jitters is to be prepared with a mental list of conversation starters. Not only will these seeds keep the dialogue moving and interesting but knowing that you are prepared will go a long way toward quieting your nerves. Keep these questions in mind, and you'll find it easy to talk to your next date:

- What do you like best about yourself?
- Who are your heroes?
- What is your greatest temptation?
- How did you come to your career?
- What kind of talent would you most like to have?
- What makes you happy?
- What kinds of things really irritate you?
- What was the craziest thing you ever did?
- What event in your life would you like to play over, and why?
- What kinds of things do you find yourself thinking about most often?

There are many other conversation starters that work well. The key is to ask open-ended questions (those that cannot be answered in one word) that explore your date's interests, likes, and dislikes. Most of us are flattered when others take an interest in us, and most of us enjoy talking about ourselves, especially if the questions stimulate our thinking. Remember to ask follow-up questions, such as, How did you come to that interest? or What do you enjoy about that?

Pose these same questions to yourself and give your answers some thought before your date. Adding your own ideas to the conversation will provide give-and-take and will serve as a great base for a flowing, lively, enjoyable conversation. What's more, bringing in your own responses lets your date learn about the real you without the pressure and anxiety of having to think on your feet.

Eight Safety Precautions

You may have had the experience of not listening to that little voice in your head called instinct. Not following your instincts, usually leads to regret. So, although dating is reasonably safe, your first line of defense is being aware of how you feel and listening to any gut feelings that may be warning you off.

If you feel uneasy, suspicious, or alarmed at any time, *take action*. While the likelihood is that your date is safe, especially if you have had opportunity to talk with and perhaps even meet briefly before your date, sometimes that internal caution flag goes up, and it is wise to have an exit plan.

- *Meet when you're emotionally comfortable.* Don't be pressured into meeting your date until you've had some email and phone exchanges that are reassuring. Pressure to rush the process is a red flag.

- *Meet in a public place.* A mini-date in a public place not only increases the safety factor but avoids the possibility of suffering through a full date if it's a poor match. Leave-taking is less likely to be accompanied by a scene. Insistence for a meet in a secluded location is a red flag.

- *Meet in familiar territory.* Going into an area you aren't familiar with can be problematic. For one thing, getting lost in an unfamiliar neighborhood is unsettling. For another, if you need to leave in a hurry, it is comforting to know where you're going! Pressure to meet where you don't want to is a red flag.

- *Travel independently.* Make your own way to the meet. Traveling independently is a must. After all, despite your predate exchanges, it makes sense to be independent at this stage. What's more, not only can you leave when you're ready but you won't be revealing where you live. Insistence on picking you up is a red flag.

- *Make your whereabouts known.* Tell someone you trust about your plans. Make sure he or she knows how to contact you, and where you'll be. Keep your cell phone turned on. Some people make arrangements for a friend to call in the middle of the date as a safety check. Pressure to ignore your phone is a red flag.

- *Easy on the Pinot Noir.* If you are used to having drinks at home, bear in mind it is not wise on a preliminary date. Drinking is tempting because it is relaxing, especially if you are a bit jittery. However, because you may be driving and you are meeting with someone you don't know well, err on the side of caution—*don't overdo it.* It is not safe to lose your ability to make safe and sensible decisions. Repeated suggestions to have another is a red flag.

- *Keep your privacy.* Don't provide home or work contact information. You don't want your date to show up when you aren't prepared for him or her; keep physical addresses to yourself. Pressure to release this information is a red flag.

- *Have an exit strategy.* For safety reasons and to gracefully exit an incompatible match, have a rehearsed basis for leaving early. For example, you may announce early in your meeting that you may have to leave early to help out a sick friend or that a problem came up at work and you may be needed. Then have a friend call you at a prescribed time; during the call you can make a decision about whether to stay on or make an early departure. Pressure to stay and forego your commitments is a red flag.

Be Real, Stay Real

When dating after 50, especially if you've been out of the dating scene for years, it is understandable to feel confused about sex, stressed about meeting new people, and concerned about safety factors. Furthermore, if you were in just one relationship for most of your adult life, it is likely that you are ambivalent about jumping into a new romance full force. Although the ultimate goal for most of us is to find a potential life partner, we also know that a committed relationship is not only comforting but also a major responsibility. Typically, boomers wade in by dating a variety of people while they warm to the dating process and, perhaps, to prevent one relationship from becoming all-important or exclusive.

Philip, a divorced 60-year-old architect, has been dating for about 8 months. His thoughts are typical of both men and women: "I hope someday to marry again, but that day is not right around the corner. I am enjoying meeting a variety of women; and frankly, after faithfully being with the same woman for 35 years, I am excited by having a variety of sexual partners. What's more, I am also enjoying the freedom of not having to answer to anyone but myself. I go to sleep when I'm tired, get up when I want to, eat what and when I want to—these may seem like minor factors, but not for me. These are the things that bring a smile to my face. I want to feel in control of my life at this point, and a committed relationship is a compromise I am not quite ready for now."

Although some may argue with Philip's point of view, most older daters want to know the truth about a potential partner's state of mind regarding commitment. It's okay to date casually but not okay to pretend that you're looking for marriage when you're not. What's more, by the time they've passed their 50th birthday, most singles hope to be dating someone mature enough to drop pretenses—someone who doesn't hide the truth to gain approval, avoid conflict, or have sex.

Kelly, a recently retired teacher who has been single for 3 years, said it well: "At midlife it's about time that each of us embraced who we are and what we want. It's about being real, telling the truth, and not pretending. Leave it to those years younger than us to hide their feelings or to pretend to be someone they're not. That phoniness is probably my biggest complaint out in the dating world. Doesn't anyone tell the truth anymore? Isn't anyone comfortable enough with who they are?"

Being real—that is, telling the truth and being authentic—takes courage, but it is ultimately attractive and signals integrity. Pretending to be someone you're not, *playing games* as it is called in the dating world, steals energy and, in the long run, doesn't work.

The following suggestions will help you stay on track:

- Be honest, but don't be mean. Being real is not an excuse to step on another person's feelings.

- Be the king or queen of afterthoughts. Sometimes it is difficult to put your real thoughts and feelings together when you're put on the spot, but remember that there is always tomorrow. If necessary, bring up the topic again and say what you really meant or felt. Better late than never.

- Remind yourself that self-acceptance is not about perfection, it is about being honest with yourself and embracing your strengths as well as your weaknesses. Admitting your faults sends a signal of self-confidence.

- If you find yourself mired in long-winded explanations in defense of yourself, stop. If you have been honest and respectful in your conversation, that should be enough.

If the date is not working out, the chemistry or fit is just not there—and that happens often in the dating scene—find a kind of way of saying so. Too many people lie because they want to protect the other person's feelings and their own—don't be one of them. Sharing your feelings on a sensitive issue like this is very difficult. Bear in mind, however, that your best hope of not getting mired in a relationship that you don't really want to be in is to be forthright. Remember, when you are on the receiving end, you want to be treated with courtesy and respect, so treat your date in the same manner.

Of course, getting real and being real are easier said than done. If this is a struggle for you, it may help to know that you're not alone; making behavioral changes is a challenge for everyone. In essence, try to identify what it is that you want, believe, and/or feel and then stick to your convictions. At the same time, don't close yourself off to views that are in conflict with yours; listen and learn rather than get defensive.

Katherine, 50, revealed her struggle to be authentic: "About a year ago I looked in the mirror, and I didn't recognize myself. It had been so long since I stood up for my convictions that I didn't know whether I still had convictions to stand up for. I hadn't been honestly myself. I didn't actually know what my real self was; I'd just been playing a lot of false roles. I even went so far as to break off an engagement with a very special man because I was sure that someone that fantastic could not possibly love me once we started to live together and he really got to know me. Instead, I sought out somebody I felt to be inferior because I was more comfortable with him. He was safer. Yet, I was dissatisfied with that relationship because I didn't really care for the guy. It seemed that when I was attracted to somebody, I'd louse it up by caring too much about pleasing them. Or I was becoming involved with men who didn't please me. In the first two years of my divorce, I continued in the same pattern: I got into relationships that I ended if I felt myself getting too close to someone who really appealed to me, or I spent more time than I wanted with men who said they were turned on to me but toward whom I felt nothing. In the past year, with the help of a psychologist, I have been 'building emotional muscle'; I have been taking the chance of being hurt, rejected, or vulnerable. With small steps I am being honest with myself and with others."

Katherine discovered that her behavior and her feelings were not genuine but created a facade behind which she had been hiding. She was surprised to learn how much of her life was guided by what she thought she *should* be rather than by who she really is. Once she recognized that she tended to respond to the demands of others rather than direct her own life, she was determined to change. She wanted to begin living her own vision, not someone else's.

Dating Success

Baby boomers find themselves newly single because of the death of their partner or because of divorce or separation. Depending on the circumstances, some people suffer deeply during the post-relationship period and require substantial time and help to recover, whereas others sprint forward almost immediately. Most individuals fall between these two extremes; but, eventually, almost all feel a desire for a new relationship.

The following guidelines can help smooth the way as you look for a compatible partner.

Don't Make Quick Judgments

Do not assume you know a person after a first meeting. It takes time to discover the wide range of feelings and behavior of another person. Because most people are wary around strangers and on a first date, your initial impression may be misleading. Relationships require time to blossom, and it is almost impossible to assess what another person is like on the basis of a brief party acquaintanceship or a dinner date. Diane will not go out with the same man twice if he doesn't prove that he is an interesting person on the first date. Steven cuts women out of his life if they do not immediately respond to his sexual advances. Although you *may* be able to uncover a deal breaker after a short conversation, if you are like Diane and Steven, you could be missing out on a great relationship because you've made a quick and superficial judgment.

Accept Rejection

Just as a snap judgment is often self-defeating, it is also foolish to pursue persistently someone who isn't interested in you. Relationships involve a complex interplay of values, interests, and physical attraction; many couples simply do not match and never will. Aside from incompatibility, some people may have other demands on their time and cannot save some for dating; other potential partners are defensive, shy, or still grieving and thus are not ready for a relationship. If your advances are rejected, it is wise to accept that the other person wishes to remain at a distance; devote your time and energy to developing relationships with people who want to get to know you, too.

Keep Your Feet on the Ground

If you have the tendency to fall head over heels in love, fight it. Give yourself time to become known to and to know your potential partner—flaws and all—before giving away your heart. Avoid the tendency to idealize your new partner, which is an issue for both women and men. Remember that all relationships go through a honeymoon phase, during which everything seems new and wonderful. When the smoke clears, and the relationship has settled in, you may feel let down when you realize that your partner is not perfect.

Committing too fast can often lead to disillusionment, especially when your expectations are unrealistic. For example, if you believe that your new lover will be able to heal your wounds, you're bound be frustrated. However, don't be too quick to abandon a relationship. If you start to sense feelings of disappointment, even subtle ones, face them instead of stewing about them. Ask yourself why you feel let down and what you expected but didn't get. Then ask yourself if your desires were realistic to begin with. If your needs seem reasonable, then discuss them with your companion; avoiding such issues is likely to perpetuate feelings of resentment, discontent, and/or mistrust.

Try not to compare your new relationship to those of your past. Most midlife daters have spent their adult life in a single committed relationship. Your new partner will not be a clone of your old one; do not expect him or her to react in the same ways. This reminder works in two directions: Your old relationship is unlikely to have been as wonderful or as horrible as you remember. As I've stressed throughout this chapter, each relationship and each person is unique. Give your potential partner a chance; don't let the slightest fallibility turn into a major betrayal.

Don't Watch the Clock

Discard any preconceived notion about how long it takes to develop a close relationship with another person. Each relationship has its own timetable. This point is particularly critical: The surest guarantee that a relationship will collapse is to impose a prescribed time period in which it should flourish.

Stay Calm

Learning to relate closely again is bound to be unsettling, and many newly single boomers are filled with anxiety. Don't let nervousness prevent you from moving forward: Do you want to go on protecting yourself or do you want to develop a new relationship? If you want the latter, it is important to recognize that intimacy always involves some risk and thus anxiety is to be expected. Most rewarding relationships do not proceed smoothly.

Focus on Your Goal

Keep your goal in mind. The purpose of a first date is twofold: fun and to decide whether you want a second one. With that in mind, plan a conversational rather than a high-activity date. A drink after work or a lunch date is preferable to a movie, for example. Bring your sense of humor and the proper perspective, which will add to the fun part of the date.

Keep Perspective

Although you would like to meet someone, your well-being doesn't depend on it. If you were doing well before the date, you'll do well afterward, even if the date doesn't work out. If you aren't doing well, forming a new relationship is not going to solve all your problems. Your state of mind is in *your* control, giving that control to someone else is always a mistake.

Remember the Golden Rule

Do unto others as you would have others do unto you. People who abide by the Golden Rule are more likely to develop satisfying relationships. Indeed, those who are chronically unhappy with other people probably are so because of a failure to see others as similar, in many respects, to themselves. Most of us want the same things in our relationships: honesty, a sharing of feelings and thoughts, empathy, support, and fun. Those of us whose relationships are lacking some of these qualities might ask, Do I myself offer these same things to others? There is no guarantee that being a model of what you want will produce positive results, but your chances of obtaining a close relationship will increase dramatically. If you open up to the other person, taking him or her into your confidence and sharing your thoughts and feelings, he or she will be more likely to reciprocate.

Have Some Trust

Although you need to keep your feet on the ground and make good judgments about others, consider that the more trusting you are, the more likely you are to be trusted by others. Research by psychologist Julian Rotter suggests that trust, like many other interpersonal behaviors, tends to be reciprocal. You are more likely to be trusted when you put some trust out there yourself.

SIZZLER #14

Hotel Date

Meredith is excited about going on her third date with Kevin. She is smitten with him, as he is with her. Kevin has reserved a hotel room and talked to the maître d' at the hotel bar, but he hasn't told Meredith. Instead, he asks Meredith to meet him in the hotel bar for a drink after work. When she walks in and asks for Kevin, the maître d' hands Meredith a note and a key to a room. The note says, "This key will open the door to an erotic evening you won't want to miss. Follow your heart upstairs."

The room is dark as Meredith enters. Kevin comes up behind her and takes her around the waist, kissing her from behind. The adult channel is playing on the TV, and Meredith can catch a glimpse of two naked people playfully chasing each other across a tennis court. It's funny and sexy at the same time.

Kevin takes some silk scarves out of his pocket and ties her hands behind her back, and then he takes another and covers her eyes, whispering that he has a wonderful surprise for her. Kevin opens the bottle of wine he's ordered from room service, and Meredith can hear the pop of the cork. He pulls off the coverlet and turns down the sheets—she can hear his hand gliding across the smooth cotton and imagines his fingers doing the same to her.

Kevin guides her into the bathroom where he has already turned on the heating lamp. The room is toasty, and as he begins to touch Meredith softly through her clothes, she can feel how excited he is. Kevin removes Meredith's shoes and then, kneeling before her, and reaching under her skirt, he teasingly pulls down her panties, then he kisses her stomach and thighs, listening to her moan softly.

He opens a bottle of body lotion and massages Meredith from her toes to her waist. When Meredith is thoroughly lubricated, Kevin takes his hands off her, leaving her in a state of high desire, telling Meredith how exciting he finds making love to her away from home.

Kevin guides Meredith to the bed and holds the glass of wine so that she can sip from it. If it spills, so much the better—he'll lick the excess off. He removes the blindfold so that Meredith can take off the rest of her clothes and help him undress.

For a while, Meredith and Kevin lie together watching the onscreen couple getting it on. The rhythm of their movements is too tantalizing to ignore, and soon Kevin and Meredith are locked together, ignoring everything in the world except the sound of their beating hearts and quickened breath.

Now it's Kevin's turn to wear the blindfold. Amazing how each touch of her hand and mouth is heightened when he can't see.

"What would you like me to do to you?" Meredith asks.

"Never stop touching me," Kevin tells her ardently. Meredith slides down and take his penis into her mouth as her thoughts of the outside world fade away.

CHAPTER FIFTEEN

Love with Another Partner

"In the last few years of my marriage, I often felt the sex was boring, humdrum, routine," says Jackie. "It reflected the relationship. After we got divorced, I didn't have sex for two years. Then, at age fifty-one, I met a man. It was clear by the second date that we were headed for an intimate relationship. I was excited and terrified. Would my body turn him off? Would I remember how to perform fellatio? What if I couldn't have an orgasm?

"I seriously thought about not having a third date so I wouldn't have to take off my clothes and put myself on the line. Being naked at fifty-one in front of a near stranger is not an easy thing to do. Parts of me have definitely gone south. When I talked it over with my best friend, she told me he was probably as scared as I was.

" 'Don't you think he's worried about whether or not his penis will work?' she asked. 'Everything pales in comparison to the big penis issue for men.'

"She was right. We were both nervous. Fortunately we did it for the first time on my living room sofa by candlelight, so I didn't have to do the complete disrobing or worry about whether or not to turn on a bedroom light. He was very passionate and very tender; and his penis did indeed work. I had an orgasm. Fellatio? Like riding a bicycle. I hadn't forgotten."

Midlife couples who have been together for many years confront their own sexual issues, but people who are starting over, starting late, or finding themselves involved in late affairs have problems, too. They aren't scanning lists of how to take the boredom out of the bedroom, but they may be standing in front of the full-length mirror agonizing about saddlebags, stretch marks, sagging breasts, potbellies, and prominent veins and the effect these signs of aging will have on new partners. Even people who are in very good shape may have temporarily lost their sexual self-confidence.

"It's one thing to make love to a trusted partner and another to test-drive your less-than-stalwart member with someone new," says Bruce, 50, who is recently out of a long-term relationship.

If you are single, widowed, or divorced, your best hedge against first-time sexual failure is prevention.

Six Keys to Staying Sexual Alone

Prolonged and involuntary celibacy can be one of the most difficult sexual conditions. When men or women lose a partner through death or divorce in middle age, they, particularly the women, will likely be alone longer than a younger person suffering the same loss. Nothing takes the place of sex, but if you break your sexuality down into its components, you can make sure each of your needs is being met in your life. In simplest terms: Sex is warmth, closeness, physical touching, and orgasm.

At this point in your life, it is more important to stay in sexual shape during celibate periods than it ever has been. Regaining sexual functioning once lost can be difficult at midlife and beyond. Don't let it go, and you won't have to worry about how to get it back when you meet your next partner.

Here are the keys to staying sexual while alone:

- *Create and strengthen intimate bonds.* Find warmth and closeness with friends and family. It's important that you not get out of the habit of relating and exchanging affection. The phrase *set in his (or her) ways* is not often applied to a sensual and sexual person.

- *Indulge your sensual side.* Candlelight is not only for shared meals. Bubble baths can be the prelude to self-loving as well as to lovemaking with a partner. Wear perfume. Buy flowers. Be romantic with yourself.

- *Fantasize.* Don't censor your sexual thoughts because you don't have a partner and/or you think you're too old for erotic daydreams. Read books and watch films that encourage sexual fantasies. Allow yourself to imagine new and creative erotic scenarios.

- *Touch.* Take your hugs where you can get them, from family and friends, even from yourself. Put your arms around yourself and hug. When you're feeling lonely, tense, or stressed, rub your hand or arm, cheek or neck. If you don't have a pet, consider adopting one.

- *Keep your hormone levels up.* If you're a man and you suffer from low testosterone, don't neglect treatment because you don't have a partner. If you're a woman, elevate your estrogen levels after menopause through hormone-replacement therapy or alternatives. Keep your vagina lubricated in preparation for intercourse through the regular use of a lubricating product.

- *Masturbate.* Regular masturbation will keep the sex organs functioning for men and women. You get all the health benefits of orgasm whether orgasm is achieved alone or with a lover. And you can use masturbation as a time to explore new ways of touching and stroking yourself, information you'll be able to share with a new partner.

If you follow these tips, you'll be ready to resume sex when you meet the person who will become your lover.

How to Become Sexually Active Again with a Partner

"I knew I was planning to make love to Kathryn when I bought the package of condoms at the pharmacy," says Ted, 56. "I felt like an elated kid and an old fool all at once. That pretty much describes the situation when you're seriously dating again after twenty years. Your emotions are up and down, up and down."

Ted had been divorced almost 2 years when he met Kathryn. He'd had two casual flings of short duration during that time. Because he did not feel emotionally involved with the women, he was able to have sex with them without worrying much about his performance.

"The first time I had sex after the divorce I felt a twinge of concern about my penis," he says, "but I told myself, 'If you have an erection failure, you just won't see her again. No big deal.'

"I knew right away it was going to be a big deal with Kathryn. I really liked her. I wanted to make love to her; and I had delayed longer than either of us wanted to wait because I was afraid of disappointing her. I could tell she was wondering what was holding me back. The day I bought the condoms was a red letter day. I wasn't entirely satisfied with my performance. My erection kept doing a disappearing and reappearing act that made me nervous. But she wasn't disappointed. She put my hand where she wanted it to be against her clitoris and had me bring her to orgasm during intercourse. I liked that a lot. It gave me confidence."

After a dry spell, becoming sexually active with a new partner can be as scary as it is exciting. Men and women share certain fears about making love to a new person at this stage in their lives.

Body-Image Anxiety

One survey of single women over 40 rated "fear of being seen naked" as their number one stumbling block to having sex again. In a society in which the prevailing image of being single is the young and beautiful cast of the now-defunct, but ever-popular HBO television series *Sex and the City*, an older, less svelte woman without a partner may believe she isn't meant to have sex again. Men, too, have more anxiety about their appearance than they did in the past, but they are less concerned than are women. A man can think he's sexy if he's overweight and out of shape; it's harder for a woman in comparable physical condition to feel good about her sex appeal.

HOW TO HANDLE: Being overly self-conscious about your appearance can sabotage sex. Remember, your partner's body isn't what it once was either. To relieve some of the anxiety, start making love with your clothes on. Feeling inside clothing for the hidden flesh and groping for buttons and zippers adds to the excitement. When you are both very aroused, cellulite concerns will fade away. Until you are comfortable with nudity, keep the lights low or off; women can wear something lacy and filmy to bed.

Comments: A 54-year-old woman says, "I bought a tube of Dermablend, a waterproof cosmetic coverup used to hide birthmarks and surgical scars. I touched up the veins on the backs of my knees and the tops of my feet. And I wore a short, sexy slip with a built-in bra that I kept on during sex the first time. The makeup and the slip gave me the confidence I needed to let go and enjoy sex."

Performance Anxiety

Women worry about whether or not their sexual technique will produce the desired results on their lover, and they worry about having an orgasm. Many women feel pressured to climax and are concerned about their performance in bed. Men worry even more about women's orgasms. They fear losing their erections or, worse, being unable to get firm and thus disappointing her. Performance anxiety is, according to a survey of single men over 40, the biggest stumbling block to first-time sex with a new partner. Women might be surprised to learn that many men delay having sex because of this anxiety.

HOW TO HANDLE: Both the man and the woman should try to be less focused on his penis. Making love in a less penis-centered way removes some of the pressure and adds to their mutual pleasure. At midlife, a man should feel comfortable asking his lover for the manual or oral stimulation he needs to become fully erect. A baby boomer woman who can show a man how to please her by guiding his hand or responding enthusiastically to his oral ministrations lets him off the erection hook. (See Chapter 5 for lovemaking tips.)

Comments: A 50-year-old man says, "The first time I made love to a new woman in twenty-five years, I said to her, 'Let me pleasure you.' I gave her orgasm after orgasm via cunnilingus. By the time she was sated,

I was fully aroused and confident enough of my erection for intercourse. If you can give a woman several orgasms, you lose the fear of failing with your penis."

Fear of Rejection

How would it feel to be rejected by your first new lover in many years? Not good. That fear keeps some people from ever having a new lover. Some midlife singles block their sexual thoughts and feelings in an effort to protect themselves from rejection. Although none of us wants to be hurt, it's important to remember that making connections with others, sexual or not, is important for our mental and physical well-being.

HOW TO HANDLE: The first step for overcoming your fear of rejection is to put passion back into your life. Chapter 2 provides some tips and exercises for building passion and boosting your self-image. Although you may have to push yourself in this area, the potential rewards of letting your partner know how you feel outweigh the risks. Even if you have sex with someone who decides not to see you again, remember that you have put yourself on the path to finding someone who *will* want to commit to you.

Comments: A 49-year-old woman says, "It's hell to be middle-aged and wondering if he's going to call or not. After I met Rick, I found myself in a bookstore glancing through that asinine book *The Rules* and briefly wondering if I should wait until a certain time period had elapsed to have sex with him so he'd call me back. Ridiculous! I talked myself out of my rejection fears and plunged ahead. It's the only thing you can do."

Fear of Intimacy

People who fear intimacy protect themselves emotionally. If they avoid getting close to a potential partner, they avoid becoming vulnerable. It is more than the fear of rejection described above. It is about having to give of themselves and become known. Some people, even if they have a guarantee that they would not be rejected, are still uncomfortable and feel vulnerable revealing themselves. People who are afraid of intimacy often act interested in another but then pull back when their partner returns their interest. Some people look for excuses to prevent the relationship from getting closer. For example, some use a fear of sexually transmitted diseases as a way to avoid sex; others find a reason to reject a potential partner before they have sex or soon thereafter.

HOW TO HANDLE: Good sex and a good relationship requires shared vulnerability. As noted in Chapter 3, sex for the older lover is more about intimacy and less about hormones. Try to work on letting go and opening yourself up to another person. Being close to another person is not the same as giving up your autonomy. (See page 38 for tips on mastering your intimacy fears.)

Comments: A 49-year-old man says, "My ex-wife often accused me of avoiding intimacy, fearing intimacy, running from intimacy. I really got tired of hearing the word intimacy in my marriage. I think she used it as a club. After the divorce, when I started sleeping with a woman I cared about, I began to think a lot about the concept of intimacy. It's not such a bad idea if a woman isn't demanding it from you."

After a man and woman have had sex, either they move forward toward a deeper intimacy and have more sex, or they don't. Some couples don't develop a relationship for good reasons: They aren't right for each other. The timing is wrong. One or both have other priorities. But some couples don't develop a relationship for the wrong reasons: They let their fears get in their way.

Overcoming the Obstacles to a New Sexual Relationship

"Matt and I became lovers on a holiday in Mexico," says Sandra, 46. "I hadn't been with a man in over a year. He hadn't been with a woman since his divorce almost a year to the day after we met. Our Mexican interlude was idyllic. The sex was wonderful. Then we went home, he to Chicago, me to St. Louis, not an impossible commute, but not convenient. Still, the relationship thrived.

"Our kids did us in. My teenagers and his adult children didn't want us to be together—with a vengeance. Not one of the four of them could deal with a parent having a sex life. We caved to the pressure and didn't see each other for three months. Now we are seeing each other when we can arrange it without the kids knowing. It's like an illicit affair. My friends say I need counseling, and they're probably right. But the sex is still wonderful. Maybe when my baby goes off to college next year, we'll work something out."

Once a new sexual relationship has been established in middle age, the participants may not get the same enthusiastic emotional support from family and friends that young lovers do. Unlike most 20-something couples, they will find a dearth of media images celebrating their love. Midlife romance is just not a major part of modern American culture. Be prepared for a range of reactions from family and friends. The following sections discuss some of the obstacles you may encounter shortly after the first series of orgasms subsides.

Teenage or Adult Children

Logically, adult children should have no effect on their single parent's sex life, but they can if you let them. Maybe they resent Dad for leaving Mom (or vice versa). Maybe they're worried about their inheritance. Perhaps they can't imagine their parents having sex—not just with each other but certainly not with someone else. Teenagers are even less capable of imagining their parents having sex with a suitable stranger. Furthermore, teenagers still require quite a bit of their parents' time, energy, and emotions.

HOW TO HANDLE: What if your kids don't approve of your having sex? As a first step, tell your teenagers that you are old enough to understand and accept the responsibilities of a sexual relationship and can make your own partner choice. If you aren't comfortable with your choice, however, they'll know it—and they'll pounce. Reassure your adult children that you know what you're doing and that you'll still have time for them and your grandchildren. Let them know that you understand their concerns, but can make your own life choices.

Don't be provocative in front of your children, especially preteens. Avoid one-night stands and avoid exposing your children to a series of lovers who spend the night. You can counter your children's objections to your sexual behavior more authoritatively if your actions are consistent with your family's values. "Do as I say, not as I do" doesn't cut it with children of any age.

Don't get into a relationship with someone who makes you feel uncomfortable. And avoid becoming sexually active to prove your attractiveness, to assuage your neediness, or to allay your fears of being left alone. Your kids won't miss those signals. They will hit you directly in the vulnerable zone. When your sexual choices aren't solid, you're more likely to have difficulty handling your kids' reactions.

Finally, remember that your children's objections to a new lover may be rooted in their unspoken wish for reconciliation between you and their other parent. Your sexual behavior is threatening because it indicates your intention of forming a new relationship. Discuss this with your children, and let them know that you can't give them the power of choosing your sex partners.

Your children should not be in charge of your life, and you should not place that burden on them.. However, this isn't to suggest you ignore your children's concerns. Quite to the contrary, the best path involves listening carefully, considering your children's concerns, communicating your understanding, and taking those concerns under advisement. The point is, after considering their concerns—and there are times when their perspective may even change your own—the final decision is yours, not theirs.

Past-Relationship Baggage
His wife was critical and domineering, so he doesn't want to hear an opinion or suggestion from you. Her husband had an affair; and she doesn't trust men anymore. In other cases, it's not about divorce and the ensuing hardship, but the death of a spouse. A spouse may have died after a long illness or suddenly. In either case, it is traumatic and the memory lingers. People bring issues from their families of origin into the first marriage. When they pack for the second, or later, marriage, they may still have the original bags, plus a whole new set. That's a heavy load to lug into the honeymoon suite.

HOW TO HANDLE: Not only do many people carry issues from a former partner into a new relationship but they sometimes choose someone who is particularly suited to their unfinished business. The woman, for example, who has trust issues, gets involved with a married man promising to leave his wife. Whether he keeps his promise or not, he's most likely trouble.

Be aware of the issues you bring into a new relationship and avoid the obvious reenactments. Stop blaming your ex for all your problems, and take a good look at yourself and your contribution to the failed relationship. When you do that, you'll be able to identify your own issues. Be open with a new partner. Discuss your issues. If you don't get a supportive response early in the relationship, you probably won't get it later.

The man or woman who lost a spouse to illness or accident may have exaggerated memories of either how wonderful or horrible the relationship was, and is wise not to jump into another relationship until an appropriate grieving process has occurred. In addition, widows and widowers need to bear in mind that they are likely to react strongly to a new spouse's health and safety conditions. It's about keeping perspective and reminding oneself not to become unduly alarmed due to past experience.

Health Problems

A 40-year-old woman married a healthy, vibrant 60-year-old man. Unfortunately, 10 years later, she is nursing him through recovery from prostate cancer surgery, a recovery complicated by his diabetes and heart condition. That dreaded scenario plays out in the minds of most middle-aged singles, but it's a particular concern for baby boomer women who get involved with men their age or older. The chances of one or both partners facing health problems early in the marriage is certainly higher than it was when they married for the first time, usually in their 20s. For some, a second relationship will involve a bigger age gap between partners than there was in the first marriage or long-term relationship. On average, with each marriage, men marry younger than they did before. If a midlife woman marries a man who is 5, 10, 15, or 20 years older, how likely is it that she will soon become his nurse? (The reverse is also true. If a midlife man marries a woman who is older, he, too, may end up becoming a nurse.)

HOW TO HANDLE: Committing to someone considerably older does increase the likelihood that the partner will become ill and need care early in the relationship. Although the future health status of anyone is impossible to predict, prevention goes a long way to living a long and healthy life. In a loving relationship, each partner has a responsibility to be supportive of the other's health. Encourage your partner to eat well, exercise moderately, get regular medical checkups to spot problems early, and manage stress effectively.

If you have a partner in ill health, you can't devote yourself entirely to caring for him or her. The challenge for partners of seriously and/ or chronically ill people is to refrain from becoming bitter and resentful. Make time for the activities and people that you enjoy because they recharge your emotional batteries. Get help with the caretaking from professionals and other family members and friends. Create a support system for both you and your partner. There are support groups for people with cancer and other diseases. Reach out for help—this makes it easier for you both to be thankful for the good years you've already had and make the most of your remaining time together.

Unresolved Personal Issues

Many people in midlife still have unresolved personal issues. Issues that can get in the way of establishing intimacy and maintaining a good sexual relationship include unresolved anger, intimacy fears, behavioral problems such as heavy drinking and overspending, and sexual hangups. In middle age, unresolved personal issues will very likely create relationship problems.

HOW TO HANDLE: As I've stressed throughout this book, practice self-acceptance. Midlife is the perfect time to embrace ourselves, blemishes and all. At this point in our lives, we've addressed many of the concerns of youth: choosing a primary career path, having children, and establishing a financial base. We have more time and inclination for reflection. Sometimes that reflection leads to harsh self-analysis.

Most of us do our best. We have good intentions and decency in our hearts. Do we have to emulate Mother Teresa before we can feel good about ourselves? No. We'll take most of our imperfections to our graves. By being more self-accepting, we can be more open, less defensive, and stop living our lives in fear of being found out. Problems such as fear of intimacy, heavy drinking, and anger decrease dramatically when we learn to accept ourselves. If you jump over these obstacles in a rush to remarry, they may mysteriously reappear in your path someday.

"Rob and I got married last year on my fiftieth birthday after a six-month courtship," says Carla. "The sex was very good until we got married, and then there was a sudden drop-off in frequency. I was interested, and he wasn't. We started fighting about when and how often to have sex. Finally, one day he told me I was just like his first wife. A bell went off in my head.

"I literally dragged him to a marital-and-sex therapist. It took us six months, as long as the courtship, to work out the issues we'd carried over from our previous marriages. We are happy now, and the sex is good again. But I would advise other couples to do this *before* the wedding, not after."

How to Avoid STDs

More than 12 million Americans will contract a sexually transmitted disease (STD) this year, and almost 20 percent of them will be over the age of 40. With the notable exception of AIDS, the great majority of these diseases are curable, most of them easily treated by antibiotics. When left untreated, some of them can lead to serious complications such as pelvic inflammatory disease in women.

Five Keys for Avoiding Midlife STDs

- Practice safe sex, using condoms during intercourse—even if the woman uses another form of birth control or is postmenopausal.

- Ask your doctor to test you for STDs during regular checkups if you are not in a monogamous relationship.

- Don't assume you can tell if a partner is likely to be HIV positive or have another STD on the basis of his or her looks, age, or previous marital status. You can't. HIV infection among men and women over 50 is a growing problem.

- If you know you're going to have a one-night stand, consider a hot session of loveplay, rather than intercourse—and use a condom.
- If you are a man planning on having only oral sex, use a condom—you can contract some STDs from fellatio.

The Late Affair

"When a man has his first extramarital affair after his fortieth birthday, everyone assumes he's in the throes of a midlife crisis," says Martin, 46. "I resent being lumped into the category of typical middle-aged man."

Having said this, Martin acknowledged that he's having an affair with his 25-year-old administrative assistant, Tiffany. To him, and presumably to his lover, they are a unique couple involved in a special relationship that has nothing in common with the cliché they undoubtedly resemble. There are, however, some commonalities in first-time midlife affairs. Often the participants invest the relationship with more meaning and take it more seriously—or convince themselves they do—than do younger first-time extramarital lovers. Often an older man seeks out a younger woman, typically a workplace subordinate. But statistics show that an increasing number of married men are attracted to their equals in the workplace, women nearer their own age. Without small children at home to motivate them to stay in their marriages, older lovers in highly emotional affairs are more likely to divorce.

"My wife and I have been ships passing in the night for years now," Martin says. "Our marriage is a property partnership. Now that our son has left for college, the two of us have even less in common than we did and fewer shared activities to attend. The sexual part of our relationship has been dead for a long time."

Tiffany believes that Martin and his wife, Georgia, never have sex. He concedes they do; but, he says, "It's not very intimate lovemaking like I have with Tiffany, but it's better sex than we've been having. I think I bring more energy to the bedroom after being with Tiffany." Will Martin leave Georgia for Tiffany? "That would be complicated," he hedges.

The odds are that Martin will break up with Tiffany, or she with him, and he will stay with his wife. Studies have shown that only about 1 in 10 people leave their spouses for their lovers. He may or may not have another affair. His marriage may or may not become close and intimate, but it probably has benefited sexually from the affair. Incidentally, Georgia may be having, or have had, an affair of her own, without Martin knowing.

Men and women become involved in affairs for the first time in middle age for many of the same reasons they might have entertained when they were younger, but their age and the length of time they've been married or in a relationship may have supplied the impetus they needed to finally act on their erotic impulses. The following sections discuss some of these reasons and their effects on the marriage.

Emotional Alienation

During the child-rearing years, a couple may be too busy to notice how alienated they are from each other. At middle age, when the household is quieter, the two look across the breakfast or dinner table and realize they have nothing to say to each other. Their sex life is probably routine and boring because they have not deepened the intimate connection between them and moved to a higher plane of lovemaking. If the children were the raison d'être for staying together, the marriage is now in trouble.

HOW IT MAY AFFECT THE MARRIAGE: Rather than working together to build a more intimate relationship, some couples choose to look elsewhere for the sexual excitement they crave. Unlike the frequent philanderer who spends a lifetime reliving the adolescent thrill of fresh attraction, the midlife first-timer is turning back sexual time in one big leap. The affair will probably be exhilarating for a while and, in a few instances, may even help the marriage. However, in my experience with couples, despite the "success stories" highlighted below, the vast majority of instances have an unhappy outcome.

Comments: A 48-year-old woman says, "I had an affair last year for the first time in a twenty-one-year marriage and for all the classic reasons. I didn't feel close to my husband anymore. We made love infrequently. I needed to feel attractive and valued by someone else. The affair lasted three months and was wake-up call for me. I got my husband into counseling. I really wanted to make my marriage better, not throw it away. He doesn't know about the affair; and I don't think he ever needs to know. We are closer now; and the sex is better."

Curiosity

Some people who married young—when they were virgins or had little sexual experience—may wonder about pleasures never tasted. They may occasionally fantasize about missed opportunities or be curious about what sex would be like with someone other than their spouse. In middle age, the sense that their erotic time is running out creates a sense of urgency in some people. Thus when the opportunity for sex with another person presents itself, the formerly faithful spouse strays.

HOW IT MAY AFFECT THE MARRIAGE: An affair motivated by sheer curiosity will probably be a low-emotional-involvement relationship and may not threaten the marriage. This may be the only taste of forbidden fruit the curious partner requires. He or she may return to the spouse, chastened, and determined to atone for the lapse by being more romantic, caring, and seductive. On the other hand, any affair can intensify, having a lasting effect on the marriage, whether it's a loss of trust or a divorce.

Comments: A 50-year-old man says, "I married my high-school sweetheart when I was twenty-two. I'd had sex with one other girl, a total of four times. Over the years, I thought about other women. I have considered using a prostitute when I traveled on business just to see what it would be like, but fear of disease kept me from it. Last year I had a fling with a woman I know at work. She's happily married, too. It was good for both of us. I felt like a real stud for the first time in my life. Lovemaking with my wife is better than it was with the other woman. She's a very good lover, and we bring a history of tenderness and passion to every encounter. But I needed to know that."

Unexpressed Anger or Hostility

Some people have affairs to get back at a spouse. That may be their subconscious agenda, no matter how they rationalize the liaison to themselves. The man or woman may have personal anger issues and be unable to express those feelings within the marriage. Or the hostility may have developed over a long period of time between a couple who express anger often and loudly, without resolving any of the problems that are making them so mad. An affair in these circumstances can be a passive-aggressive act of revenge.

HOW IT MAY AFFECT THE MARRIAGE: Anything can happen, including divorce and remarriage, when a middle-aged person with a big emotional agenda has a first extramarital affair. It's possible the affair may remain undiscovered and will lessen some of the feelings of resentment toward the spouse. The marriage and the sex may improve. On the other hand, the affair may be exposed, leading the openly hostile couple into another battle and the repressed-anger couple into a confrontation. Neither couple is likely to resolve the issues and rebuild the marriage without some counseling, but the possibility for a stronger marriage is there if they do get help.

Comments: A 48-year-old man says, "My wife was the church secretary, PTA president, and all-around loyal woman. A year ago she got involved with another man. Now we are in the process of getting a divorce so she can marry him. She tells me that she learned in therapy she'd been angry at me for twenty years because I was a workaholic and emotionally withdrawn from her. Interestingly, she wants her cut of the money I earned through my workaholic ways. The new guy doesn't make as much. Do I wish I'd paid attention to her unexpressed feelings and needs a long time ago? Yes. The truth is I always knew something was wrong. I just didn't ask what. I figured she'd tell me if it was important."

Desire for More or Different Sex

After 20 years of making love to a partner who won't or can't indulge an erotic desire, a man or woman may finally look elsewhere. The desire may be for more frequent sex or oral sex or for more sexual variation such as anal sex, bondage, or light S&M. In some cases, a partner seeks another who will indulge a kink his or her spouse finds distasteful, such as foot fetishism. Very often, a man or woman is simply looking for a partner who will be more creative and spontaneous in bed. At this stage in life, the unfulfilled partner may think that he or she has waited long enough and is now ready to find someone who wants the same things in bed.

HOW IT MAY AFFECT THE MARRIAGE: The affair may become an ongoing sexual outlet with low emotional involvement and may coexist with the marriage. Sometimes, this kind of affair *removes* stress from the marriage, particularly if the partner who can't comply sexually has medical reasons for not doing so. Or the sexual seeker may discover that once his or her fantasy or desire has been met, it is no longer appealing.

Comments: A 48-year-old man says, "My wife is not as highly sexed as I am. Nor is she as interested in exploring sexual variations. She will do things for me, like agreeing to tie me up, but she won't get into them. I accidentally discovered that a coworker was interested in some mildly kinky forms of sex when I overheard her talking to a friend on the phone. After thinking it over a long time, I made my move. I haven't regretted it, and I hope I can keep the affair going without my wife ever finding out. She thinks I've 'outgrown' some of my sexual ideas and is happy with our life together."

Ego Boost

The one-night stand, the out-of-town fling, the brief affair with an attractive subordinate—all may be nothing more than shots of testosterone to the ego. That doesn't mean every ego getting an illicit sexual boost is male. Women can have affairs rooted in the need for an ego boost, and their libidos are also fueled by testosterone. When a couple has been together a long time, they may have stopped giving each other the positive emotional feedback most people need. The midlifer seeking another partner may actually be looking for compliments, romantic gestures, and lust-filled glances that say, "You are sexy and desirable."

HOW IT MAY AFFECT THE MARRIAGE: An ego-boost affair typically does not evolve into a long-lasting emotional relationship. The effect on the marriage will probably be minimal and may even be positive—if discovery is avoided. Sexual battery recharged, the errant lover is often in the position to then give his or her spouse a needed ego boost.

Comments: A 49-year-old man says, "I was tired of being taken for granted by my wife and by my kids away at college who had no interest in me beyond the answer to the question, Dad, did you send a check? It had been a long time since a woman touched my hand or my arm and looked into my eyes while we were talking. This woman did. And she was a very classy and beautiful woman. I felt like a new man after our little fling."

Avoidance

Some people are beset by myriad problems at midlife. Corporate downsizing, hitting the glass ceiling, dealing with aging parents, unexpected health problems, living with teenagers, and paying for college are some of the big issues that seem to accompany receding hairlines and growing waistlines. If the marriage is suffering from sex problems at this stage in life, one or both partners may be too stressed to see that the solutions lie in adapting their lovemaking styles and deepening their intimate connection. They avoid facing such issues by having an affair.

HOW IT MAY AFFECT THE MARRIAGE: For some people, the temporary sexual diversion and respite from marital problems helps them gain a new perspective and tolerance. The affair may enable them to keep the marriage intact through the difficult period. If they become very emotionally involved with a lover, however, they may decide to leave the marriage, believing (likely falsely) that they'll be leaving all their problems behind, too.

Comments: A 52-year-old woman says, "Last year I had an affair that saved my marriage. We had my terminally ill mother-in-law staying with us when our daughter returned home pregnant and not married; and I had to take a pay cut to stay employed. My husband and I were at each other's throats all the time. I had an affair with a friend who'd also been downsized and was having marital difficulties. We called it our little vacation from reality. Both of us did go back to reality because we helped each other be able to cope."

Dull the Pain of Loss

Traumatic loss brings some couples closer together; but it drives many others apart, sometimes temporarily, sometimes not. The death of a loved one, an empty nest, or a devastating career blow produce feelings of pain and loss. A man or a woman who can't share painful feelings with a spouse may find it easier to open up to and seek comfort from someone with whom there is more emotional distance. This disclosure can lead to the bedroom.

HOW IT MAY AFFECT THE MARRIAGE: Much depends again on how emotionally involved the lovers become. Most affairs are low-emotional-involvement relationships. If the bond between the lovers becomes intense, a middle-aged man or woman coping with significant loss may seize on the relationship as salvation.

Comments: A 52-year-old woman says, "After our son was paralyzed in a diving accident three years ago, my husband had an affair with his secretary. After all these years and at a time like that, he had an affair. I was devastated. For a while he thought he was in love with her. He realized he wasn't and begged me to take him back. I want the marriage to stay together, but I don't really think I've forgiven him yet. When I first found out about the affair, I had the hottest sex with him I've had in years. But we've had problems off and on since then, with his erections, my low libido. Maybe time will heal."

In many cases, there is more than one reason motivating a man or woman to have an affair. Although reliable statistics are hard to find, affairs are certainly more common than they were in the past. When a first-time affair happens at midlife, however, emotions can easily be magnified. If you or your partner is having an affair or has recently ended one, talk to a therapist. Most affairs, if discovered, and many are, leave the aggrieved spouse devastated. Couples, including the offender and aggrieved, definitely could use help in putting things back together again and in building a more solid foundation.

Should You Have an Affair?

If you are tempted to have an affair, only you can weigh the pros and cons for your particular situation. No one can make that choice for you. In my practice, I discourage unhappy spouses to have an affair. Instead, I suggest that he or she deal with the relationship issues first. Ask yourself why you are considering an affair. If you answer this question truthfully, you may discover the root causes for your present dissatisfaction. Once the issues are revealed, you can work on dealing with them, if possible. Remember that an affair is usually yet another complication rather than an answer. On the other hand, you may find good reasons to give in to temptation and seek another lover.

If you are still tempted to have an affair, first ask yourself the following questions:

What do you want from an affair?

Review the common reasons for midlife affairs discussed in this chapter. Are you looking for intimacy, a different kind of sex, more sex, an ego boost, or escape from the pain of a midlife loss? Could you get what you need from your mate if you asked? Sometimes we assume that our partners won't be willing to listen, change, or compromise, when in fact they would be if only they had the chance. Before looking outside the marriage for what you need, talk to your mate about your dissatisfaction. Don't threaten to have an affair if your needs aren't met.

Do you have a hidden agenda?

Anger, resentment, emotional alienation, and other factors are often the subtext of an extramarital affair, particularly at midlife. The feelings have fermented inside you for years. Having an affair may be a way of letting the feelings out. But is it the best way? Is it fair to you, your spouse, or your prospective lover? An affair can be a means of avoidance: You can avoid working on your marriage, facing your personal issues, and dealing with common midlife fears and concerns. Some people manufacture dissatisfaction with their marriage as an excuse for having an affair that is really motivated by a poor self-image or by the fear of growing old.

Are your lover's expectations for the affair the same as yours?

Having an affair with another unhappily married person who has no plans to divorce, for example, is different from having an affair with a single person who hopes you will leave your spouse and remarry him or her. Some people are content in emotionally limited marriages. They may seek out a lover from time to time, but they enjoy the safety and security of their marriage. Which kind of person are you? What kind is your lover?

What are the risks inherent in this affair?

Will you fall in love? Will your lover? Would your spouse leave you if the affair were discovered? What other repercussions might befall you? Trouble at work? Confrontations with teenage or young adult children? Financial consequences? Emotional wreckage? When weighing the risks of the affair, don't forget to consider the emotional ones. When people get involved in highly emotionally charged affairs, they report conflict and pain on discovery or separation. A casual affair may coexist with a marriage, but an intense amour competes with it. Are you prepared for the outcome should the extramarital relationship become intense?

Are you prepared for the mistrust that will exist between you and your spouse if the affair is discovered and then ended?

Even a casual affair can have a strong effect on a marriage. The consequences run the gamut from destructive to enhancing. After a brief undiscovered affair, you'll likely become more open, loving, and receptive to your spouse. Discovery, on the other hand, generally leads to at least some negative and complicated situations. One of the principal consequences of a discovered affair is mistrust. Once you have broken the bond of intimacy between you and your spouse, you'll likely find trust is gone. Even an undiscovered affair can result in mistrust; straying partners distrust themselves and/or their spouse. "If I cheated, so can he (or she)" is a comment I've often heard from patients in the aftermath of an affair. And they may also say, "If I cheated once, I'm afraid I'll do it again. I don't trust myself anymore."

Is your spouse physically unable to be a sexual partner?

If your spouse is suffering from a debilitating or terminal illness that precludes sexual activity, the decision to have an affair is complicated. Among other hardships, you are probably grieving for your partner's loss of sexuality as well as your own enforced celibacy, and it may be difficult for you to see solutions. (See page 235 for suggestions for maintaining intimate contact during illness or disability.) Then schedule an appointment with a therapist to talk about your needs and desires. In such circumstances, I advise my patients to be very clear about what they are doing before they seek another lover. Besides the common effects presented in this chapter, healthy spouses who stray must deal with different guilt and self-image issues from those of other unfaithful partners. They typically need some help facing the emotional problems that accompany an affair under these circumstances.

Should you have an affair? Keep in mind that, in the aftermath of an affair, mistrust can contribute to the unraveling of a marriage. Only you can analyze your motives and weigh the risks. Only you can decide if you should have an affair or not.

Consequences of the Affair: Should You Leave Your Partner?

One of the toughest questions you may have to face is whether to leave your partner because one of you has had an affair. Finding an answer can be difficult and depends on who—you or your partner—has found another lover.

Should You Leave Your Partner for Your Lover?

As mentioned earlier, few people leave their spouses to marry their lovers. The consequences of divorce are frequently as hard on the person who seeks it as they are on the other partner, particularly at midlife. Divorce can lead to financial hardship, emotional distress, and all the problems associated with angry teenage or adult children and extended families. Embarrassment over divorce is more common among people over 50 than among those who are younger.

Even if your marriage is unsatisfactory, you can expect a great deal of sadness and upheaval upon deciding to end it. Discomfort accompanies any loss, and the end of a longstanding marriage is a major loss.

Although divorce may be the best choice for a couple, the decision should not be made in anger or haste, especially if the couple has been together for many years. See a counselor before leaving your spouse. And take all the time you need in making a decision. Don't be hurried by an impatient lover.

The difficulties of starting over with a new partner may be greater than you are imagining now, particularly if the partner is much younger than you. A younger woman may want children, but the man may feel his child-rearing days are over. A younger man may be heavily involved in his career just when an older woman is ready to retire and travel.

Before making a final decision about divorce, go through the following checklist:

- *I have considered the financial consequences of the divorce, and I am dealing with them.* Talk to your lawyer, tax accountant, and financial planner. Unless you are wealthy, a midlife divorce will almost surely mean a reduction in lifestyle for both partners.

- *I have anticipated the emotional effect of the divorce, and I am getting help to deal with it.* Too many people assume they will be happy once they get the divorce they want. Before experiencing happiness, they will almost inevitably go through periods of grief, guilt, anxiety, and doubt.

- *I have done everything I can to be fair to my spouse.* Some people get angry at the partner they're leaving because they need the anger as an impetus to action. Assigning full blame for the failure of the marriage to your partner is unfair and unrealistic. You will be able to move on with your new life faster if you accept responsibility for your own part in the dissolution of your marriage—and if you treat your spouse fairly, both emotionally and financially.

- *I have communicated my feelings to my children, but I haven't tried to put them in the middle of the divorce.* If your children are teenagers or older, they need and deserve some kind of explanation from you. Without going into the details of your sex life, you should be honest with them. Don't attack the other parent. And don't force your children into a position in which they feel they have to take the side of one parent against another. If they're angry at you, understand and leave the emotional doors open for them.

- *I have been fair to my lover, too.* It isn't fair to let your lover be blamed for the breakup of your marriage. If you were committed to the marriage, you wouldn't be getting a divorce. The third party makes a convenient target for the ex-spouse, children, other family members, and friends. In their view, the marriage may have been perfect until the "home wrecker" came along. Don't play into that myth. If you're seeking a divorce, you're doing it for *you*; otherwise, you shouldn't be getting one.

Should You Leave Your Partner Over an Affair?

If your spouse has strayed but doesn't want a divorce, you have to decide if you want to rebuild your marriage, leave, or even accept a nonmonogamous relationship. You need to make this decision based on what *you* want, not on what friends or family tell you to do. Don't make a choice based on immediate hurt and anger. You may choose divorce as an act of revenge; but the hurt and anger won't magically go away once the final decree is stamped.

In the aftermath of your spouse's affair and before seeking a divorce, follow these suggestions:

- *Don't say anything you don't really mean.* Threatening to get a divorce puts you in a corner. Issuing an ultimatum weakens your position. If you say, "I'll leave if you don't stop seeing him (or her)," then you have to leave or lose your bargaining power when your spouse doesn't end the affair.

- *See a therapist.* If your mate won't go with you, go alone. You need to work through a process of grieving that will probably include blame and self-pity. And you will need to learn how to reestablish communication with your partner. A communication breakdown typically accompanies the discovery of an affair.

- *Expect the healing process to take some time.* If the marriage is to be healed, the betrayed spouse has to work through feelings of resentment and animosity before he or she can examine the problems that have led to the affair. This will likely take months rather than weeks. The situation didn't develop overnight, and it won't be resolved that quickly either.

- *Consider a temporary separation.* For some couples, a temporary separation provides an important time-out period. The difficulty in separation lies in how it is used. Often, rather than employing a brief separation constructively, the betrayed spouse withdraws, and the straying spouse continues the affair. Set up some ground rules. And continue talking, preferably with the help of a counselor.

- *Define your terms.* What do you want from your spouse? What are you willing to give in return? What accommodations must each of you make to put the marriage back on solid ground? The obvious first issue is whether the straying spouse will give up his or her lover. If not, are you willing to live with that situation? If your partner wants to end the relationship and heal the marriage, he or she must be willing to work at reestablishing trust.

An extramarital affair typically does not end a marriage. In some cases, it can be, in retrospect, good for the relationship. Before deciding to leave a marriage because of an affair—yours or your partner's—give yourself at least 6 months to consider your options. At midlife, the stakes of divorce can be quite high. You have invested most of your adult life in the relationship and thus you have a lot to lose.

RECONCILIATION: If you decide to reconcile you must rebuild the trust between you and your partner. This can be a delicate matter, filled with pitfalls. Here are some guidelines to help you along the way:

- *Take small steps.* A great many attempts at repair and change fail because they are too sweeping in nature. The couple is impatient and attempts to fix all the problems at once. This generally leads to disillusionment and despair. Try to face your problems one at time;

and even then, break each one into smaller issues. Change will be more successful and less overwhelming, if it is made gradually and in small steps.

- *Expect resistance.* Compounding the difficulty we all have with making changes, is that change in relationships involves the risk of moving closer to another person. Most of us want the rewards of that closeness, but you or your spouse may fear the increased vulnerability and possibility of hurt that accompany such intimacy. And the loss of trust may increase the resistance one or both partners have to opening up the other.

- *Expect some testing.* Both parties can be expected to test the sincerity of each other's efforts to change. Testing may take the form of provocation, questioning of motivation ("You're doing this only because you're afraid I'll leave you"), expressing feelings of hopelessness ("These changes seem artificial and trivial"), and/or a return to earlier behaviors. Recognize that these reactions are a natural part of the change process and continue trying to instigate the restorative behaviors. By moving past temporary discouragement, you and your partner can set a new precedent.

- *Be positive.* It is much easier to increase positive behavior than it is to directly eliminate negative behavior. For example, instead of trying to suppress a tendency toward excessive criticism, focus on increasing the number of compliments and supportive comments you give each other. Research in behavioral science suggests that undesirable behavior is more effectively controlled when confronted in a manner that cannot be interpreted as negative.

- *Take action.* Although feelings and beliefs are critically important to the repair of trust, neither carries as much significance as action. *Telling* your partner you love him or her does not have the immediacy and potency of a demonstration of that love. It is what you do, not what you say, that will ultimately heal your relationship and build trust.

New Beginnings

Anne was widowed in her early 40s when her beloved husband died of cancer. For 5 years after his death she didn't have a date. Then she had a flurry of arranged first dates with men who either didn't call back when she wished they had or did call back when she wished they hadn't. Finally she met Ted, also a widower. He was everything she wanted in a man. She desired him, and the feeling came as a shock.

"I feel like Sleeping Beauty's grandmother," she joked to friends. "To experience lust stirring in my loins again is a strange experience." And—she didn't add—very scary.

Underneath her bravado, Anne was as frightened of making love to Ted as she was desirous of doing so. His hands on her body when he caressed her during good-bye kisses at her door promised something she wanted him to deliver. But what if seeing her body fully unclothed turned him off? After they'd had several dates, she knew the inevitable big moment was coming. She planned a big seduction dinner, complete with candles, flowers, his favorite meal, and soft music; and she wore a new and flattering hostess gown.

Anne knew she was drinking too much wine, but couldn't seem to stop herself from gulping it down. Ted picked up on her nervousness and that steadied his own nerves. Her fearfulness gave him more courage than he thought he had. He, too, wanted to make love but was afraid of disappointing her. Would she measure him against her late husband, the man she remembered in his erotic prime? Had there been other men in between—and had they perhaps been younger, more virile than he?

After dinner, they sat side by side on the sofa, her hand in his, while they listened to soft jazz playing on the stereo. He let go of her hand, put his arm around her shoulder, and pulled her closer to him. First he kissed her hairline; then her cheeks, nose, and chin; and finally her lips. His hand caressed her breast. Emboldened by the heat of her body beneath her dress, he pressed harder. She pulled away.

"Did I hurt you?" he asked, surprised and confused by her response.

"No!" she exclaimed, grabbing his hand and clasping it to her chest. Her heart was pounding; and her face was flushed. "I was just..."

She couldn't finish the thought, so he added his own interpretation: She was just shy. He kissed her, thrusting his tongue into her mouth. Her girlish behavior made him feel like a young buck. He felt his penis stirring hopefully. For her part, she was imagining the look of disgust on his face as she removed her clothes, exposing less-than-perfect flesh. She wasn't the woman she'd been all those years ago when she'd first experienced sex. Again, she pulled out of his embrace.

"What's wrong?" he asked.

"I can't," she said, and she began to cry.

Her tears doused the flames of his passion. After briefly trying to comfort her, Ted made a hasty retreat. Alone in her misery, she drank the coffee she'd intended to share with him. What was wrong with her? Surely other women were able to start over again despite bodies that had known their share of wear and tear.

Anne made up her mind to invite Ted over to consummate their relationship the moment he called. But he didn't call. Days, then weeks passed. She didn't hear from him. Mutual friends hinted that Ted, considering himself rejected by her, was never going to call her again.

Now she couldn't get Ted out of her mind. She lay in bed some nights, with her hand clamped between her legs, fantasizing about him. More than once, she reached for the phone. Once or twice, she even dialed his number but hung up on the first ring. "You're a coward," she told herself.

Fortifying herself with a small brandy, she punched in Ted's phone number, held her breath, and willed herself to let it ring. When he answered, she didn't hang up. He was happy to hear her voice.

"I'm lying alone in my bed, naked, thinking carnal thoughts about you," she said.

"Share them by all means," he replied, and she did.

She told the story of Sleeping Beauty's grandmother who'd allowed her vanity regarding her physical imperfections to keep her imprisoned in a celibate state. Then she described her longing, allowing her fingers to play with her clitoris as she spoke. Her voice grew huskier, her breath more jagged.

"I want you to come," he said, and she did.

Later that night she came again and again after he'd joined her in bed.

CHAPTER SIXTEEN

Keeping the Romance Alive Forever

"Can you keep the romance alive?" Janet asked wistfully. At 52, she and her husband have just reconciled after a separation. The romance is very much alive again, and they would like to keep it that way.

"We took each other for granted and drifted apart," she says, "like too many couples do. He had an affair, and I found out. We had been separated for six months when we started dating again. We've been through marital counseling, and we're taking a second honeymoon. This time I want it to last for the rest of forever."

When romance is missing from people's lives, they may not feel loved and desired by their partners. They might be open to an affair or closed to sexual activity. Romance keeps the doors connecting a man and a woman open. Some evidence suggests that mature couples may actually be more romantic than are younger ones. At midlife, men and women are better matched sexually and emotionally and, in this state of simpatico, are more likely to speak the tender words and make the thoughtful gestures of romance. As discussed earlier in the book, romance is more important to men over 50 than it is to younger men.

Friendship: The Hidden Component of Romance

Few of us are surprised when friendship turns into love, yet we may not realize that friendship remains an important component of a love relationship, particularly a long-term one. Like romantic love, friendship has an arc. The young partners before children are close friends who explore each other's likes and dislikes, feelings and beliefs through long discussions. As their lives become more complex, the friendship may be less close. The birth of children, the acquisition of a home, career development, and the pull of other emotional ties work together to diminish the amount of time the couple can spend having long, intimate conversations about the meaning of life. If the friendship matters to them, however, they will make the time to be intimate with each other, verbally as well as physically.

When a husband and wife speak to each other only about their schedules, duties, and chores, they are putting their friendship as well as their passion at risk. These are the couples who at midlife discover they have nothing to say to each other now that they once again have the time to talk. How likely is it that they'll have romance in their relationship if they don't have even conversation?

A lasting relationship is, among other things, a friendship agreement. Even with sexual feelings, a successful division of family responsibilities, and mutual respect, a couple who does not have companionship at midlife will probably have a less satisfying sexual and romantic life than they would like. If the romance has gone out of your relationship, try to put the friendship back in first.

Six Steps to Reviving Friendship

- *Don't say, "You never talk to me."* Blaming an uncommunicative partner will only put him or her in a defensive position. If the lack of real conversation disturbs you, initiate dialogue by snuggling up and musing, "Honey, do you remember when we used to talk into the wee hours of the morning?"

- *Ask questions.* If you simply tell your spouse to talk to you, he or she is likely to answer, "What do you want me to say?" Instead ask questions, and be sure your questions show both your knowledge of and interest in your partner's life apart from you. Pretend you've just met someone shy and use your wiles to draw the other person out. Ask open-ended questions that can't be answered in one or two words. A "Yes, Dear" or a "No, Dear" will not start a conversation.

- *Don't assume you know the other like the back of your hand.* People change and grow and don't necessarily tell others about every little thing. Good friends don't let that happen. When you think of it, share your newfound beliefs or changed ideas. Don't assume you know where your spouse stands on political issues; just because he or she was an antiwar protester when you first met doesn't necessarily mean he or she hasn't had a change of heart. Ask each other what you think about such issues.

- *Talk and you will be talked to.* Share information. In the beginning, you told your partner everything. Maybe you called each other at work several times a day. Now one or the other is often chagrined at being the last to know that a neighborhood couple is splitting, their daughter is scheduled for a sonogram, or the pastor is leaving the parish.

- *Show your friend you care.* Do a favor without being asked. Go out of your way to get tickets to a game or play that your spouse wants to see. Share companionable silent activities. Remember when you used to sit side by side on the sofa—one of you reading, the other watching TV—just because you enjoyed being together?

What Romance Is—And Isn't

Once you've reconnected as friends, add a little romance to the mix. There is a difference between romance and the romantic love phase of sexual attraction. Romance is not the same as sexual passion or employing romantic gestures to seduce a partner.

- *Romantic love stage.* This is a period of euphoria lasting from 3 to 6 months at the beginning of a love relationship, a time in which the lovers idealize each other. This euphoria plays an important role in the early development of an intimate and lasting relationship. To reinforce the bond, the body produces a chemical cocktail that creates a natural high, sometimes known as a *lovesick feeling.* The primary ingredient in the love cocktail is phenylethylamine (PEA). In the euphoric days, the lovers crave each other's company because their PEA levels rise when they're together. Love sickness is nothing more than the pangs of PEA deprivation. Eventually, the body's PEA production returns to normal, and the romantic love stage ends.

- *Sexual passion.* Romance does help keep sexual passion alive, but passion ebbs and flows throughout any healthy, ongoing relationship. In contrast, romance can remain constant.

- *Expression of love.* Romance is an ongoing expression of love between two people. Through words and actions, the partners demonstrate their love, affection, and respect for each other. And this can last forever.

Five Midlife Romantic Misconceptions
Many midlife couples have misconceptions about the longevity of romance. Once you see through the following fallacies, you'll be on your way to keeping romance in your relationship forever.

- Many believe romance can't endure because they equate *romance* with an image of youth and beauty and/or the euphoria felt during the romantic love stage.

- Some give up on romance when they think their partner is less than a romantic ideal.

- Others assume that it isn't possible to sustain romance over decades of togetherness.

- Many think that full knowledge, disclosure, and understanding of each other kill romance, because the mystery is gone.

- Some refuse to ask for the kind of romantic words and gestures they crave because they believe true romance allows their partner to intuit their desires and to fulfill them.

If these misconceptions have been keeping the romance out of your life, banish them and get romantic.

The Romance Quiz

How much romance do you have in your life? Take a few minutes to assess the romantic aspect of your relationship. Whether you want more sex, more closeness, better communication, or increased intimacy, you'll increase your chances of getting it if you try a little romance. Heartfelt romantic words and gestures smooth the path to your relationship goals.

1. When was the last time you said, "I love you," and under what circumstances?

2. Can you remember the most recent *unrequested* favor you did for your mate? What was it?

3. How often do you offer to give your partner a back rub?

4. How long has it been since you looked deeply into your partner's eyes and held his or her gaze while having a conversation?

5. When was the last time he brought home flowers for no special reason?

6. How often do you dine by candlelight using the good china for the two of you alone?

7. When did you last buy the other a no-occasion little gift?

8. How long has it been since you rushed home to freshen up before the other arrived?

9. How long has it been since you listened to music alone together and danced by firelight in the living room? Or rented a movie and cuddled up together to watch it?

10. When was the last time you took a shower or bath together?

11. When did she last buy new lingerie?

12. When did you last write your partner a love note, letter, or poem or add an endearment to the bottom of a greeting card?

If most of your answers to these questions are "I can't remember," it's time to recapture the romance.

Ten Steps to Rediscovering Romance

"I equated romance with the jittery feeling you have when you first fall in love," says Joan. "I thought it was gone, long gone, after twenty-two years of marriage. My husband said we needed a little romance in our lives; and I thought he meant more sex. I'm an avid consumer of pop psychology, but nothing had quite prepared me for the changes that have come over him in the past few years. He wants to talk. He wants to cuddle. Now, he wants romance.

"As a joke, I sent flowers to his office. He was thrilled. The sex was better that night than it had been in months. He worshiped my clitoris. I am learning how to be a romantic woman, which was never my style. But I'm enjoying this new phase of our lives. It's sexy."

Rediscover your lost romantic side, and you may recapture some of the sexual passion you thought had subsided, too. Here are some tips:

• *See each other as lovers again.* After a couple has settled well into marriage, the partners view each other as husband and wife, father and mother. Some married couples even call each other Mom and

Dad. Try this simple exercise: Look at your partner with fresh eyes and *see* your lover.

- *Use each other's names or occasional terms of endearment.* Stop calling each other Mom and Dad. Go back to the days when you were Harry and Sally and all that that implied.

- *Tell your partner how special he or she is.* Choose your words carefully. Although you appreciate your mate for all the stalwart qualities that enable him or her to share the load of family responsibilities, don't mention them now. What are the qualities that first attracted you, that made this person more special to you than others you'd known? Were you drawn by your spouse's warmth, charm, wit, intelligence, or beautiful smile?

- *Be affectionate but not as a prelude to lovemaking.* If a hug, a kiss, or a caress are immediately interpreted as a sexual invitation, the romance has seeped out of your relationship. Get physical. Holding hands—publicly and privately—is a very romantic thing to do. Small gestures of affection in public say, "I'm proud to be with this wonderful person."

- *Take time to do things for each other.* Some couples have daily power struggles over the small chores, like who will pick up the cleaning, stop at the supermarket, or mail the bills. Stop confronting your partner as if the two of you were opposing sides in a labor negotiation. Do something thoughtful and unexpected, such as stopping at an out-of-the-way market to buy the raspberries your partner craves in the early days of the season.

- *Buy love gifts.* Love gifts are little tokens of romantic esteem given when no occasion demands them. Do you need some ideas? Try a single red rose wrapped in tissue and tied with a ribbon, a miniature box of fine chocolates, a bag of gourmet jelly beans, a paperback book, a stack of magazines, a snowglobe paperweight of a sentimental scene, an ornament for the Christmas tree, or even a silly souvenir from the ballpark. A 52-year-old woman who has been married 30 years still remembers the big bottle of hand lotion her husband brought her from a grocery-shopping trip their first year of marriage. He was in the army, and they were "broker than broke." The hand lotion represented his spending money for two days.

- *Date each other.* Call your partner and ask him or her out on a date. You take charge of the reservations, getting directions, or whatever planning needs to be done. Put the same effort into your appearance that you did when you were first dating. Suggest that your partner make the next date. After a few dates, ask your lover to go away with you for the weekend.

- *Don't neglect the accouterments of romance.* Light candles at the dinner table when the two of you are dining alone. Buy fresh flowers as often as you can afford. Use fragrance again, if you've stopped. Buy some new lingerie for her and silk robes for both of you.

- *Accompany your partner somewhere you really don't want to go.* At midlife, many couples feel comfortable enough to go their separate ways to sporting events, concerts, movies, plays, and other events if they don't share each other's tastes. Independence is a good thing. No one is suggesting you face life like conjoined twins, but it is romantic to occasionally accompany your partner to an event just because it's special to him or her, even if you aren't interested yourself.

- *Say "I love you" often.* That three-word sentence is the most romantic thing you can say.

If you try all 10 suggestions, you will almost surely rekindle your romance. Having regained the feelings of excitement and discovery, you won't want to lose them again.

How to Keep the Romance Alive

"Whenever people talk about working on a relationship, I want to yawn," says Chuck, 48. "I know I'm in for a boring conversation about their earnest approach to relating. Why not try playing at a relationship for a change? In our Puritan society, everything is work. Marriage is work. Sex is work. Work is work. I think there's a lot of room for play in life. You can get your job done well and enjoy doing it. You can have a good relationship without approaching it like the plans for a nuclear reactor. And you can certainly have better sex if you learn to lighten up. Adults have forgotten how to play.

"My wife gave me the greatest compliment recently. She told me I'm the most romantic guy she's ever known because I can always make her giggle. She said, 'Chuck, sometimes you make me feel like I have champagne bubbling up inside.' What a sexy thing to say to a man."

Romance is not all soft lighting and candles any more than sex is always a deeply emotional and intimate experience. A takeout pizza eaten in bed can be the most romantic dinner a couple has shared in months if it leads to exciting sex or a feeling of closeness. The ability to make a lover laugh can be the most romantic quality anyone possesses. How can one measure the value of a partner who can lighten each day with smiles?

To keep the romance alive in a long-term relationship, you need the right mind-set. Without it, you'll always be consulting a romantic calendar for the suggestion of the day. Romantic spontaneity is a product of seven indispensable attitudes.

- *Empathy.* True romantics are able to put themselves in their partner's place. They can see and feel the world as he or she does. Empathy makes it possible for them to personalize the words and gestures of love and to give what their partner desires, not what they themselves would like to give.

- *Adventurousness.* Excitement, adventure, and risk cause the body to produce PEA, the potent hormone that gives the romantic love stage its power. If you want to duplicate the feeling of falling in love, take a hot-air balloon ride or go hang gliding together, travel to foreign countries where you've never been and can't speak the language, or explore New York City by subway. Be sexually adventurous, too.

- *Affection.* Affectionate gestures and words are the basic communication components of romance. As a relationship deepens, the gestures of romance will likely be more varied and creative than the gift of a single red rose. A romantic man or woman says words and makes gestures that reflect intimate knowledge of the beloved. These small daily doses of affection reinforce the bond of intimacy.

- *Flirtation.* Flirting is both playful and sexy, a way of making your partner feel desired as he or she was in the beginning of love. Contrary to what many think, flirting is not the province of the young. Romantic couples continue to flirt throughout their lives.

- *Humor.* Lighthearted lovers have the gift of romance. Most people take sex, relationships, and life far too seriously. Sex is supposed to be fun, and sometimes it's funny, too. Romantics who have the humorous touch can be irresistible to their partners. They put the spontaneity and joy into being together.

- *Sensuality.* Romantic people revel in all the senses: taste, smell, sight, touch, and sound. They are good lovers because they know that lovemaking is more than technique and genital connection, more than orgasm. When both partners are focused on sensual pleasure, they experience everything—from a shared sunset to sex—more fully.

- *Generosity.* In romance as in sex, those who are able to give and share enhance their own and their partner's experience. The soul of romance is generosity. Empathy cannot exist without it. It is difficult for a miser and a romantic to exist in the same person.

How Some Couples Never Lose the Magic

Mike and Barb are an attractive and sexy couple in their early 50s. They fell in love in high school; married when she was 20 and he was 21; and evolved separately into secure, exciting, interesting individuals and together as a warm and charismatic couple. People like to be around them because they have never lost the aura of magic that we usually associate with the young in love.

"We've had our problems over the years like every couple who's been married a long time and raised a family together," Barb says, "but we never stopped loving each other or being romantic with each other. In our second year of marriage, Mike's father, a volunteer sheriff, was shot to death trying to resolve a domestic dispute; and a few months later, I miscarried our first child. I remember waking up in the hospital after the miscarriage. Mike was gently applying lip gloss to my lips. He'd run out to buy a tube while I was sleeping because he'd noticed my lips were dry and wanted to make me comfortable in any way he could. I knew then everything would eventually be all right.

"For my fiftieth birthday, Mike took me to a resort for the weekend. We had a beautiful suite. He'd arranged for a lovely bouquet of flowers and chilled champagne. And he gave me diamond earrings, an extravagance I didn't know I wanted so much until I held them in my hand. It was like our wedding night all over again."

A friend who has known them since they were engaged says, "They always have and still do radiate sexual energy. And they have a good time together. I've watched them go through hard times and good times, and I've never known them to lose their ability to laugh easily or fail to comfort each other. I like to be with them. It cheers me up to be around them."

Mike and Barb embrace the seven indispensable romantic attitudes. After 30 years of marriage, the magic lingers.

Ellen and Dick, in their 70s, recently celebrated their 50th anniversary, and they, too, display the seven indispensable attitudes, creating magic. Like Mike and Barb, they have a wide circle of family and friends who find joy and comfort in being around them.

"We have a good time, even in the bad times," Ellen says. "My heart still beats a little faster when he comes into the room if we've been apart for the day. I can't imagine what my life would have been like without him." Dick retired before Ellen did, and in her last year of working, he had dinner waiting when she came home. "One of the nicest things he did for me last year was plant hundreds of bulbs, irises and tulips. He knew they would be blooming around the time of my retirement, and he wanted me to have something to look forward to in those first days of missing my job. We had lunch on the porch on warm days and admired the flowers."

Dick adds, "Life with Ellen has never been dull, not one moment since I met her over fifty years ago at a ball park. I was playing amateur ball. She came with a girlfriend to the game. I was attracted to her hair; she had beautiful long, wavy hair that shone with burnished highlights in the sun. After the game I got someone to introduce us, and I asked her out. We were married six weeks after we met. We just knew right away that we wanted to be together for the rest of our lives."

These two couples and others like them have a special relationship that attracts others to them. Most of us like to be around lovers. We want to believe in the magic; and we can because their magic is real.

If your partner is not as romantic as you would like, don't despair. Here are some ways you can encourage the development of romantic attitudes:

- *Start with yourself.* Change your own attitudes and behaviors to more positive and romantic ones. You have to give romance to get it. Without realizing that you are, you might be sabotaging the romance in your relationship by not appearing to be open to it.

- *Give positive reinforcement.* Show appreciation for any romantic gesture, no matter how small or how generic. A handful of flowers that aren't your favorite. A brief good-bye kiss. A heartfelt thank-you for a favor done. Don't wait for your partner to behave like your romantic ideal before you melt.

- *Withhold criticism.* Criticizing someone for not being romantic won't make the loving words and gestures flow. People do not respond romantically to being criticized or nagged.

- *Give your partner what he or she needs to feel loved.* The best way to inspire romance is to show your partner that you really understand his or her desires. Personalize your own display of affection.

The Last Words

- *Live a life outside the bedroom that is vital and adventurous.* Stay out of ruts. Avoid stale routines. Expand your experiences. Live a counterphobic lifestyle and take chances. Then bring this bold attitude to the bedroom.

- *Yes, living with the same person for decades really is boring.* So don't stay the same person you were when you met and married. Change. Evolve. Grow. You have a responsibility to your partner to do that. Expand your personal boundaries. Keep learning. An active, curious mind is a sexual turn-on.

- *Keep your relationship emotionally open.* Don't become one of those couples who have nothing substantial to say to each other because they've eliminated so many issues of discussion over the years. Retain the sexy openness that new lovers share. It's a form of verbal foreplay.

- *Remember that good sex involves friction and fiction.* Stay sexually stimulated by watching erotic films, reading sexy books, indulging your fantasies. Don't be afraid of a good fight.

- *Accept that you and your partner's sexuality evolves and changes over the years.* Adapt your lovemaking style to the changes. Be flexible; rigidity is deadly, especially in the bedroom. Find the good in the changes, and make the most of each new phase of life.

- *Stay active, fit, and healthy.* You probably can't maintain a good sex life unless you do.

- *Remember that attitude is everything.* When you approach life with hope and enthusiasm, you make the best of the bad days and enjoy the good ones to the fullest. A good attitude creates sexual energy. By midlife, negative people are too tired and defeated to enjoy sex.

If you think you can, you can.

SIZZLER #16

The "Like" Connection

For their 35th wedding anniversary, Matt presented Carol with an elegant diamond necklace. She gave him a new set of golf clubs. Carol doesn't care much for diamonds, and Matt hasn't played enough golf to wear out his old set of clubs. Family and friends teased them about their gift choices at the surprise party their sons threw for them.

"Do you two even know each other?" Carol's sister asked.

Sudden tears welled in Carol's eyes. Another question had sprung to mind: Do we even *like* each other? She, the aging girl next door, and he, the poor boy who made good by adapting a veneer of carefully cultivated sophistication now seem a world apart. From across the room, he saw the look on her face, and his own face fell in response.

After the party, they had a serious discussion about their marriage. Neither wanted a divorce, but neither felt happy anymore.

"Maybe we expect too much?" he mused. "What does *happy* mean at our age anyway?"

So they agreed to work harder on their relationship and to try to put some romance back in their life. Toward that end, each made stereotypical gestures. He brought roses and fine chocolates home. She lit candles and served his favorite meals.

"Matt's probably right," she confided to her sister. "We expect too much. Romantic gestures aren't very meaningful when you already live as well as we do."

"The accouterments of romance aren't as meaningful as the thought behind them," her sister replied, but Carol looked at her doubtfully.

That night Matt told her she'd be receiving several large boxes soon, but she wasn't to open them until he gave her permission. Her interest piqued, she tried to get him to tell her what the secret cartons would contain. He wouldn't. When they arrived later in the week, she was baffled.

"Can we open them now?" she demanded as soon as he came home.

"No. They sit here untouched for two weeks from this Friday. Block four days off the calendar then, by the way."

"It's going to take us four days to open these boxes?" she asked incredulously.

"In a manner of speaking," he said.

She hadn't seen him have so much fun with a surprise since one Christmas when the children were small. He'd earned his first major bonus and had covered the floor of the small living room in their old house with gifts for her and them. Seeing him like this reminded her of how much Matt genuinely enjoyed giving. She thought guiltily of the unworn diamond necklace in its blue velvet-lined box and put her hand instinctively to her throat. He met her eyes, and she could swear he knew what she was thinking. How long had it been since she'd felt he could read her mind?

He didn't go into the office on the day scheduled for the opening of the boxes. Eagerly, she tore open the first one and pulled out—a backpack. Mystified, she looked at him with raised eyebrows. A backpack?

"There should be another one of those," he said offhandedly.

There was. And a tent and all the accompanying gear, including fishing rods and waterproof disposable cameras. They were going camping for four days. She'd long ago stopped asking him if they could take a drive to a nearby national park, pitch a tent, and relax. Now they were doing it.

"Oh, Matt," she cried, throwing her arms around him and hugging hard. "I don't know what to say."

They were ebullient on the drive to the campground. He proved so much more adept at pitching a tent than she'd expected that she was suspicious.

"Where'd you learn how to do this?" she asked.

"I took a seminar at the sporting-goods store," he said sheepishly.

Again she threw her arms around him. In the middle of the forest, with the sound of a trout stream and birds chirping, it seemed as if the years fell away. She was young again. So was he.

After eating the dinner they'd prepared on the campfire, they retired to the tent. They were awkward at first, fumbling with zippers and buttons, fingers trembling. She pulled her turtleneck sweater over her head. The diamond necklace gleamed in the soft light inside the tent.

"I've never loved you more," he said; and everything else was said with their bodies.

CONCLUSION

You're Still Sexy

Many variations of sex that were considered taboo when we were younger are now well accepted. Oral sex, masturbation, anal sex, and even many forms of kinky sex such as spanking and bondage have come out of the closet. Women can have partners younger than themselves—as men always could have; and women are not penalized for being sexually active before marriage. The "virgin clause" isn't part of the marital contract anymore. Enlightened people no longer regard homosexuality or bisexuality as evil or perverse.

One taboo, however, has outlasted the others: elder sex. An individual's definition of *elder* seems to depend, of course, on his or her own age. We know that 20-year-olds probably think we are very old, and it wouldn't surprise me to hear they don't think sex is possible after the age of 40, if not 35. On the other hand, a 70-year-old man who is still sexually active with his wife of 48 years told me he considers *old* to be 15 years older than whatever age he currently is. With laughter in his eyes, he said, "Obviously, I will never get old." He added, "And as long as Paul Newman is still sexy, so am I." It's a good thing to think of yourself: sexy, not old.

As I noted in the introduction, the baby boom generation—with another one of its members turning 50 every 7 or 8 seconds—has changed and will continue to change the way our society views aging and sexuality. Eventually the age taboo will seem silly as believing brides must be virgins or that oral sex is perverse does to us now. Meanwhile, subscribing to that belief is the one major obstacle standing between you and great sex at this stage in your life. Don't let yourself fall into a sex-negative mind-set or your body will follow you into the shutdown mode.

Sex does change as we age. And aren't we fortunate that it does? Like fine wine and art masterpieces, great lovers appreciate in value and are more appreciated by their partners as time goes by. In your 20s, passion was everything, but passion—for both sexes—didn't always lead to pleasure. Young men long for the kind of ejaculatory control that mature men take for granted, and young women strain to reach orgasm when that response comes easily to a mature woman.

Older is not only beautiful but better. Men are more tender, women more physically responsive. Each has the wisdom and experience to celebrate the other.

Resources

Books
I hope you will refer to this book whenever you need help over a rough patch, need a new approach to lovemaking, or want a reminder that you're still sexy after all. Here are some other books that you may find useful or inspirational in maintaining a sex-positive frame of mind:

Aphrodite, a memoir of the senses by Isabelle Allende
The Autobiography of My Body, a novel by David Guy
Best American Erotica, a collection of erotic short stories
Boomer Babes, a self-help guide by Linda Stasi and Rosemary Rogers
An Erotic Beyond: Sade, poem and essays by Octavia Paz
Herotica, a four-volumes collection of erotic short stories
His Secret Life, a study of male fantasies by Bob Berkowitz
Inventing Memory, a novel by Erica Jong
Kama Sutra, the classic guidebook; buy the illustrated edition for the art
Little Birds: Erotica, erotic short stories by Anaïs Nin
My Summer with George, a novel by Marilyn French

Sex: An Oral History, interviews with real people of all ages about their sex lives, by Harry Maurer

Vox, a novel by Nicholson Baker

And don't forget my previous books:

The Art of the Quickie: Fast Sex, Fast Orgasm/Anytime, Anywhere
Secrets of Better Sex

Catalogs, Stores, and Websites

Adam & Eve Catalog
800-765-ADAM
www.adameve.com

The photos are more explicit than in other catalogs. Their bestsellers include Dr. Ruth's Eroscillator, a smaller, streamlined, and quiet vibrator with detachable heads for different kinds of stimulation. The Power Rabbit is also a big seller. Adam & Eve co-produces and markets high-quality erotic films and instructional videos. If you see their name on the box, you can be sure it's a good product.

Good Vibrations
800-BUY-VIBE (800-289-8423)
415-974-8980
www.goodvibes.com

Catalog illustrations tend more toward the soft and pretty, with a lot of drawings mixed among the photos. An ordering plus: The company guarantees they will not give, sell, or trade your name to other mail-order businesses. They sell books, videos, and sex toys and probably have a greater range of G-spot vibrators and informational material than other catalogs. Check out *The New Good Vibrations Guide to Sex: Tips and Techniques from America's Favorite Sex Store*, by Cathy Winks and Anne Semans. There is a retail store in San Francisco.

Toys in Babeland
800-658-9119
www.babeland.com

This women-owned and -operated company produces a catalog for toys, books, videos, and safe-sex supplies. There are retail stores in the New York area and in Los Angeles; see the website for store locations.

The Xandria Catalog
800-242-2823
www.xandria.com

This company guarantees not to give, sell, or trade your name to other mail-order businesses. Their catalog is an interesting combination of the tasteful and the slightly raunchy (although exuberantly raunchy). In addition to the standard mix of books, videos, and sex toys, they also market excellent publications on such topics as sexuality and cancer and sexuality and disability. These booklets contain information on where to buy specialized products to aid sexual expression, other resource information, and fine illustrations on adapting sexual positions and skills to specific situations.

Other Resources

There are many good erotic and instructional videos available. In addition to the Adam & Eve label, look for Candida Royalle's Femme Productions erotic videos and instructional videos in *The Better Sex Video Series* by the Townsend Institute and in the Sinclair Institute series.

Increasingly, novels and some films feature older characters involved in romantic relationships. Look for them. Teenagers aren't the only ones who can benefit from spending time with good role models.

Keeping Informed

It's also important to keep up with the latest and most accurate information available in the areas of medicine, general health, diet, and exercise. As you now know, everything you take into your body can have a potential effect on sexuality. Every week it seems, some study appears contradicting the results of a previous study. You have to evaluate carefully what you read. Often an explosive headline introduces an article that barely summarizes the research and the scientific conclusions can be distorted by the popular press. Thus it is important to stay abreast of current developments and read everything with an open and analytical mind. As the population ages, more antiaging products and "miracle aging cures" will compete for our dollars and our hopes. You'll have to be a careful consumer of both information and products.

It's unlikely that the "cure" for aging will be discovered in our lifetime, but the secrets of enduring sexuality are already available to you—in this book. I'll leave you with a quote from the actor Jack Nicholson, a comment made on his 55th birthday: "I feel exactly the same as I've always felt: a lightly reined-in voracious beast." If that doesn't make you feel good about your age, has anyone told you that music icon Tina Turner of the glorious legs is now well into her 60s and is still rockin'?

Index

About the Author

Joel D. Block, Ph.D., is an award-winning psychologist practicing couples and sex therapy. A diplomate of the American Board of Professional Psychology, Dr. Block is a senior psychologist on the staff of the Long Island Jewish Medical Center and an assistant clinical professor at the Albert Einstein College of Medicine. He is the author of numerous magazine articles and books, including *Secrets of Better Sex*, *The Art of the Quickie: Fast Sex, Fast Orgasm, Anytime, Anywhere*, and his debut novel, *The Wrong Schwartz*. For more information, visit his website at www.drblock.com or email him at drblock@drblock.com.